SPIRITS OF DEFIANCE

Spirits of Defiance

NATIONAL PROHIBITION AND
JAZZ AGE LITERATURE, 1920–1933

Kathleen Drowne

The Ohio State University Press
Columbus

Copyright © 2005 by The Ohio State University.

Library of Congress Cataloging-in-Publication Data
Drowne, Kathleen Morgan.
Spirits of defiance : national prohibition and jazz age literature, 1920–1933 / Kathleen Drowne.
    p. cm.
Includes bibliographical references and index.
ISBN 0–8142–0997–1 (alk. paper)—ISBN 0–8142–5142–0 (pbk. : alk. paper)—ISBN 0–8142–9075–2 (cd-rom) 1. American literature—20th century—History and criticism. 2. Drinking of alcoholic beverages in literature. 3. Prohibition—United States—History—20th century. 4. Bars (Drinking establishments) in literature. 5. Drinking customs in literature. I. Title.
PS228.D74D76 2005
810.9'358—dc22
                    2005018493

Cover design by Dan O'Dair.
Type set in Adobe Garamond.
Printed by Thomson-Shore, Inc.

9 8 7 6 5 4 3 2 1

For Patrick and Genevieve

CONTENTS

ILLUSTRATIONS

ACKNOWLEDGMENTS

When National Prohibition was repealed in 1933, happy drinkers resurrected the peppy 1929 Tin Pan Alley song "Happy Days Are Here Again" to mark their celebration, even adding new lyrics to attest to the joys of drinking legal beer. Now that I've reached the end of this project, I'd like to resurrect this song myself and add some new lyrics to honor the extensive network of wonderful, smart, talented people who helped me bring this book into being. Over the years I have relied heavily on the wisdom, advice, and support of professors, colleagues, friends, and family, and I feel deep debts of gratitude not only to those generous individuals who read and commented on drafts of this book, but also to many people who never read a single page of my manuscript but who also never hesitated to offer steady encouragement and kind words when I needed them most. It is because of them that, for me, happy days are here again.

First I wish to thank Linda Wagner-Martin, my mentor, friend, and former advisor at the University of North Carolina at Chapel Hill. She taught me sound scholarly methods, reminded me to keep my project in proper perspective, and helped me retain my sense of humor. While a UNC-CH graduate student, I benefited enormously from the expertise of Fred Hobson, Townsend Ludington, Trudier Harris, and James Coleman. I am particularly indebted to William L. Andrews, an academic mentor and my former boss at the journal *a/b: Auto/Biography Studies,* who taught me so much about the professional world of academia.

I also wish to thank the organizations that have provided me with financial and institutional support at various stages in this project: The Center for the Study of the American South at the University of North Carolina at Chapel Hill; The Graduate School of the University of North Carolina at Chapel Hill; and especially the W. E. B. Du Bois Institute for Afro-American Research at Harvard University. My year as a resident fellow at the Du Bois Institute (1999–2000) was surely the most stimulating academic experience of my life, and I remain indebted to Henry Louis Gates, Jr., Jill Salk, Carli Coetzee, Emily Bernard, the late Richard Newman, and the many other people I met there who made my time in Cambridge so rewarding.

For assistance with permissions and with compiling the illustrations for this book, I am grateful to Lynn Wolf Gentzler of the State Historical Society of Missouri, Columbia; John Monahan of the Beinecke Rare Book and Manuscript Library, Yale University; Tom Featherstone of the Walter P. Reuther Library at Wayne State University; the Schomburg Center for Research in Black Culture, New York Public Libraries; the Harry Ransom Humanities Research Center at the University of Texas at Austin; and the Photoduplication Service of the Library of Congress.

My colleagues at the University of Missouri-Rolla enthusiastically supported my work on this project, especially my fellow writing group members, Liz Cummins, Brenda Hammack, Patrick Huber, Anne Goodwyn Jones, and Kris Swenson, who all read portions of chapter 5 and offered valuable suggestions. Throughout the revision process, Larry Vonalt was particularly generous with his time and his encouragement, and Lorraine Woolsey and Cynthia Tharp kept everything running smoothly at the UMR Writing Center in my absence. I am also grateful to the tireless librarians at the Wilson Library, University of Missouri-Rolla, especially Jane Driber, Marsha Fuller, Jim Morisaki, Scott Peterson, Virginia Schnabel, and John Seguin, for their sage advice and for their cheerful assistance in acquiring interlibrary loan materials.

I will always be thankful for the unwavering support of Stephen and Karin Drowne, Michael and Michelle Gorra, Jennifer Halloran, David Leeming, Kelly Reames, Jean Sanborn, Karen Santoro, Scott Walker, and Shannon Wooden. Jennifer Haytock graciously read the introduction to this book and offered many helpful suggestions. I offer a special word of gratitude to Anne Goodwyn Jones, a wonderful friend and mentor who critiqued many portions of this book and who helped me to clarify my thinking about issues of culture and influence. It has been a genuine pleasure to work with Heather Miller and Sandy Crooms, my acquisitions editors at The Ohio State University Press.

Above all, the love and support of my parents, William and Joanne Drowne, and my grandparents, Eugene and Barbara Schutz, have sustained me in my work and in my life. My final word of thanks goes to my wonderful husband and colleague, Patrick Huber. He carefully read drafts and revisions of every chapter, offered countless valuable suggestions, tracked down obscure but wonderful bits of Prohibition-era history, and all the while remained infinitely positive, patient, and caring. His own thoughtful scholarship in the history and popular culture of Jazz Age America improved my work immeasurably, and so I gratefully dedicate this book to him and to our beautiful daughter, Genevieve. Only they know how much I truly owe them, and only I know how much they have blessed my life.

Introduction

Prohibition and American Literature, 1920–1933

"'Tis simple," said the Man from Minn.,
"To cure the world of mortal sin—
        Just legislate against it."
Then up spake Congress with a roar,
"We never thought of that before.
        Let's go!"
        And they commenced it.
—Wallace Irwin, "Owed to Volstead" (1922)

On April 15, 1919, more than nine months before National Prohibition was to go into effect, a *Wall Street Journal* headline made a dire prediction: "Bone-Dry Literature Coming." "The modern writer," the article announced, "has a new problem to face. National Prohibition will make literature 'dry.'" The article went on to explain, facetiously, that due to the approaching prohibition on alcoholic beverages, scheduled to go into effect at midnight on January 16, 1920, "The [literary] hero may still flick the ashes from his cigarette, but when the time comes for him to take a drink he must order a chocolate soda." The article also spoofed the kinds of seduction scenes that readers could soon expect to find in Prohibition-era novels: "She sipped her buttermilk slowly and calmly noted its effect. After the second bottle she was a woman emancipated. She reached across the table and untied her handsome admirer's cravat."[1]

The *New York Times* published a similarly satirical article, also in 1919, under the lengthy headline "Must We De-Alcoholize Literature? How Shakespeare, Rare Ben Jonson, Robert Burns, and Omar Khayyam Will Sound if They Are Revised to Fit Those Sober Days Soon to Come." This article noted that "[o]ne of the first means of enforcing national prohibition . . . will be the suppression of all advertising of alcoholic drinks," and that temperance reformers might easily consider those "convivial" passages in literature that describe episodes of drinking to be a form of advertising.

If so, the article reasoned, then censors may attempt to expurgate or revise famous literary works by Chaucer, Shakespeare, Dickens, and others to eliminate all references to "exhilarating beverages."[2] This article, like the previous *Wall Street Journal* piece, offered tongue-in-cheek speculation on the impact that Prohibition laws might have on American and even world literature. Underneath the humorous tone and witty examples, however, these articles also revealed a real sense of uneasiness about the potential consequences and far-reaching effects of the new liquor legislation. Certainly nobody would seriously attempt to "de-alcoholize" Shakespeare's Jack Falstaff or Dickens's old Fezziwig, yet a sense of apprehension and uncertainty clearly existed regarding the future of American life and, more particularly, American literature in a dry nation.

National Prohibition obviously did not result in the creation of a "bone-dry literature" in which heroes drank chocolate soda, women behaved brazenly under the influence of buttermilk, and Mr. Pickwick was bereft of his favorite punch. History also proves specious the solemn claim of British novelist and Cambridge professor Sir Arthur Quiller-Couch, that "under enforced prohibition the United States will never produce a great literature," which the *New York Times* reported in a 1922 front-page article. During a debate with a teetotaling academic, Quiller-Couch actually went so far as to declare, "high literature, both in its creation and its full enjoyment, demands total manhood of which a teetotal manhood is obviously a modification," and that few if any non-drinkers have ever become great poets or critics.[3] In hindsight we recognize that, contrary to Quiller-Couch's oddly gendered prediction, the era of enforced Prohibition coincided with an enormous outpouring of acclaimed American literature that remains unparalleled today. Some of the most celebrated works by William Faulkner, F. Scott Fitzgerald, Ernest Hemingway, Langston Hughes, Sinclair Lewis, Dorothy Parker, Claude McKay, and Zora Neale Hurston first reached the shelves during Prohibition, as did many now-forgotten but once-popular novels, such as Elinor Glyn's *It* (1927) and Upton Sinclair's *The Wet Parade* (1931). Interestingly, as Quiller-Couch noted, many of our most highly prized writers of the Prohibition era were, themselves, enthusiastic drinkers who felt little compulsion to obey the new liquor laws. Their blatant disregard for Prohibition surfaces in many works of fiction from this period, sometimes overtly and sometimes obliquely.

National Prohibition did exert a profound influence on American literature, but not in the ways that any of the above observers predicted. Critics of the time, though, remained ambivalent about what to make of its effect on American letters. For example, in a 1923 *New York Times* review of Ednah Aiken's forgettable and largely forgotten novel about

Prohibition, *If Today Be Sweet,* the anonymous reviewer vehemently discounted the very attempt of contemporary writers to wrestle with the cultural significance of the Eighteenth Amendment. "We are still in the midst of the vast overturning that the prohibition amendment occasioned and it is altogether too soon to draw from the situation any large truths which carry conviction," the reviewer declared firmly. "Years hence it will possibly be an engrossing and instructive matter to consider from a fictional viewpoint the era in which America shifted from wet to dry. But at the present moment it is a dubious matter until the generation directly affected (both socially and financially) has passed away and given place to a new and impartial one."[4] This reviewer failed to acknowledge, however, that dozens of fiction writers, as well as historians, reporters, politicians, artists, musicians, movie directors, and even cartoonists, had already begun drawing conclusions about Prohibition—some of them, like Sir Quiller-Couch, even before it went into effect—and they continued their analyses well beyond Prohibition's 1933 repeal. National Prohibition ranks as one of the most hotly debated political controversies of the 1920s, and its reverberations extended into nearly every aspect of American popular culture; few public figures who had the ear of the nation declined an opportunity to comment upon its great wisdom or its immense folly.

Not surprisingly, many novelists and short-story writers added their voices to the chorus by incorporating into their works their experiences with and opinions about National Prohibition. Some writers who believed that Prohibition was unnecessary, inappropriate, and ultimately futile used their fiction to promulgate these views. In *To Make My Bread* (1932), for example, Grace Lumpkin offers compelling evidence to support how the Prohibition laws unjustly punished the struggling farmers of southern Appalachia. And Wallace Thurman, in his graphic portrayals of inebriated Harlem nightlife in *The Blacker the Berry . . .* (1929) and *Infants of the Spring* (1932), articulates his disdain for the hopelessly ineffective dry laws. In fact, the "wet" politics of many writers surfaced in their sympathetic depiction of characters who defy the Prohibition laws and their unsympathetic censure of characters who support the Prohibition cause.

It would be far too reductive, however, to accept the idea that, in the American literature of the 1920s and early 1930s, violating Prohibition is always perceived as morally superior to obeying it. In fact, many of the popular novels and stories of that era, most of which have now been largely forgotten, take precisely the opposite stance. Mass-circulation magazines and popular novels catered to a conservative, middle-class readership deeply invested in the eventual success of Prohibition, and for us to assume that Americans were united in their common loathing of the liquor laws would deny the vigorous support that the laws received in hundreds of thousands of American homes. It is interesting to note, however, that the fiction of this era that has been incorporated into the American literary canon over the past seventy years is, for the most part, anti-Prohibition. And in those works that include overt commentary on the Eighteenth Amendment, illegal drinking is portrayed as a highly symbolic and meaningful behavior that allows writers to explain—and justify—their characters' legal and moral transgressions.

More often, however, literary depictions of unlawful drinking appear without any authorial comment, explanation, or justification regarding the politics of National Prohibition. In such scenes, drinking is portrayed as an apparently neutral activity, a common pastime to be enjoyed by ordinary adults. This lack of explicit alcohol-related commentary has led many readers to accept these drinking scenes as, indeed, politically and morally neutral. In fact, readers unfamiliar with the details of Prohibition often do not even realize that these characters are breaking any laws whatsoever in their pursuit of a cocktail or a bottle of gin. Yet one of Prohibition's major social effects was to politicize what had previously been essentially apolitical events. During the 1920s and early 1930s, house parties, nightclub get-togethers, luncheons, and other ordinary social gatherings became politically charged, depending on the presence (or absence) of alcohol. Readers attuned to this important cultural context recognize that scenes of Prohibition-era carousing do carry moral and political weight that often complicates the text in significant ways.

Characters such as clever bootleggers and wily moonshiners, settings such as dingy speakeasies and raucous cabarets, and the shadowy influence of "the law" in general and revenue agents in particular surface in many works of American literature produced during National Prohibition. Yet the history of those nearly fourteen years, during which the nation underwent, in the words of President Herbert Hoover, "a great social and economic experiment, noble in motive," has been relegated to a footnote—if that—in most literary studies of the era. This omission is both surprising and unfortunate, especially given the many insightful journal articles and books that have been published about the alcoholic tendencies of writers including Faulkner, Fitzgerald, Lewis, Thurman, and Hemingway, as well as about the cascade of transformations that reshaped American popular culture during the Jazz Age. *Spirits of Defiance* seeks to fill this gap in American literary studies by demonstrating how understanding the culture surrounding National Prohibition can lead to a deeper, more meaningful, and more nuanced understanding of the many literary works written and published between 1920, the year the Eighteenth Amendment went into effect, and 1933, the year it was repealed.

In its broadest strokes, then, *Spirits of Defiance* aims to identify and

explain elements of Prohibition culture that permeate literary texts produced during this era. Bootleggers, moonshiners, and revenuers seldom
populate twenty-first-century fiction, but they were familiar—sometimes
even stock—characters in the fiction of the 1920s and early 1930s. The
sheer number of uniquely Prohibition-era characters that enliven such
works as F. Scott Fitzgerald's *The Great Gatsby* (1925), Carl Van Vechten's
Nigger Heaven (1926), Claude McKay's *Home to Harlem* (1928), William
Faulkner's *Sanctuary* (1931), and literally dozens of other Jazz Age works
suggests the widespread public awareness and even acceptance of such figures at the time. However, few of today's readers are sufficiently attuned to
the culture of Prohibition to recognize subtle connotations associated with
these characters. For example, in *The Great Gatsby,* Jay Gatsby's involvement with a chain of drugstores would not register as a relevant aspect of
Prohibition culture to readers unfamiliar with the ways that pharmacies
funneled money for large-scale bootlegging operations during the 1920s.
Such details actually offer useful information about the origins of Gatsby's
mysterious fortune and the nature and scope of his business with his
gangster-mentor, Meyer Wolfsheim. To cite another example, readers
unacquainted with the "buffet" and other "good-time flats" of Prohibition-
era Harlem may not fully appreciate the extent to which Jake Brown, the
protagonist in *Home to Harlem,* immersed himself in the outlaw culture of
bootleg liquor, gambling, and prostitution. By clarifying these sometimes
obscure elements of everyday life during Prohibition, *Spirits of Defiance*
will help readers achieve a more sophisticated understanding of the literature produced between 1920 and 1933.

Treating fictional works as lenses through which we can better appreciate history can be admittedly a complicated maneuver. Nevertheless, I
argue that the authors included in this study have composed novels and
short stories that realistically portray and, as a result, help to illuminate
particular facets of American life under National Prohibition. Realism
itself is a slippery literary term, and it is not my intent to debate the nature
of literary representation as it pertains to the material world. Nor would I
argue with literary critics who classify writers such as William Faulkner not
as realists but as modernists. The scope of this project lies solely in fictional representations of Prohibition culture that have been corroborated by
nonfiction sources, particularly newspaper and magazine articles and
scholarly historical studies. Collectively, the works of fiction addressed in
this book offer a realistic, historically accurate picture of how different
kinds of Americans responded to the legal, social, and cultural changes
wrought by the passage of National Prohibition.

Of course, writers told the "truth" about Prohibition in a number of
ways. In a few instances, such as in Upton Sinclair's pro-Prohibition *The*

Wet Parade, the merit of the Eighteenth Amendment as a noble and worthy ideal takes center stage as the primary subject of the story. In contrast, the challenge and appeal of participating in the culture of Prohibition by purchasing and consuming illegal alcohol provided some writers with the foundations for various other plot lines. For example, stories such as Dorothy Parker's "Big Blonde" (1930) and Sherwood Anderson's "A Jury Case" (1933), as well as scenes in Sinclair Lewis's *Babbitt,* Wallace Thurman's *The Blacker the Berry . . .* and *Infants of the Spring,* and Grace Lumpkin's *To Make My Bread,* infuse with drama those moments when characters choose to step beyond the protection of the law and participate in an illicit, liquor-drenched world. In F. Scott Fitzgerald's *The Beautiful and Damned* (1922) and *The Great Gatsby,* Carl Van Vechten's *Nigger Heaven,* Zora Neale Hurston's "Muttsy" (1926), and Claude McKay's *Home to Harlem,* scenes of Prohibition-era drinking and carousing offer important and meaningful backdrops to the primary action. Subtler still are works such as Walter White's *The Fire in the Flint* (1924), Langston Hughes's *Not Without Laughter* (1930), and William Faulkner's *Sanctuary,* in which Prohibition provides an opportunity for the authors to present much broader commentary on the class and racial conflicts that riddled American society.

Although all the works included in this study are set against the colorful background of National Prohibition, it is important to recognize that, with the important exception of Sinclair's *The Wet Parade,* these authors were not deliberately writing political propaganda to support or attack the liquor laws. For the most part, they left the debate surrounding Prohibition to the newspaper editors, magazine writers, politicians, and reformers who wrote and published literally millions of words during the 1920s and early 1930s about the wisdom and efficacy (or lack thereof) of the Eighteenth Amendment. The writers discussed in this book did, however, absorb the realities of life under National Prohibition, and by portraying the underground world of drinking they were, to a degree, politicizing their fiction. For example, in Dorothy Parker's "Just a Little One" (1928), the female narrator accompanies her male friend to a speakeasy, and during the course of their increasingly drunken conversation she downs no fewer than half a dozen cocktails. Before Prohibition this would have been an unlikely scene indeed, for respectable middle-class women rarely patronized public drinking establishments. But in this story, not only does the woman unapologetically patronize the speakeasy, but she also assertively orders multiple drinks, even to the point of her public inebriation. Speakeasy culture, the increased presence of women drinking in public, and the details surrounding the quality of Prohibition-era liquor (her frequent comments about the delights of drinking "real Scotch," for example) are critical elements of "Just a Little One." Furthermore, the lack of authorial censure of this woman or her surroundings identifies the story politically as one that celebrates the lawlessness of Prohibition-era life and the freedoms that women enjoy, ironically, as a result of this prohibitive legislation. The absence of commentary about the actions of this couple further suggests that this scene portrays relatively typical behavior among young men and women in 1928 New York. In other words, even works such as "Just a Little One" that do not overtly comment on the political aspects of Prohibition are often caught up in the small but revealing details of life under the influence of this legislation.

From time to time in this study I refer to "Prohibition culture," by which I mean the social forces, trends, phenomena, influences, language, attitudes, and behaviors that emerged in the 1920s and early 1930s as direct or indirect responses to the federal laws restricting alcoholic beverages. Elements of Prohibition culture do not always relate to drinking explicitly, although they are often linked. Rather, Prohibition culture encompasses all the ways that Americans assimilated the Eighteenth Amendment and its attendant legislation into their daily lives, including the new morals and attitudes that Prohibition helped to foster, particularly among members of the younger generation. One obvious example of Prohibition culture is the rapid proliferation of speakeasies, blind pigs, roadhouses—all the illicit watering holes that appeared on the American landscape to provide customers with illegal drinks. Other, less observable elements of Prohibition culture include the personal and economic relationships that developed between otherwise law-abiding citizens and their bootleggers and other purveyors of alcoholic beverages, including messenger boys, hotel bellhops, soda jerks, pharmacists, and even doctors and priests (in fact, one of William Faulkner's own personal bootleggers was allegedly a young New Orleans priest who took his customers' orders in the belfry of the St. Louis Cathedral). For example, during the years of Prohibition, doctors increased the number of medicinal alcohol prescriptions they wrote for their patients by almost a hundred times the level of previous years. Bellhops in hotels survived almost entirely on the tips they made by delivering liquor to guests, and soda jerks served up fountain drinks that hardly resembled soda. Formerly lawful places such as doctor's offices and soda shops were frequently transformed into illegal fronts behind which the black-market liquor economy thrived.

Another facet of Prohibition culture involves the dozens of popular Tin Pan Alley, jazz, blues, and hillbilly songs that directly addressed the alcohol controversy. These songs brought the highly controversial and politicized issue of National Prohibition into the realm of casual entertainment. The proliferation of radios and phonographs during the 1920s, along with the mass marketing of mail-order records, made it possible for youth across the nation to sing along and dance to such topical numbers as "Prohibition Blues" (1919) or "If I Meet the Guy Who Made This Country Dry" (1920), regardless of their personal politics. Similarly, dance crazes such as the Charleston, the fox-trot, and the Black Bottom became part of Prohibition culture because they were wildly popular at speakeasies, nightclubs, roadhouses, cocktail parties, and other venues that arose directly because of Prohibition. And certain widespread and transgressive behaviors that became popular during the 1920s, such as women drinking, petting, smoking cigarettes, and dressing more alluringly, also sprang, to a degree, from the social climate that resulted in part from Prohibition legislation.

A more subtle layer of Prohibition culture is also critical to this study. The Eighteenth Amendment and the accompanying Volstead Act, also passed in 1919, represented a blatant attempt by the U.S. government to impose a standard of common morality on its citizens by criminalizing what had never before been considered a federal offense. The average American was profoundly concerned with the Prohibition laws because, as historian Herbert Asbury claimed in *The Great Illusion: An Informal History of Prohibition* (1950), they "interfered with his personal habits and appetites and pleasures, and threatened to abolish the means of procuring them." Some zealous "dry" leaders and government officials wanted liquor violators to be penalized in much the same way as murderers, burglars, and drug peddlers, while "wets" pleaded with the courts that liquor violations in no way approached such violent or antisocial crimes. In fact, few "wets" could be convinced that they or their bootleggers were criminals at all; rather, as Asbury explained, the typical American drinker during Prohibition believed that "the man who sold him his liquor was 'good old Joe, a fine fellow'" (165). Nevertheless, the Volstead Act authorized a schedule of fines and prison terms that left no doubt that all activities related to manufacturing, selling, and transporting alcoholic beverages were indeed considered by the federal government to be criminal behaviors. In fact, in 1929 the Volstead Act was supplemented by the Jones Act, which increased the maximum penalty for Prohibition violators to five years in prison and $10,000—even for first offenders—and made any liquor violation a felony. Not surprisingly, the Jones Act intensified the public's criticism of the government's efforts to curtail the drinking habits of its citizens.

This unprecedented government intervention into saloons, restaurants, clubs, and personal liquor cabinets created for millions of Americans a moral conflict that was much more complicated than merely whether or not they would choose to drink alcoholic beverages. Prohibition led countless citizens to violate federal laws on a regular basis, which historians argue led to a lack of reverence for certain forms of authority, particularly legal authority. Every time Americans patronized a speakeasy, bought a pint of gin from a bootlegger, asked a doctor for an unnecessary prescription for "medicinal alcohol," or otherwise dodged the provisions of the Volstead Act, they chose to follow their own principles rather than allow the U.S. Constitution to determine for them what was "moral" behavior. Small as they may seem, these acts were repeated thousands of times an hour during the nearly fourteen years of Prohibition. These commonplace violations of the Eighteenth Amendment eroded Americans' long-cherished sense of patriotism; one important consequence of Prohibition that began during the 1920s and resonated long after repeal was the general citizenry's overall loss of respect for the power and wisdom of the government. Literary scholar John Erskine commented in 1927, "the growing disrespect for law is the most serious menace to our society" (42), and this disrespect flourished, he argued, in both "dry" and "wet" camps. Prohibition supporters were disillusioned by the government's inability to enforce a law they so fervently believed in, while Prohibition opponents resented the government's interference in the first place. Virtually no one was satisfied with the government's performance regarding Prohibition.

Effective legal enforcement of Prohibition proved impossible in part because the thriving temperance movement in the United States had originally been based primarily on moral issues, not legal ones. The Eighteenth Amendment, as well as the hundreds of local, county, and state dry laws that were passed prior to 1919, were ratified largely in the spirit of morality—because abstaining from alcohol was the right thing to do, the correct way to teach children, the righteous path, the quickest road to spiritual salvation, and the surest way to alleviate human suffering. Members of the Anti-Saloon League, the Woman's Christian Temperance Union, and other reform-minded organizations endeavored to convince their fellow Americans that abstaining from alcohol carried with it its own intrinsic rewards, not to mention a home life that was less violent and more financially stable. But after National Prohibition went into effect in 1920, legal arguments against alcohol rapidly replaced moral imperatives; in other words, the claim that all Americans must abstain from alcohol simply because federal law requires it superseded any claim of temperance as its own moral reward. In 1924 Mabel Walker Willebrandt, the assistant U.S. attorney general, essentially abandoned moral justifications for Prohibition when she asked members of the Woman's National Committee for Law Enforcement to "become a positive force to inspire obedience to law" and thereby set an example of good behavior for their communities to follow. President Calvin Coolidge echoed Willebrandt's appeal, calling for adherence to liquor legislation not because of any moral, spiritual, or even financial benefit to be gained from resisting alcohol, but out of respect for the U.S. Constitution and the gravity of its amendments (Murdock 100). Yet many Americans found even this legal argument unconvincing. As one Columbia University student explained to his professor, "They say we should cultivate respect for the prohibition law because they fixed it so it can't be repealed. Queer reason for respecting a law!" (Erskine 48).

Of course, millions of Americans casually violated the Prohibition laws because they saw no connection between morality and drinking alcohol. Others drank in defiance of National Prohibition because breaking these laws allowed them to make a political statement. In many contexts, defying Prohibition became a socially acceptable way for people to rebel, to define themselves in opposition to their government, and to convince themselves that they were independent of, or even above, the law. Those who reached their teens and twenties during the 1920s seemed particularly susceptible to this line of thinking. Historian Norman Clark notes in *Deliver Us from Evil: An Interpretation of American Prohibition* (1976) that for young people during Prohibition, "the raised glass rejected any authority higher than individual pleasure. And it was easy. If a young person in the United States chose to transport or sell a bottle in the back seat of his automobile, this was a matter for which the risks were far outweighed by the promised rewards in prestige and status" (152). In other words, the "individual pleasure" pursued by these drinkers resided less in the taste of alcohol (which tended to be pretty awful during Prohibition) or even the feeling of inebriation, but rather in the social esteem that came with casually partaking of the forbidden. Martha Bensley Bruère, a well-known social worker and writer of the late 1920s and early 1930s, summed up this youthful attitude by commenting that during Prohibition, "drinking by young people was 'an adventure, a gesture of daring, a sign of revolt, an illusion of power, part of the game they call life'" (Clark 152).

Spirits of Defiance focuses on a variety of novels and short stories, all written and published between 1920 and 1933, including many works currently included in the American literary canon. I have chosen to limit the time span in this way so as to identify how writers incorporated Prohibition culture into their work during the actual years these liquor laws were on the books, without benefit of hindsight or constitutional repeal. In order to recover this culture of Prohibition and bring it back into view, I have relied heavily on social histories of the era, biographies, cultural studies, and newspaper and magazine reportage. And, since neither white nor black writers wrote in isolation from one another, I have juxtaposed their works within chapters despite their often-differing political and artistic agendas. While this is not a biographical project, some authors' life experiences and personal politics do bear on their literary representations of Prohibition culture, and I have tried to remain sensitive to these cases without overstating their importance. I have found that Prohibition permeated so much of American popular culture during the 1920s that I could have replaced any of my selected works with others that would have been equally illuminating. My choice of texts, then, is meant to be representative, not comprehensive.

Chapter 1, "Remembering the Culture of National Prohibition," offers a brief overview of the social and cultural history of the Prohibition era; the remaining chapters investigate various aspects of Prohibition culture that appear in literary works of the 1920s and early 1930s. The second and third chapters profile characters associated with Prohibition who populate the literature of the era. Chapter 2, "Outside the Law: Liquor Providers of the Prohibition Era," closely examines the literary presence of moonshiners, bootleggers, and revenue agents, and explores the ubiquitous liquor trafficking that took place in the biggest of cities and the smallest of towns. From William Faulkner's *Sanctuary*, in which the operations of rural moonshiners lead to rape and murder, to Rudolph Fisher's *The Walls of Jericho* (1928), in which a ruthless bootlegger threatens the security of all of Harlem, to Upton Sinclair's *The Wet Parade*, in which an honest revenue agent is martyred to a hopeless cause, these works and others depict the various figures who were responsible for perpetuating or combating the underground liquor economy.

Chapter 3, "These Wild Young People: Drinking and Youth Culture," profiles the figures of the "sheik" and the "flapper"—the emblematic young male and female revelers of the Prohibition era—and examines their roles in shaping the youth culture of the 1920s. Langston Hughes's *Not Without Laughter*, for example, portrays a flapper whose manners and morals could have come straight from the pages of a sophisticated New York magazine, but she actually hails from a rural African American community in the long-dry state of Kansas. In contrast, the sophisticated flappers who crowd the fiction of F. Scott Fitzgerald and Sinclair Lewis sometimes reveal an innocence of spirit seldom attributed to the radical "new woman." This chapter also briefly examines the "dry" opponents of these devoted drinkers: the reformers and teetotalers, many of whom are depicted by Prohibition-era writers far more uncharitably than are the charming, irresponsible scofflaws.

Chapters 4 and 5 map several of the locations where many people drank and socialized during Prohibition and discuss the ways that these sites mark the literature of the age. Chapter 4, "Hidden in Plain Sight: The Drinking Joints," explains the origins of and distinctions among relatively public places such as speakeasies, roadhouses, and cabarets—locations where people could drink, for the most part, unmolested by law enforcement officials. Speakeasies adorn the pages of much Prohibition-era fiction, peeping from Harlem alleyways in Fisher's *The Walls of Jericho* and from the streets of midtown Manhattan in Parker's short stories; roadhouses hide down unmarked dirt roads in Hughes's *Not Without Laughter* and Lewis's *Babbitt;* cabarets and nightclubs glitter along Seventh Avenue in Van Vechten's *Nigger Heaven* and McKay's *Home to Harlem.* These locations provide writers with settings freighted with social and political meaning merely by virtue of their outlaw existence.

Chapter 5, "'Let's Stay In': The Prohibition-Era House Party," examines how Prohibition transformed the simple house party into the site of some of the wildest spectacles of drunken revelry in the entire Jazz Age. With the aid of helpful bootleggers and the participation of anywhere from a handful of close friends to a mansion full of strangers, hosts and hostesses opened their homes to both quiet, private transgressions against the liquor laws and full-scale bacchanals that rivaled the festivities at the most ostentatious cabarets. The sophisticated, upscale cocktail parties depicted in Fitzgerald's *The Beautiful and Damned* and *The Great Gatsby* and in Countee Cullen's *One Way to Heaven* (1932) provide revealing counterparts to the simultaneous desperation and celebration of the Harlem rent parties described in Wallace Thurman's *The Blacker the Berry . . .* and *Infants of the Spring.* Most debauched, scandalous, and thrilling of all are the scenes describing the "good-time flats" in McKay's novel *Home to Harlem.*

One final note: the novels and short stories included in *Spirits of Defiance* represent a wide range of American literature; the categories often used to differentiate discrete areas of literary study (southern, African American, modernist, realist, feminist, etc.) have not proven particularly useful constructs for this project. National Prohibition was, indeed, a truly national situation, and while this legislation certainly did not affect every individual in the same way, its far-reaching effects permeated everyday life throughout the nation. Separating authors based on their geographic backgrounds, their race, their gender, or their style of writing misses the point: writers of every stripe wrestled with the contradictions and consequences of National Prohibition. The writers discussed in this book, like their fellow citizens in general, offered no single overriding response to the Eighteenth Amendment; Americans spoke not with one voice about how best to address the issue of alcoholic beverages, but rather with a cacophony of many disparate voices. Thus, it seems fitting that the authors included in *Spirits of Defiance* be allowed to speak for themselves, to articulate their own attitudes toward National Prohibition, and as a result help readers learn to appreciate the many ways their fiction absorbed, interpreted, and reflected the powerful cultural influence of National Prohibition.

CHAPTER 1

Remembering the Culture of National Prohibition

"What makes we New Yorkers sore is to think they should try
and wish a law like that on Us. Isn't this supposed to be a government of the people, for the people, and by the people?"
"People," I said. "Who and the hell voted for Prohibition
if it wasn't the people?"
"The people of where?" he says.
—Ring Lardner, *The Big Town* (1925)

Today, more than seventy years after it was repealed, National Prohibition continues to exert some influence on the collective memory and popular culture of Americans. For example, a recent television commercial for Michelob beer shows a wagon full of Prohibition officials raiding a bootlegger's warehouse during the 1920s. In the commercial, shot in black and white, the officers handcuff the surprised perpetrators, enthusiastically smash barrels of beer, and then topple a shelf of bottles to the floor. Shattered glass and illegal liquor fly everywhere. But when the officers come upon a stash of Michelob, they put down their axes, forget about the captive bootleggers, and gleefully tiptoe away to share their confiscated barrel. While the point of the commercial is that the officers salvage the treasured Michelob rather than the other brands of inferior-tasting beer, the historical context of Prohibition suggests that the men rescue—and drink—the beer at the expense of the national law, and possibly (though not probably) their own jobs. The commercial turns the Eighteenth Amendment into a kind of gag—something to be subverted even, and perhaps especially, by those entrusted to enforce this very law.

This widespread image of the corruption, futility, and frivolity of Prohibition, based on our limited exposure to the era and its few enduring symbols, encapsulates our common understanding of American life in the 1920s. It is easy to envision Prohibition as a national joke—an easy target for modern-day spoofs such as the Michelob commercial. Even a 1997 episode of *The Simpsons,* "Homer vs. the Eighteenth Amendment," depicts a "dry" Springfield in which Moe the bartender runs the neighborhood speakeasy, Homer smuggles bootleg whiskey inside bowling balls, and Rex Banner, the straitlaced Prohibition agent, becomes the whole town's enemy. Prohibition also functions in our popular culture as an entertaining, exciting backdrop against which authors and filmmakers set stories about gangsters, moonshiners, flappers, and other elements of the glamorous Jazz Age. Throughout the late twentieth century, movies about life during the "Roaring Twenties"—*The Great Gatsby* (1974), *The Cotton Club* (1984), *The Untouchables* (1987), and *Bullets Over Broadway* (1994), among many others—emphasize the excitement of the era by drawing on stereotypes generated at least as much by a shared mythology of Prohibition as by anything found in the historical record. More specifically, we remember the almost fourteen years of National Prohibition not as the culmination of decades of widespread social reform, religious evangelizing, and sophisticated political agitation, but rather as a fun-filled time during which young pleasure seekers and wily bootleggers matched wits against sneaky federal agents and humorless teetotalers in a "noble experiment" that was utterly doomed to fail.

Our common Prohibition-era iconography—flappers and gangsters, joyriding and jazz—has obscured many of the darker and more complex sides of American culture in the 1920s. When we imagine life during Prohibition, we see beautiful women with bobbed hair and long beaded necklaces dancing the Charleston and drinking gin punch. We see rural Appalachian moonshiners huddling around their corn-liquor still hidden high in the hills. We see exuberant partygoers in Harlem cabarets passing around a flask. We see Eliot Ness squaring off against Al Capone, machine guns blazing. We see glamour and violence, freedom and mayhem, but we sometimes fail to recognize the powerful social forces that led Americans to alter the Constitution so that selling a drink meant breaking the law. Nor do we fully grasp the pervasiveness of this legislation and how deeply it affected American society and culture.

Today, Prohibition seems to most of us a foolhardy endeavor. The idea that Americans would ever accept the federal government intervening in their private behaviors based on such a narrow definition of morality is practically unthinkable. But it is important to realize that the drinking culture in America before World War I was far different than it is today. Public drunkenness was a serious problem, and women especially lived in fear that their husbands' and fathers' heavy drinking put themselves and their children in immediate danger of impoverishment, violence, and abandonment. Indeed, in many cases they were absolutely right; as Madelon Powers explains in *Faces Along the Bar: Lore and Order in the*

Workingman's Saloon, 1870–1920 (1998), in the eighteenth and nineteenth centuries, excessive drinking was an American cultural norm to a much greater degree than it is now. Instead of concentrating on changing the behavior of drinkers, though, Prohibition supporters concentrated on banning the drink itself, earnestly believing that if the alcohol supply dried up, then drinkers would, too. The argument that laws banning liquor could eliminate Americans' desire for alcoholic beverages did in time prove spurious, but to many well-intentioned reformers of the Progressive Era it seemed a reasonable course of action. Unfortunately for these reformers, the fervor, intensity, and passion with which "dry" Americans fought for the passage of the Prohibition amendment was easily matched by "wets" who wished to subvert the new legislation.

In December 1917 Congress adopted and sent to the states the Eighteenth Amendment to the U.S. Constitution, which read, in part, "After one year from the ratification of this article the manufacture, sale, or transportation of intoxicating liquors within, the importation thereof into, or the exportation thereof from the United States . . . for beverage purposes is hereby prohibited." In hindsight, it is easy to see that one of the law's major flaws was already embedded in its language; neither buying nor drinking alcohol was outlawed—only making, shipping, and selling liquor were deemed criminal behaviors. As literary scholar John Erskine wrote in 1927, "The amendment is too vague, and it does not forbid drinking. If drinking is not wrong, we shall never feel that the manufacture of drink is wrong" (52). In January 1919, the required thirty-sixth state ratified the amendment. That October, over the veto of President Woodrow Wilson, Congress passed the National Prohibition Act, more commonly known as the Volstead Act (after its sponsor, Republican senator Andrew Volstead of Minnesota). The Volstead Act defined "intoxicating liquors" as any beverage that contained at least one-half of one percent alcohol, established fines (up to $1,000) and jail sentences (up to six months) for various violations, outlined provisions for medicinal and sacramental alcohol, and invested the Bureau of Internal Revenue—a federal office—with the authority to enforce these measures everywhere in the United States. At midnight on January 16, 1920, National Prohibition became the law of the land and remained so until it was repealed, by the Twenty-First Amendment, on December 5, 1933.

Though it officially began and ended on specific dates, it would be a mistake to think of Prohibition as merely a blip on the radar screen of American history, visible for just shy of fourteen years and then gone with the stroke of President Franklin D. Roosevelt's pen. The culture surrounding the legal limitation of alcoholic beverages spans a much longer time period and resulted from decades of persistent and highly organized temperance agitation. This social movement began in the early days of the Republic and climaxed with Americans' desperate post–World War I desire for "a return to normalcy."

Dry legislation proliferated across the country in the years immediately before World War I for a number of reasons, mostly due to the efforts and influence of temperance and reform societies. Small associations in antebellum America had been agitating for restrictive liquor laws since the Second Great Awakening, and by the late nineteenth century both the Woman's Christian Temperance Union (formed in 1874) and the Anti-Saloon League (formed in 1893) had gained national political influence. Until World War I, however, these anti-alcohol reformists mostly concentrated their efforts on state elections and local options, whereby individual counties, and occasionally states, could decide for themselves whether or not, and to what extent, to go "dry." By 1915, nineteen of the nation's forty-eight states, most of them located in the South and Midwest, had voted complete prohibition into law (the details of which were defined by these individual states), and almost half of all Americans lived in areas of the United States that had outlawed the practice of selling liquor by the drink. But as U.S. involvement in World War I escalated, temperance supporters saw an opportunity to broaden their arguments and bring their dry agenda to a wider audience. Seeing the American citizenry respond to the overseas war effort with a combination of loyal self-sacrifice, noble patriotism, and tremendous fear, the temperance societies stepped up their campaign. Reformers painted for the public a compelling political equation suggesting that federal legislation prohibiting the manufacture and sale of alcoholic beverages would result, inevitably and swiftly, in a more sober, efficient, and thrifty America.

The prohibitionists, however, would never have succeeded by basing their argument solely on an idealized vision of America. World War I offered temperance supporters a unique opportunity to exploit Americans' fervent patriotism by linking their dry cause to the concrete experience of self-sacrifice on the home front. For the first time, the federal government imposed civilian systems of rationing and conservation. As William Leuchtenberg explains in *Perils of Prosperity* (1993), the Fuel Administration limited coal and oil, instituted "heatless Thursdays," adopted daylight savings time, and closed down many nonessential factories for one day each week. In 1917 the government implemented a highly successful system of voluntary food rationing; Americans everywhere were encouraged to conserve as much as possible in order to increase food shipments to the Allied forces in Europe. Restaurants served shark and whale instead of their regular seafood offerings, bakers made coarser breads in order to conserve wheat, and grocers limited the sale of sugar to two pounds per individual per month (34–35).

Perhaps as an inevitable extension of this rationing, prohibitionists were quick to accuse breweries and distilleries of wasting grain that could otherwise be used for food. Thus a powerful alliance between temperance and patriotism was forged. In May 1917 Congress made it illegal for American servicemen to be served intoxicating beverages under any circumstances, and later that same year it forbade the manufacture of distilled alcoholic beverages from grain or any form of food, thus effectively halting the legal manufacture of spirits. Prohibitionists believed that every bottle of beer represented a potential meal for American soldiers in Europe; Maude Radford Warren, a popular novelist of the 1910s and 1920s and an ardent reformer, echoed the sentiments of many self-sacrificing Americans when she claimed, hyperbolically, that "Every man who works on the land to produce drink instead of bread is a loss in winning the War; and worse, he may mean a dead soldier" (Rogers xiii).

Anti-alcohol sentiment also fanned the flames of rising anti-German sentiment, much of it focusing on breweries and their often-German owners, workers, and patrons. Anything smacking of Germany aroused rancor; in the years surrounding World War I, many Americans were quick to associate the culture of the German American community, particularly beer brewing and drinking, with sinister alliances with the Kaiser. This antipathy became so oppressive that many loyal Americans of German descent changed their surnames in order to protect themselves from unfounded accusations of disloyalty or even treason. At times, the purging of German influence devolved into the truly ludicrous: public performances of Beethoven's music were banned in Boston, pretzels were outlawed in Cincinnati, and sauerkraut and dachshunds were to be referred to, respectively, as "liberty cabbage" and "liberty pups." Wayne Wheeler, leader of the powerful Anti-Saloon League, perpetuated destructive anti-German propaganda by insisting, in 1917, "the liquor traffic is the strong financial supporter of the German American Alliance. The purpose of this Alliance is to secure German solidarity for the promotion of German ideals and German Kultur and oppose any restriction or prohibition of the liquor traffic" (Merz 27). Naturally, many German Americans did oppose Prohibition legislation, both because of their cultural traditions and, in some cases, because the source of their livelihood actually was connected to the brewing industry. These German Americans were acutely aware of the complicated position that the war created for them; one pre-Prohibition postcard depicts a bleak cartoon of three Germans being hanged from a tree with a closed brewery in the background. In an ironic play on Benjamin Franklin's famous warning, the caption reads, "If this town goes dry, us Germans vill hang togeder [sic]."

The hostility of native-born Protestant Americans toward immigrants and foreigners extended well beyond Germans to include profound resentments toward the Irish, Italians, Greeks, and Poles. These cultures represented, to many Anglo-Americans, a culture of drinking and, in many cases, Catholicism, both of which threatened white Protestant worldviews. Political cartoons of the period typically employed the stock character of the Irishman drunk on beer and the Italian drunk on wine; the mocking stance of these cartoons thinly veiled the fear that these supposedly drunkard foreigners elicited, and prohibition propaganda of the time directly advocated suppressing the intemperate culture of these unwelcome interlopers.

Prohibitionists also championed the ideal of the efficient American worker in order to sway voters to their dry cause. Asserting that many laborers were severely impaired by their drinking habits, and that overall efficiency was drastically hampered by Monday morning absenteeism, temperance advocates persuaded business owners to vote dry in order to keep liquor out of the hands of their workforce. Feeling threatened by the flood of immigrant populations and the "Great Migration" of black southerners to northern industrial centers, industrialists such as Henry Ford enthusiastically embraced Prohibition as a much-needed measure to control the intemperate behavior of the working classes and, at the same time, perpetuate their own white middle-class values of sobriety, economy, and thrift.

The combination of all these sources of inspiration allowed dry advocates to ramrod the Prohibition amendment through Congress with amazing speed during World War I. As a result of the ultimate U.S. triumph overseas, many patriotic citizens were eager to face their grand destiny as leaders of the free world and were therefore amenable to legislation that appeared to position America as the world's moral leader. "The suppression of the drink traffic," wrote newspaper tycoon William Randolph Hearst in a 1919 editorial, "is an expression of the higher morality upon which we are now embarking" (Clark 1976, 140). Without realistically considering many of the possible negative consequences of Prohibition legislation, the nation's leaders naively assumed that U.S. citizens would embrace this interference in their private behavior for the collective good of the nation and of future generations. Indeed, less than two weeks before enactment John F. Kramer, the first Prohibition commissioner, earnestly declared, "among drunkards themselves prohibition, sooner or later, will be strongly and sincerely indorsed [sic]."[1]

What most lawmakers did not realize, of course, was that this amendment to the Constitution would become one of the biggest domestic policy fiascoes in American history. Almost completely unenforceable, National Prohibition greased the wheels of organized crime on every level,

Figure 1
Customers making their last purchases at a liquor store in Detroit before Prohibition goes into effect. Courtesy of the Walter P. Reuther Library, Wayne State University.

from the multimillion-dollar syndicates of Al Capone and George Remus to the penny-ante violations of small-town moonshiners and bootleggers. Even more significantly, Prohibition created a nation of lawbreakers out of a generally obedient citizenry, almost literally overnight. Prohibition drastically lowered the bar when it came to legal and moral transgression; millions of Americans from the president of the United States to the lowliest garbageman had his or her own favorite bootlegger, in direct violation of constitutional law. This sweeping pattern of violations set the stage for ordinary Americans to commit even further legal and moral transgressions; Congressman George Schneider of Wisconsin recognized this in 1925 when he asserted, "vice, crime, immorality, disease, insanity, corruption, and a general disregard for law, directly traceable to the unenforceability of the Volstead Act, are increasing with alarming rapidity" (Cashman 53). While Schneider's claims may be slightly overstated, he is correct in his claim that many legal and moral transgressions may have never occurred had it not been for the radical precedent set by Americans' blatant disrespect for Prohibition legislation.

Despite, or perhaps because of, the government's general failure to enforce the liquor laws, the effects of the Eighteenth Amendment on

Americans of every stripe were so far-reaching that it is hard to imagine a contemporary equivalent. While the law directly targeted adult male drinkers—the general saloon clientele—one certainly did not have to be an adult, a man, or even a drinker to be deeply affected by Prohibition legislation. Prohibition influenced practically everything about American culture in the 1920s: economics and crime, advertising and fashion, music and dancing, drama and film, education and religion, political and reform movements, even the kinds of crops raised by American farmers. In short, although Prohibition legislation remained "news" for only a brief time, for nearly fourteen years newspapers and magazines across the country were filled with daily stories detailing the sweeping consequences of Prohibition. Newspapers in particular "discussed incessantly drink's threat to youth and morality," explains historian Catherine Murdock. "By the end of the [1920s] the *New York Times* reserved a full page each day for stories on hijackings, speakeasy raids, bootleggers, and wet and dry speeches. Drys complained that such sensationalism affected citizens' faith in the amendment, which is probably true. But as one writer at the time pointed out, Prohibition was 'essentially the stuff of which news is made'" (93–94). It was Prohibition's pervasiveness as a source of both news and entertainment that led to the development of a distinct "culture of Prohibition."

Congress enacted Prohibition legislation during a time when America was struggling to define its national character and identity in the wake of World War I. Partly as a result of the domestic turmoil the country experienced during the Great Migration, the revival of the Ku Klux Klan, and the return of the American soldiers from overseas, Prohibition became, for many, a highly racialized issue. Many whites saw Prohibition as a vehicle by which they could control the behavior of intemperate blacks—a stereotype greatly strengthened by prohibition advocate D. W. Griffith's influential 1915 film *The Birth of a Nation*. Griffith's film about the redemption of the Reconstruction South, which was ultimately viewed by more than fifty million Americans, portrayed black people as drunken criminals and sexual beasts whose alcoholic sprees threatened to upset the social order of the entire nation. Critic Joan Silverman argues that one of Griffith's overarching messages in *The Birth of a Nation* was that a nationwide prohibition amendment was the country's best chance to forestall racial violence and miscegenation; according to Griffith's racist vision, Silverman maintains, when black people "have access to liquor, they give themselves airs, seize political control, [and] prey on white women. When they have access to liquor they stop working and go on rampages" (29).

The Birth of a Nation not only encouraged a return to the antebellum days of white supremacy, but it also helped inspire the reemergence of the Ku Klux Klan, a secret terrorist organization that had lain largely dormant for the preceding two generations. On Thanksgiving night in 1915, sixteen white men from Atlanta swore their allegiance to the Invisible Empire atop nearby Stone Mountain, and they soon received a charter for their society from the state of Georgia. By 1924 the Ku Klux Klan boasted more than two million members nationwide. Klan members, most of whom were Protestant fundamentalists, feared the political, social, and moral influence of Catholics, Jews, African Americans, political radicals, and immigrants of almost every variety. Klan members also mistrusted many manifestations of the "modern" lifestyle, and they believed in particular that women smoking, dancing, petting in automobiles, wearing short skirts, and drinking signified the diminishing of traditional conservative American values. In *The Ku Klux Klan in the City, 1915–1930* (1967), historian Kenneth Jackson explains, "The Invisible Empire unhesitatingly affirmed that it stood four-square for law enforcement [of Prohibition] and against bootleggers, moonshiners, and 'wild women'" (18). The Klan also traded largely on the image of drunken black men assaulting innocent white women in order to rally their forces and promote legalized prohibition, among other social causes.

Of course, Klansmen's voting behavior and their drinking behavior were not necessarily consistent. Significantly, one part of the pledge of allegiance to the Klan was never to turn in a fellow Klansman to the police except in cases of murder, treason, or similarly serious offenses. With this built-in protection system, members were free to engage in the illicit liquor trade as much as they liked. Walter White, African American novelist and long-time field secretary of the NAACP, offers a revealing portrayal of this side of the Ku Klux Klan in his 1924 novel *The Fire in the Flint,* in which a young, idealistic black doctor returns to his South Georgia town to find that the Klan has taken over the community and, ironically, moonshining has become a leading local industry. The Klansmen loudly articulate their standard pro-temperance position in public but all the while spend their free time drinking moonshine and seducing black women in the roadhouses on the outskirts of town.

Of course, one did not have to be a card-carrying member of the Ku Klux Klan to believe that Prohibition would be a useful tool in the continued civil and social subjugation of African Americans and immigrants. In a conversation between several characters in Sinclair Lewis's *Babbitt* (1922), Lewis reveals the prevailing paternalistic and self-serving attitudes of average white businessmen who vote dry in order to control the behavior of other groups of people, yet remain themselves as wet as ever. Over a pitcher of cocktails, Babbitt and his middle-class cronies discuss the endlessly fascinating subject of Prohibition and its supposed goals:

"... no one got a right to invade personal liberty," said Orville Jones.

"Just the same, you don't want to forget prohibition is a mighty good thing for the working-classes. Keeps 'em from wasting their money and lowering their productiveness," said Virgil Gunch.

"Yes, that's so. But the trouble is the manner of enforcement," insisted Howard Littlefield. "Congress didn't understand the right system. Now, if I'd been running the thing, I'd have arranged it so that the drinker himself was licensed, and then we could have taken care of the shiftless workman—kept him from drinking—and yet not've interfered with the rights—with the personal liberty—of fellows like ourselves."

They bobbed their heads, looking admiringly at one another, and stated, "That's so, that would be the stunt."

"The thing that worries me is that a lot of these guys will take to cocaine," sighed Eddie Swanson.

They bobbed more violently, and groaned, "That's so, there is a danger of that." (102)

"Fellows like ourselves" ought to be exempt from such prohibitive laws, goes their logic, since such upstanding, successful white men clearly deem themselves capable of deciding for themselves how to behave. Yet they believe that it is perfectly fine and even desirable for the government to intervene in the lives of the "shiftless workman"—that is, any fellow not "like ourselves," including African Americans, immigrants, and other people who were routinely denied the full benefits of American citizenry. Lewis's satire of these men and their self-important, self-indulgent perspectives is plain, yet the ideas articulated by these characters about Prohibition were widespread.

White racism did not abate with the passage of Prohibition. Racial tensions ran high throughout the years of Prohibition, and Jim Crow segregation reigned supreme in the South and much of the Midwest. In certain cases, however, Prohibition did function as a somewhat unifying force between white and black Americans. Some loyal drys did combine racial forces through temperance organizations that welcomed both black and white members. But because so many people agreed on the futility and foolishness of Prohibition, frequent interracial alliances (between black moonshiners and white patrons, for example) were more often forged through common disdain for the Eighteenth Amendment and common desire for liquor. Prohibition also spawned such a large underground economy that a number of black and white workers found themselves employed at the same bootlegger's warehouse or on the same fleet of drivers. The urban social scene during Prohibition also accommodated more interracial mingling than had been common previously; although speakeasies and cabarets in white neighborhoods still denied black patronage, such underground establishments in black neighborhoods often accommodated a mixed-race clientele. This white tourism to black hot spots did engender resentment and distrust on the part of many black locals, but nevertheless these examples of black and white drinkers socializing together would likely not have occurred so frequently without the influence of National Prohibition.

Another often-overlooked consequence of Prohibition legislation was the deep and painful ideological schism that it caused within African American communities. The issue of Prohibition posed serious challenges to the leadership of Harlem and other black areas and exacerbated volatile conflicts between the old and the new guard. Most prominent African American clergymen, educators, and social reformers were ardent prohibitionists who argued that temperance should be a goal of not just black America, but of any self-respecting community. For example, Kelly Miller, a minister, newspaper writer, and sociology professor at Howard University, railed against the failure of the dry experiment in America's black urban districts in his weekly columns that appeared in black newspapers across the country. Ashamed of the intemperance they witnessed in many black communities, Miller and other black intellectuals, including writer, editor, and activist W. E. B. Du Bois, journalist Edgar Grey, and the Reverend Adam Clayton Powell, Sr., warned that violating the Prohibition laws seriously jeopardized black citizens' already tenuous standing in American society. Often, these leaders focused their attacks on the highly publicized goings-on in Harlem, both because of this area's importance as the newly established cultural capital of black America, and because of its growing reputation, by the mid-1920s, as a bootlegger's paradise.

In hindsight, it seems somewhat peculiar that old-guard black leaders supported Prohibition so vehemently, considering that the national battle for Prohibition had been fought mainly by white temperance soldiers who followed strict segregationist policies and at times even allied themselves with the Klan. Yet many black leaders chose to overlook the racist ideology that tainted the Prohibition movement, believing that the greater good of racial uplift would ultimately be accomplished if dry politics prevailed. Miller, Grey, and Powell, among many others, promoted the theory that the dry experiment would foster a moral renewal of America that would lead directly to increased respect for the civil rights of African Americans. They also believed that strict enforcement of the Prohibition Amendment would, by implication, strengthen the Fourteenth and Fifteenth Amendments, which guaranteed civil and voting rights for African Americans but which were frequently ignored during the 1920s, especially in the South. The idea of Prohibition repeal particularly frightened some black intellectuals; according to historian Michael Lerner, at least one black politician publicly expressed his fear that repealing the Eighteenth Amendment would initiate a domino effect that might lead the nation to repeal other amendments, including the Thirteenth, which had abolished slavery (298).

Because these black dry leaders perceived so much at stake for African Americans regarding Prohibition, they frequently lashed out at their fellow black citizens who openly violated the liquor laws. Editorials in the *Amsterdam News,* a black New York newspaper, referred to anyone involved in the liquor trade as a "race traitor" and harshly excoriated women, who were commonly believed to support Prohibition more ardently than men, for any transgression of the Volstead Act (Lerner 298–99). To such conservative black leaders as Miller and Powell, Prohibition offered a "long-awaited opportunity to present the urban African American community as orderly, respectable, and temperate" (Lerner 299). They were profoundly disappointed to see this opportunity squandered by careless young partygoers.

While the moral leaders of Harlem raged against alcohol from pulpits and editorial pages, vehemently condemning both the customers and the traffickers of demon rum, many African Americans blithely continued their ongoing love affair with bootleg liquor. This cultural disconnection within the African American community often surfaced along generational lines. The conservative old-guard leaders of Harlem had come to power during the Progressive Era of social reform, while the younger population was largely made up of southern migrants who had relocated to Harlem during the Great Migration of the 1910s and 1920s. During the 1920s, these newly arrived southerners made up more than two-thirds of the African American population in New York (Lerner 301). Thousands of these Harlem newcomers believed that drinking was neither a sin nor a negative reflection on the race as a whole; rather, they embraced drinking culture as one important component of the newfound social freedoms they were able to enjoy in the North. Perhaps not surprisingly, relatively few migrants were willing to sacrifice their freedom to participate in Prohibition-era drinking culture because of the rebukes of Kelly Miller and other conservative critics.

Ultimately, the contentious issue of Prohibition enforcement pressed Harlem's old-guard leaders into untenable political positions. As Michael Lerner explains, the *Amsterdam News* and the *New York Age*—both African

American newspapers—"advocated stronger Prohibition enforcement in Harlem, with the *Age* going as far as to print open challenges to U.S. Attorney Emory Buckner by printing the addresses of dozens of speakeasies and asking why Buckner had not moved to close them." Moral leaders charged that the lax police presence above 125th Street was a deliberate strategy designed "to concentrate vice in the black districts" of the city. Yet when the police raided Harlem cabarets and arrested black bootleggers and their customers, these same papers alleged that law enforcement officers were unfairly targeting black citizens. In the end, Lerner asserts, the opinions of Powell, Grey, Miller, and other old-guard Harlem leaders "proved too contradictory and too alarmist to hold any weight in the Harlem of the 1920s" (336). Their oft-repeated jeremiads that disaster would befall violators of the Eighteenth Amendment were simply too exaggerated for people to take seriously, and eventually such claims significantly weakened these leaders' authority in the black community.

This inability of conservative moral and social leaders to dictate the general behavior of African Americans in Harlem added to the overall scope of Prohibition's grand failure. Many of Harlem's intellectuals, professionals, and even churchgoers defected to the wet side, marking a serious blow to the old-guard leadership of Harlem. While conservative ministers and writers continued to publish their strongly worded protests against liquor in particular and Jazz Age culture in general, new voices also emerged from within the Harlem community that rejected the old-fashioned moralism of the previous generation. These new writers vehemently denied the supposed social benefits of Prohibition and calmly accepted that drinking and vice were an inevitable part of life in the modern city. In 1925 Winthrop Lane, a writer for the *Survey Graphic,* downplayed the ability or desire of the cabaret lifestyle to exploit the average African American in Harlem:

> No doubt people are fleeced a bit in paying for their entertainment, no doubt some people are swept along pretty rapidly on a current of erotic pleasure, a current of uncertain direction and ambiguous goal. But they come there of their own accord; they seek the cabaret. As an instrument of exploitation the cabaret does not touch many people. Its scope is the scope of a retreat for devotees. (694)

David Levering Lewis concurs, arguing that most people "rose in Harlem each day to go to work, many of them before the last white revellers had careened homeward. The great majority never saw the interior of a night club" (211). True as these claims may be, plenty of Harlem residents did manage to find their way into local cabarets, and Harlem Renaissance writers including Langston Hughes, Wallace Thurman, Claude McKay, Zora Neale Hurston, and Rudolph Fisher took on the artistic and political challenges of portraying the intemperate side of Prohibition-era Harlem. As a result, they have left behind a literary legacy that offers a realistic vision of black urban life and allows readers to glimpse the inner workings of Prohibition culture in Harlem.

Many accounts of Prohibition culture have emphasized the schism between the older generation and the younger one in both black and white communities.[2] It is important to remember, however, that much of what young people of the 1920s knew about the world, they learned from their elders. Indeed, young adults constituted only a fraction of the total number of Volstead violators during Prohibition—their parents and grandparents made up the rest. In an *Atlantic Monthly* article of November 1926, "Our Dissolving Ethics," James Truslow Adams suggests that "whatever we may say of the individual of either generation . . . the responsibility of the older as a whole to the younger as a whole is—to use a liquid measure—just about in the ration of dad's quart bottle to son's half-pint flask" (577). And in Booth Tarkington's 1929 short story "The Neck, and Bush Thring," which appeared in the *Saturday Evening Post,* a young man stuns his girlfriend's father when he admits, "most everybody of my age feels that the worst of the whole prohibition evil is the way the older people seem to be showing more and more disrespect for the law and the Constitution, the older they get" (163). Despite common notions that it was the younger generation that consistently flouted the law, considerable evidence suggests that Prohibition violators came from virtually every age bracket.

Although Prohibition legislation may have affected youth and adults in somewhat different ways, drinkers of every age had some common experiences as they adjusted to life in a "dry" nation. Many urban and suburban adult male drinkers in 1920 were likely dismayed to see their corner saloon close its doors on January 16 of that year, but a number of illicit speakeasies surfaced fairly quickly to replace the outlawed saloons. Gaining access to these speakeasies was fairly easy, especially for those regular drinkers whose faces were known around the neighborhood and who clearly were not federal Prohibition agents, or "revenuers." And even far away from home, according to historian William Leuchtenberg, "in wet cities such as New York and San Francisco, the easiest way for a stranger to locate a speakeasy, it was said, was to 'ask the nearest cop,' who could usually point one out to him just a few doors away" (216).

Figure 2
A stylish young woman models a tiny garter flask, 1926.
Courtesy of the Library of Congress.

Prohibition-era drinkers soon found that, after the enactment of the new legislation, the prices of their favorite drinks skyrocketed. Of course liquor prices varied depending on geographic region, the kind of establishment one frequented, and the quality of the drink itself, but in many cases a glass of beer that typically cost a pre-Prohibition nickel would cost a post-Prohibition half-dollar, or even more. Good beer became increasingly hard to get, and many drinkers resorted to drinking highballs of low-grade whiskey or gin mixed with ginger ale or club soda, which helped to mask the taste of the alcohol. Another alternative source was medicinal whiskey; drinkers who could convince (or pay) a doctor to write a prescription for a pint of whiskey could then go to any drugstore and purchase it. Finding a bootlegger to help keep home liquor cabinets stocked seldom posed serious problems for Prohibition-era drinkers, and it was usually a fairly simple, albeit expensive, endeavor to secure a bottle or even a case of bootleg liquor. In fact, the *New Yorker* brazenly listed current bootleggers' street prices as well as popular new cocktail recipes.[3]

While people who lived in rural America necessarily responded to Prohibition somewhat differently than their urban counterparts, Prohibition permeated their culture on just as many levels. Even in the driest of rural counties, some people recognized the substantial money to be made at the expense of the Eighteenth Amendment. For example, many opportunistic farmers began to plant corn, wheat, hops, and grapes—all fermentable and therefore potentially lucrative products—instead of cotton, hay, or beans. Rural dwellers also developed their own version of the speakeasy: the country roadhouse. Usually situated just off a remote country lane, roadhouses served moonshine liquor to all who could walk, ride, or drive there. They provided rural people a place where they could drink, dance, talk, listen to music, and even conduct business. And long before 1920, moonshiners realized that the sparsely populated countryside provided countless hiding places for corn-liquor stills, and the "white lightning" that these stills produced garnered a substantial price during Prohibition.

Anyone with enough money in the 1920s could usually secure whatever kind of liquor he or she desired, although bootleggers frequently adulterated real scotch, rye, and gin, diluting them with water and adding coloring, flavoring, and additional alcohol. Obtaining genuine liquor became a challenge during Prohibition; in fact, the phrase "the real McCoy" may have originated as a reference to the impeccable reputation of Bill McCoy, a rumrunner who never sold anything but the purest smuggled whiskey. A favorite strategy of unscrupulous bootleggers was to buy empty bottles with the labels intact, fill them with inferior liquor, and charge premium prices to anyone they could trick. Those without ample means or good connections still found ways to dodge Prohibition regulations and acquire alcoholic beverages, however primitive, foul-tasting, or even dangerous. Historian John Kobler explains some of these home-grown responses to Prohibition:

> Midwestern farmers favored pumpkin wine, prepared by emptying a pumpkin, introducing cider, alcohol, or fruit, sealing the opening with wax and letting the mixture ferment for a month or so. In Kansas, another poor man's drink was white line, alcohol diluted with water; in Washington and the contiguous sections of Maryland and Virginia, panther whiskey, which had a perilously high percentage of fusel oil; in the Virginia hinterlands, jackass brandy, reputedly distilled from peaches, but likely to erode the intestines; in Philadelphia, happy Sally, jump steady, and soda pop moon, all loaded with violently toxic industrial alcohols [often isopropyl alcohol]; in Chicago, yack yack bourbon, flavored and colored with burned sugar and iodine. Skid row bums everywhere drank rub-a-dub (rubbing alcohol) and other potions containing wood alcohol, thereby courting blindness or death. Some of them would recover a few mouthfuls by squeezing Sterno through a sock. (314)

Law or no law, money or no money, a great many Americans in the 1920s were far from willing to give up alcohol, and they regularly risked blindness, paralysis, and even death to acquire their outlawed but much-beloved drink.

In fact, poisoned alcohol killed thousands of people during the 1920s—mostly poor people who could not afford to buy their liquor from reliable bootleggers. Some of Prohibition's poorest victims became permanently paralyzed after drinking poisoned "jake," or Jamaican ginger extract, which in 1930 destroyed the health of more than fifty thousand working-class and farming people in Kansas City, Wichita, Oklahoma City, Cincinnati, and the surrounding rural areas. Those poisoned were permanently paralyzed; most never walked again without canes, crutches, or walkers. They dragged their feet, rocking from one side to the other to swing their weakened legs forward, slapping their shoes to the pavement. This peculiar gait became known as the "jake walk" and the illness was called the "jake leg." In 1930, and for a short time after, both black and white southern musicians recorded more than a dozen songs referring to the jake leg tragedy; many of them either knew victims or were themselves victims. One former jake drinker recalled, "It was liquid fire, the wildest, most horrible drink you can imagine. I tried some once, just to show off, in Texas where the mark of a man was not to cut your jake with water but toss it down straight. It stoned you into a weird type of intoxication, a violent, brawling, broad-chasing insanity" (Kobler 310). It also led to the largely untold suffering of tremendous numbers of poor people of both races.

Beyond the obvious impact that Prohibition had on many Americans' health and drinking habits, the effects of this legislation permeated virtually every aspect of American popular culture, including language, music, movies, social customs, and literature. After World War I ended, Americans had something entirely new to occupy their energy and imagination: how to evade the Volstead laws successfully. Judging by the proliferation of newspaper articles and editorials, pulp fiction stories, vaudeville acts, songs, and movies that dealt with the culture of Prohibition, it seemed an inexhaustible topic for popular debate and amusement. Of course, some lost patience with this ubiquitous topic sooner than others. "Thoughtful drys, as well as wets, deplored the debasement of social intercourse resulting from prohibition," notes historian John Kobler. "Ceaseless chatter about liquor monopolized attention at dinner tables, clubs, business and professional gatherings, where to get it, how to make it, whose bootlegger sold the best stuff" (339), to the great dismay of many prohibitionists who had hoped the passage of the amendment would bring discussions of alcohol, as well as drinking itself, to a permanent end.

Just as the topic of Prohibition monopolized conversations around the country, the language of Prohibition infiltrated American English, changing in distinctive and interesting ways how people talked about their world. Colorful expressions, many of them now long passed out of use, enlivened discussions about drinking. Some terms have remained with us through the almost seven decades since repeal; we may still hear liquor referred to as "hooch" and an intoxicated person described as "stewed" or "loaded." But the amazing proliferation of terms used to describe alcohol-related experiences during the Prohibition years attests to the pervasive presence of alcohol in the national imagination. "New terms and expressions having to do with alcoholic drinks and their consumption have arisen since the adoption of national prohibition and the passage of the Volstead Act," asserted Achsah Hardin in a 1931 article in *American Speech*. "In many instances words already in existence have been given new impetus or new significance, while in other instances new words have been coined. . . . *Booze* and *bootleg* largely have replaced drink and liquor, while *speakeasy, blind pig,* and *blind tiger* have replaced saloon and bar." Hardin compiled long lists of words and phrases to describe everything from party organizations ("Drys" and "Wets" in varying degrees, "Repealers," "Weaslers," "Escapists"), enforcement agents ("Dick," "Flatfoot," "John Law," "Slewfoot," "Wheeler"), drinkers themselves ("Barrel house bum," "Jake hound," "Sponge," "Tank"), illegal drinking venues ("Boosery," "Moonlight inn," "Red Nugget," "Sample room"), liquor dealers ("Duck," "Legger," "Pour-out-man," "Shiner"), terms used for acquiring liquor ("Get a load of pig iron," "See a man about a dog"), liquor itself ("Boxcar," "Corn juice," "Giggle water," "Juniper juice," "Monkey swill," "Mountain dew," "Nose paint," "Panther sweat," "Rookus juice," "Squirrel dew," "Tonsil bath," "White mule"), and the state of being or getting drunk ("Drench the gizzard," "Hit the hotbozel," "On a bender," "Seeing snakes," "Frazzled," "Methodistconated," "Piffled," "Snozzled," "Spifflicated," "Woozey").

Other linguists and language enthusiasts also documented the transformation of the American vocabulary; H. L. Mencken devoted several pages of his seminal *American Language* to the examination of what Hardin called "Volstead English." Edmund Wilson adds, in *The American Earthquake: A Documentary of the Twenties and Thirties* (1958), that in the new language of social drinking, "more nuances are nowadays discriminated than was the case before Prohibition," and that regarding the vocabulary of excessive drinking:

> It is interesting to note that one hears nowadays less often of people going on *sprees, toots, tears, jags, bats, brannigans* or *benders.* All these

terms suggest, not merely extreme drunkenness, but also an exceptional occurrence, a breaking away by the drinker from the conditions of his normal life. It is possible that their partial disappearance is mainly to be accounted for by the fact that this kind of fierce protracted drinking has now become universal, an accepted feature of social life instead of a disreputable escapade. (91)

Throughout the music, movies, and literature of the era, references to drinking, drinkers, and their opponents were made all the more vivid and lively by the liberal use of these terms.

Prohibition stimulated the creation and circulation of dozens of songs about liquor and drinking, most often against, but occasionally in favor of, the legislation. This music, often parodies of already popular tunes with new Prohibition-related lyrics, chronicled the culture of Prohibition on a number of levels and for a number of audiences. Most of these songs had their roots in the new canons of jazz, blues, and novelty songs that enjoyed frequent airplay on the radio and vigorous record sales across the country. Songs with titles such as "The Prohibition Blues," "How Are You Going to Wet Your Whistle (When the Whole Darn World Goes Dry?)," "Bootleggers' Blues," "Moonshine Blues," "You Drink Too Much," and "Everybody Wants a Key to My Cellar," to name only a few, indicate the widespread popularity of Prohibition as a topic both of debate and of at least some amusement. Lively social music intended to be played at parties and dances frequently took witty swipes at the inefficacy of the Prohibition laws, while comparatively few popular songs of the 1920s counseled young people to obey the law and remain sober.

Like popular music, motion pictures displayed images of Prohibition culture to audiences across the country. Film historian Lewis Jacobs claimed, in his 1939 study *The Rise of the American Film*, that movies were "a powerful medium for disseminating new ideas and attitudes toward government and society, standards of taste, conduct, morals, canons of convention and culture" (Silverman 23). Moviemakers during the 1910s offered the public a steady diet of moral melodramas such as the famous *Ten Nights in a Bar-Room* (1913), based on Timothy Shay Arthur's 1854 novel, which presented a strong temperance message via the terrible fate that met drinkers. But glimpses of the high-spirited, glamorous, Fitzgerald-style response to Prohibition were in high demand from moviegoers of the 1920s, and images of wild speakeasy revelry became far more common on the silver screen than scenes of anti-saloon meetings or temperance prayer services. In fact, according to historian Catherine Murdock, movie heroes and heroines "drank far more often than bad guys" after the passage of the Prohibition laws. Murdock notes in *Domesticating Drink*

(1998) that on screen, "glamorous parties in nightclubs or country clubs featured highballs, cocktails, fancy glassware—a world apart from the lives of the audience. Images of tippling heroines merged with those of young collegians, wealthy urbanites, and daring radicals to promote drinking as a positive quality" (94).

These trend-setting movies literally taught people about current fashions, trendy dance steps, modern courting rituals, new Volstead language, and the latest cocktail recipes. They also taught viewers new and interesting ways to outmaneuver revenue agents. Historian Frederick Lewis Allen recalled how the producers of one picture advertised their film by highlighting a number of quintessential and largely appealing facets of Prohibition culture: "brilliant men, beautiful jazz babies, champagne baths, midnight revels, petting parties in the purple dawn, all ending in one terrific smashing climax that makes you gasp" (84). This trend of disregarding the legal and moral consequences of violating Prohibition laws led the Motion Picture Producers and Distributors of America to decide, in 1926, that "recent movies had dealt too frivolously with the Volstead Act, and members [of the MPPDA] instructed the president of that organization, Will H. Hays, to strike from films any 'word, phrase, clause, or sentence that directly or indirectly encourages the slightest disregard for the law.' In films made thereafter, liquor was not to be 'brought in unnecessarily in any way which might be construed as being for an ulterior purpose or which in any way promotes disrespect for the law'" (Clark 1975, 166–67). The movie producers, however, knew what the public wanted. Not surprisingly, producers continued to glamorize Prohibition lawbreakers in their popular and profitable features. In fact, according to one 1930 survey, "three out of four films referred in some way to liquor; whereas the hero drank in two out of five films and even the heroine in one out of five, the villain did so in only one film out of ten" (Barr 238). To appease their governing body, however, moviemakers often tacked on a transparent obligatory moral suggesting that drinking in violation of the law, as was so jubilantly demonstrated in the film, would ultimately lead to unhappiness and tragedy.

Like music and movies, American literature of the 1920s and early 1930s was indelibly influenced by the culture of Prohibition. Fiction of the time often doubled as cultural reportage, depicting incidents peculiar to the Prohibition era with a high level of realistic detail. Scenes in novels and short stories often take place in cabarets, speakeasies, roadhouses, buffet flats, or other venues primarily defined by their role of distributing alcohol. Literary reflections of Prohibition often include male characters who are bootleggers or rumrunners (or else are their regular customers), enthusiastic speakeasy patrons, or even government revenuers. Female

characters commonly enjoy gin or other liquors, smoke and dance in public, and otherwise embody certain elements of the liberated, stereotypical
"flapper" lifestyle. In literature, as in life, even the private consumption of
alcohol takes on political and social meanings; if the hero of a novel set in
1925 drinks a glass of whiskey, even without comment from the narrator,
the reader knows that this character probably engaged a bootlegger somewhere along the way. The author silently but powerfully sets that character
against the Prohibition cause and then asks the reader to interpret the
meaning of that transgression. Claude McKay's *Home to Harlem* (1928), F.
Scott Fitzgerald's *The Great Gatsby* (1925), Sinclair Lewis's *Babbitt* (1922),
and William Faulkner's *Sanctuary* (1931), to name only a few, all render
very different visions of Prohibition culture, but each contains elements of
Prohibition reportage.

Prohibition literature spawned stock characters that had never existed
before—indeed, there had been no real reason for them to exist prior to
1920. For example, while Prohibition did not invent organized crime, it
certainly contributed to the rise of the gangster figure in the popular imagination. His characteristics were fleshed out first by newspaper reportage
about Al Capone, George Remus, "Bugs" Moran, "Lucky" Luciano, "Big
Bill" Dwyer, Casper Holstein, and other real-life figures, but soon movies,
music, and literature began churning out gangster figures of their own.
Similarly, the bootlegger was another character borne of temperance
reform but refined by the literature, both fiction and nonfiction, that
sought to commodify his life for the reading public. The speakeasy and
other illicit drinking venues sprang into action in response to Prohibition.
But these too were co-opted by movies and novels that endeavored to teach
people how to participate in Jazz Age culture by not just reflecting but also
defining popular trends and fashionable behavior. In a similar manner, the
causes of the Harlem rent party of the 1920s—high rents, low wages, and
few good jobs—may not be directly attributable to Prohibition, but the
existence of Prohibition made it possible for hard-pressed people to raise
funds by selling illegal liquor, and for Harlem Renaissance writers to capture these gatherings in all their intensity. In all these cases and many more,
literature both imitated life and perpetuated strategies by which Americans
of every race and class evaded the Prohibition laws.

CHAPTER 2

Outside the Law:

LIQUOR PROVIDERS OF THE PROHIBITION ERA

The average self-respecting young man will shudder with disgust at
the mere thought of hunting up a sneaking bootlegger.
—*Cyclopedia of Temperance and Prohibition* (1891)

On January 4, 1920, just twelve days before the Eighteenth Amendment
went into effect, John F. Kramer, the first U.S. Prohibition commissioner,
promised the American people that soon, alcoholic beverages would be
neither manufactured, "nor sold, nor given away, nor hauled in anything
on the surface of the earth nor under the sea nor in the air" (Merz 123).
This boast returned to haunt Kramer and other guardians of the law, as
Americans quickly and easily found ways to dodge the new Prohibition
legislation. Many opportunistic citizens, when faced with the constitutional ban on their favorite beverages, promptly went into the business of
providing themselves and other thirsty individuals with the drinks they so
ardently desired. Of course, some serious risks accompanied such an
undertaking; while enforcement agents were few, and honest ones were
fewer, anyone caught and convicted of manufacturing, transporting, or
selling liquor faced fines of up to one thousand dollars and six months in
jail for a first offense. Subsequent convictions could cost as much as ten
thousand dollars and five years in prison. Nevertheless, thousands of
enterprising folks entered the illegal liquor game, believing that the potential financial gains far outweighed the risks. The identity of these people
was a poorly kept secret in most communities; despite the illegality of
their business, bootleggers and moonshiners became common and well-
known figures.

The terms *moonshiner* and *bootlegger* are often used interchangeably in
both fiction and nonfiction sources from the 1920s to describe a purvey-
or of illegal alcohol. There are, however, some general differences that distinguish the two. In broad strokes, we can imagine moonshiners as the
often-rural producers of illegal alcohol, and bootleggers as the often-urban

distributors of this liquor. Moonshiners were most often rural people, usually men, who worked their stills secretly—often, as the term suggests, by
the light of the moon. They generally distilled corn whiskey ("moonshine"
or "shine") but were also known on occasion to make and market ferment-
ed drinks such as beer and wine. While moonshiners regularly catered to
the local trade, they would also sell their whiskey to bootleggers, who
would then transport it to another city or town for resale. The term *bootlegger* originated in the nineteenth century to describe the illicit transporting of liquor in flasks hidden in the tops of tall leather boots. During the
years of National Prohibition, bootleggers specialized in the illegal transportation of liquor from one place to another; legendary bootleggers such
as George Remus owned entire fleets of powerful souped-up cars that
could outpace most police or federal agents' vehicles. Bootleggers, generally a more urban crowd than typical moonshiners, also distributed liquor
they bought from "rumrunners" (liquor smugglers), and sometimes they
even produced their own hooch by transforming various forms of toxic
alcohol into less lethal mixtures by boiling out poisons and adding flavors
and colors.

Both moonshiners and bootleggers feared interference by law enforcement agencies, but they coped with this threat in different ways.
Moonshiners went to great lengths to keep the location of their stills a
secret, often relocating the entire contraption periodically. Their best
defense against the law was to avoid detection in the first place, since few
moonshiners could afford to pay for protection from arrest. Bootleggers,
however, often interacted more brazenly with the law, and in many cases
they paid police and federal agents handsomely to look the other way during liquor deliveries to speakeasies and private homes. Bootleggers who
owned their own speakeasies or cabarets almost always had to pay police
and federal agents to prevent them from raiding the joint and smashing up
the business. While there are, of course, many variations on these basic pat-
terns, these are the essential strategies by which moonshiners and bootleggers conducted their liquor operations during Prohibition.

Despite the long shadow they cast over the illegal liquor trade, federal
revenuers generally did not pose a huge threat to the welfare of most
moonshiners and bootleggers, largely because the government had vastly
underestimated the number of agents required to enforce the Volstead Act.
In 1920 the government employed a mere 1,520 men as Prohibition
agents nationwide; ten years later that number had climbed to only 2,836.
Many of these drastically underpaid men proved eager to augment their
meager salaries with graft money from wealthy bootleggers and mob bosses. Cultural historian Frederick Lewis Allen noted (with benefit of hindsight) that the government should have foreseen the inevitable corruption

of this pitiful regiment, for "anybody who believed that men employable at thirty-five or forty or fifty dollars a week would surely have the force of character to resist corruption by men whose pockets were bulging with money, would be ready to believe also in Santa Claus, perpetual motion, and pixies" (208). Anecdotes from the period recall Prohibition agents who rode to work in chauffeured limousines and dressed their wives in luxurious fur coats, ostensibly on their weekly forty-dollar paycheck but in reality purchased with protection money paid by business-savvy bootleggers.

The advent of National Prohibition catapulted moonshiners, bootleggers, and their nemeses—the police and federal Prohibition agents—into the collective national imagination. These figures became highly visible during this era largely because newspapers across the country reported daily on the moonshiners whose stills were found and destroyed by federal agents and the bootleggers whose warehouses or speakeasies were raided by police. Magazine writers, movie producers, and Tin Pan Alley songsters also contributed to the celebrity of these illegal liquor providers by featuring them as the subjects—and often the heroes—of articles, films, and popular songs. And perhaps most importantly, moonshiners and bootleggers were personally important to countless individuals who became their regular customers, handing over top dollar for usually substandard liquor. Understandably, these outlaw personalities fascinated a number of authors writing during the 1920s and early 1930s; William Faulkner, F. Scott Fitzgerald, Sherwood Anderson, Rudolph Fisher, and Grace Lumpkin, among others, portray moonshiners and bootleggers as integral figures in Prohibition-era America. Sometimes these agents of the underground liquor economy merely lurk in the background of a particular story, while in other works they are of primary importance. But the pervasiveness of these characters in the literature of the era suggests that bootleggers and moonshiners rather quickly became full-fledged icons of American culture and were widely recognized during the years of National Prohibition as an inescapable, often useful, and always interesting part of life.

The Moonshiner

> Oh the moonshiners in the mountains, they operate the stills,
> They're true blue to each other, what they say they'll do, they will,
> They all carry six-shooters, shot guns, and bowie knives,
> And the man who tries to raid them is sure to lose his life.
> —"Prohibition Is a Failure" (1930) by Lowe Stokes and His North Georgians

Moonshining thrived in rural areas long before Prohibition became the law of the land. For centuries, even when and where the manufacture of alcoholic beverages was legal, moonshiners covertly operated their stills to make enough whiskey for themselves and their local customers and thus avoid the taxation and licensing fees that accompanied regulated liquor production and consumption. As dry laws spread into many counties and states in the late nineteenth and early twentieth centuries, moonshining became an increasingly common livelihood for those willing to risk fines and imprisonment to supply local drinkers with homemade spirits. Local and federal agents tried to enforce these liquor laws long before the Eighteenth Amendment made the whole country dry; between 1876 and 1920 Bureau of Internal Revenue agents seized nearly seventy thousand commercial stills across the country—an average of more than fifteen hundred each year. But with the advent of National Prohibition, illicit stills became an important source of alcohol nationwide, and thus moonshiners began to operate on a much wider scale. Everyone, it seemed, wanted to get in on the act, but inexperienced moonshiners proved far less adept than the old-timers at concealing their activities from the law. In only the first six months of National Prohibition, agents seized nearly ten thousand commercial-grade stills (Kobler 241).

Illegal distillation, however, was not confined to large-scale operations in the mountains and forests of rural America. Easily concealed portable copper stills, designed to produce one gallon of distilled spirits at a time and available in hardware stores for as little as five dollars, became immensely popular in urban and suburban areas during Prohibition. Early in 1920 New York City's federal Prohibition administrator, Charles O'Connor, warned, "Any person caught with one of these stills in his possession will be proceeded against at once. I advise everybody who has one to bring it to my office immediately," or else risk jail time. In response to this threat, New Yorkers surrendered not one single still. Everyone knew that most stills could be concealed quite easily from the law—little kitchen ones in homes, big commercial ones in outlying areas. Enforcement agencies simply lacked sufficient manpower to curb the practice of liquor distillation. Even the author of the Eighteenth Amendment, Texas senator Morris Sheppard, was embarrassed to learn that moonshiners had hidden a commercial still with a daily capacity of 130 gallons on his farm near Austin (Merz 54–55).

The underground liquor economy provided an important source of income for many rural people who farmed where land was poor and wage jobs were scarce. This outlaw economy was rooted in the hardships of rural America, and both literature and history suggest that a country moonshiner's life held very little glamour and contrasted sharply with the extravagant, decadent nightlife enjoyed by many wealthy urbanites during the 1920s. Living outside the law and beyond city limits, risking jail time and steep fines in order to produce whiskey that was at times barely palatable, most rural moonshiners' lives were marked by isolation and, in many cases, intense poverty. Despite their role as producers of liquor in an age when virtually no liquor was to be made legally, moonshiners remained relatively powerless figures throughout the Prohibition years, far removed from large liquor syndicates and subject to the whims of their local buyers. Those moonshiners who supplied city bootleggers with corn liquor were paid far less than their liquor was worth in urban areas, and thus the bootleggers were the ones who made the most significant profits. And many country moonshiners found themselves scraping by on the little money they brought in from friends, neighbors, and small roadhouse owners, and doing their best to hide from or outrun the law.

Writers familiar with the operations of rural, penny-ante moonshiners knew that these local distillers added to the collective experiences of many small-town folks living in dry districts before and during Prohibition. For example, in his novel *The Fire in the Flint* (1924), Walter White tells the story of an idealistic black doctor, educated in the North, who returns to his small hometown in Georgia to practice medicine. White's primary story line has little to do with Prohibition as such, but he includes details about the practices of local moonshiners not just to add regional flavor but also to indicate to the reader how even the seemingly upstanding, law-abiding citizens of Central City participated in this illicit culture of drinking. White explains how "the initiated" townspeople "drove out to certain lonely spots [and] deposited under well-known trees a jug or other container with a banknote stuck in its mouth. One then gave a certain whistle and walked away. Soon there would come an answering signal. One went back to the tree and found the money gone but the container filled with a colourless or pale-yellow liquid" (39). This system may have protected the small-town moonshiner from eyewitness identification, but it was a slow way to make money, and the fellows responsible for filling those jugs were surely not living lives of luxury.

National Prohibition had serious social and economic consequences for rural communities that, by and large, went unappreciated by urban dwellers. For many upper- and middle-class Americans living in cities and larger towns, violating Prohibition was seen as a kind of game—a thrilling endeavor to outwit the law and partake of something clearly forbidden. Defying the liquor laws often provided a sense of liberation from traditional standards of morality and propriety and made the transgressors feel powerful, independent, and modern. This spirit of "ain't we got fun" was frequently misapplied to rural dwellers, resulting in numerous depictions

in popular culture of moonshiners as happy-go-lucky, carefree, unsophisticated country bumpkins. For example, several musicians, including Gid
Tanner and his Skillet Lickers and Fiddlin' John Carson, recorded songs
and comedy sketches based on the presumed antics of wily southern
Appalachian moonshiners. The Skillet Lickers released a fourteen-part skit
on seven records about free-spirited hillbilly moonshiners, "A Corn Licker
Still in Georgia" (1927–30); the first record alone reportedly sold more
than a quarter of a million copies. John Carson's famous record series of
irreverent "Moonshine Kate" sketches (1928–30) also sold well; these
humorous narratives featured a clever moonshiner and his beautiful, sharp-
tongued daughter who repeatedly outsmarted the bumbling revenuer or
the corrupt local sheriff. But for many poor rural moonshiners,
Prohibition was no joke. The stakes were high for struggling country people for whom distilling corn liquor was one of the few means available to
supply the income needed for food, taxes, and other basic necessities.

Grace Lumpkin captured the plight of the impoverished rural moonshiner in her highly acclaimed 1932 proletarian novel *To Make My Bread.*
Heralded as one of the foremost literary chronicles of the famous 1929 textile strike in Gastonia, North Carolina, *To Make My Bread,* in the words of
critic Lisa Schreibersdorf, is a form of testimonial that "introduce[s] characters who voice 'first person' experience to provide evidence" for real-life
arguments about labor relations and the role of political activism (309).
Lumpkin incorporates into her novel a character, Bonnie, based on Ella
May Wiggins, a well-known unionist and strike balladeer who was murdered on her way to a union meeting on September 14, 1929. The inclu-
sion of this historically based character, along with Lumpkin's realistic portrayal of the miserable labor conditions that sparked the Gastonia strike,
compelled many contemporary reviewers to praise the novel for its authen-
ticity and "truth-telling." Lumpkin's ability to use fiction to recount actual historical events is not limited, however, to the circumstances surrounding the textile strike. She also paints an accurate picture of the conditions
pertaining to rural moonshiners living on hardscrabble farms in southern
Appalachia without, as one reviewer wrote in the *New York Times,* "[tak-
ing] refuge in moralistic asides."[1]

To Make My Bread has traditionally been interpreted as a commentary
on the difficulties that mountain people encountered in attempting to
make the transition to industrial life in the mill towns.[2] While this is certainly true, critics have largely overlooked the role that National
Prohibition played in contributing to the plight of already hard-pressed
rural families such as the McClures, the main characters of the novel. With
few income options available and debts at the village store mounting, the
elderly patriarch of the McClures, Granpap Kirkland, decides to team up

with the McEacherns, a local moonshining family, to generate a little money. Granpap leaves home for days at a time, carrying heavy bags of sprouted corn down the mountain and into the next state, where it is ground into sweet meal to feed the McEacherns' whiskey still. "The revenue men were thick through the mountains," the narrator notes, and the risk of capture was high. "If Granpap was caught with the sprouted corn he would be arrested. And he got very little money for the risk. The McEacherns took most of the money because they owned the still and peddled the liquor. That, of course, was most dangerous, for it meant going down into the outside" (14). The "outside" is a frightening place for these mountain people, and one that the McClures and their neighbors desperately try to avoid. Finally, the economic depression that battered rural America during the 1920s forces the McClures to descend into the nearby textile town to seek work in the mills.

Granpap represents a particular kind of moonshiner during the 1920s—the kind who turns to the illegal liquor economy as a last resort. Although he enjoys his whiskey and feels no remorse at disobeying Prohibition as a drinker, he agrees only reluctantly to disobey the laws as an actual moonshiner. But the traditional masculine role of breadwinner weighs heavily on Granpap's shoulders, and when his children and grandchildren are in danger of literally starving to death, he feels no compulsion to obey any law that denies him a way to support them. When his daughter, Emma, begs him to give up moonshining, Granpap points out that it is the law that is criminal, not the moonshiners themselves:

> "We've got a right," Granpap said, "to make money in the best way we can. You need the money—you and the young ones. How much would the bags of corn bring me if I sold them to Swain? Made into whisky I get more. We need the money, and we've got a right to make hit."
>
> "I'm not a-talking about rights," Emma insisted. "We've got a right. But the Law's got the power."
>
> "We've got the hills."
>
> "Yes. But hit's not like it was. Seems every year the outside creeps nearer. Look at that peddler, Small Hardy. The first time he come was some winters ago and now he comes every spring and always talking about the outside. And if the outside creeps nearer, the Law does, too." (71)

Like many rural moonshiners, Granpap Kirkland believes that the government has robbed him of his right to support his family, and this essentially invalidates the idea of law for Granpap altogether. Emma thus articulates a revealing tension between "the Law," which admittedly has the power, and justice, as the rural hill folks define it. Lumpkin makes clear that, in this community, the idea of justice trumps any legislation that makes it harder for a man to feed his children. Thus in this situation, breaking the law is seen as merely a legal transgression, while adhering to the law and allowing his family to starve as a result would be a far more serious moral transgression. This important distinction between the legal and moral implications of National Prohibition also surfaces in other 1920s and early 1930s texts, including Fitzgerald's *The Beautiful and Damned,* Lewis's *Babbitt,* and Faulkner's *Sanctuary.* For Lumpkin's Granpap and others like him, both in southern Appalachia and elsewhere, to obey the newly established and erratically enforced liquor laws would be a far worse sin than to break them.

Unfortunately for Granpap and the rest of his family, the law, as immoral as they believe it to be, prevails. One day a neighbor comes to Emma's door with the dreaded news: "the Law's got your pap" (82). Emma's son Kirk understands the sacrifice that Granpap has made for his family, but his self-centered brother Basil, who desperately wants to abandon his mountain life to become one of the educated and "civilized" townspeople, can hardly contain his bitterness. Focusing solely on how people from town will perceive his grandfather's imprisonment, Basil condemns Granpap's decision to moonshine with the McEacherns:

> "Hit's a disgrace," he said.
>
> Emma raised herself. "Hit's not a disgrace, Basil McClure, unless you make it so."
>
> "Granpap's broke the law."
>
> "For you and the others, to get money to feed ye."
>
> "He had a right," Kirk said, looking jaunty under his bandage, and very sure of himself.
>
> "Hit's a disgrace," Basil repeated. "Up at the settlement they'll look at us and say, 'The law's got Granpap Kirkland.'"
>
> Emma looked at him. "And there'll be plenty to say he had a right," she told Basil. (82)

Although Kirk and Emma understand Granpap's actions as adherence to a code of justice that supersedes the power of the Volstead Act, Basil's preoccupation with the illegality (and therefore disgracefulness) of Granpap's actions obscures, for him, the difficult moral dilemma that his grandfather faced. The elderly moonshiner is sentenced to two years in prison, but before the court remands him, Granpap angrily declares to the judge that "he'd fought in the Confederacy, and he'd done his duty and he had a right to make money when his folks needed money. No government could take that right away" (87). Granpap's futile courtroom outburst echoed the feelings of many Americans, impoverished or otherwise, who believed that the government's effort to outlaw an economic opportunity as important as whiskey production was both cruel and unjust.

A similar scenario, but with far less overt political rhetoric, appears in Sherwood Anderson's short story "A Jury Case," collected in *Death in the Woods* (1933). Although the collection met with mixed reviews when it was first published, reviewer Louis Kronenberger pointed out that in these stories "there are evocations of phases and moments in American life which, as things go, are the real thing."[3] "A Jury Case" revolves around three rough mountain men living in an undefined rural area who pool their money to buy a still and go into the moonshine business together. The most ruthless of the men, Harvey Groves, had a father who was a notorious moonshiner in the area. The elder Groves, the narrator relates admiringly, was "one of the kind that can make pretty fair whisky out of anything. They make whisky out of potatoes, buckwheat, rye, corn or whatever they can get—the ones who really know how" (189). At the age of twenty-five, Harvey enters his father's "profession" with Cal Long and George Small, each paying one-third of the cost of a small copper still. The narrator describes how the moonshiners in the area made "moon whisky in a small still—it's called 'over-night stuff'—about fourteen gallons to the run, and you make a run in one night. You can sell it fast. There are plenty of men to buy and run it into the coal mining country over east of here. It's pretty raw stuff" (191). Harvey, Cal, and George set about running their new still, and are beginning to make a success of it, when Harvey decides to cheat his partners:

> [O]ne night after they had made and sold two runs, Harvey stole the still from the other two.
>
> Of course Cal set out to get him for that.
>
> There wasn't any law he and George Small could evoke—or whatever it is you do with a law when you use it to get some man.
>
> It took Cal a week to find out where Harvey had hidden, and was operating, the still, and then he went to find George.
>
> He wanted to get Harvey, but he wanted to get the still, too.
> (194)

Cal and George approach Harvey's hideout, and Cal manipulates George, the weaker man, into shooting and killing Harvey. The sheriff apprehends the two shortly afterward, and George is arrested for Harvey's murder. But unlike the judge in *To Make My Bread,* who sends Granpap Kirkland to prison for two years, in Anderson's story the mountain folk refuse to let the law interfere with their notions of justice. The narrator comments at the end of the story that if any local jury tries George Small, "even though the evidence is all against him . . . the jury will just go it blind and bring in a verdict of not guilty" (200).

While Lumpkin portrays Granpap Kirkland as a positive, well-meaning character who is unfairly victimized by the Prohibition laws, Anderson's moonshiners in "A Jury Case" are all deeply unsympathetic characters. Both lawless and merciless, they mistreat their families and their business partners, and they stop at nothing to exact revenge on one another. Nevertheless, even though Cal and George are clearly guilty of not just moonshining but murder, jurors from that remote mountain county would rather allow a known killer to go free than submit to outside judgment and obligations to a law that they do not support. Furthermore, the story suggests that Harvey's murder was, to some extent, justified; he was attempting to rob Cal and George of what was seen in their community to be a legitimate livelihood. In this way, the moonshiners in Anderson's story, like Granpap in Lumpkin's novel, occupy a space beyond not just the Prohibition laws, but beyond "the Law" in general. And although Anderson certainly does not depict Harvey, Cal, and George as moral heroes, they are actors in a highly moral system that privileges independent living and responsible local decision making over remote federal legislation and the sort of "justice" found in court.

While "the Law" exists far beyond the isolated mountain hollows of *To Make My Bread* and "A Jury Case," it occupies a much more central role in *Sanctuary* (1931), William Faulkner's consummate novel about Prohibition culture. The action is divided among several settings, including a rural moonshiner's hideout, a small town in Mississippi, and the city of Memphis; the story focuses on the privileged daughter of a judge, Temple Drake, and a doomed court case in which an innocent man is convicted and lynched for a murder he did not commit. Although Faulkner at times dismissed *Sanctuary* as merely "a cheap idea . . . deliberately conceived to make money" (Singal 154), in fact the novel represents the foremost literary depiction of rural Prohibition culture in our contemporary American canon. While the novel seldom refers to the liquor laws directly, virtually every element of the plot is concerned, in some way, with specific aspects of the culture of Prohibition. The characters of Temple Drake and her ill-chosen boyfriend, Gowan Stevens, could not have been conceived before the Eighteenth Amendment began to influence the behavior of young collegiate men and women. Popeye, the malevolent bootlegger, offers readers a glimpse into the sordid underworld of Memphis fueled by the profits made from illegal liquor sales. Lee Goodwin and the other misfit moonshiners who manufacture and sell whiskey out at the "Old Frenchman place" provide illuminating examples of outlaws living on the fringes of small-town southern society. And Ruby Lamar, Lee's long-suffering common-law wife and former Memphis prostitute, singles out Prohibition as the cause of much of her considerable misery.

A 1931 *New York Times* review of *Sanctuary* praised Faulkner for his ability to evoke "the southern underworld of decaying poor whites, of moonshiners, of half-wits and harlots and madames," and the powerful way in which he tells "a complicated story of human evil working out its strange and inevitable destiny."[4] Indeed, none of the characters is spared a ruthless interrogation of his capacity for evil, and often this evil is linked to the influence of alcohol. From the very first scene, Faulkner establishes the context of the story as one steeped in the culture of drinking and shrouded in antisocial criminality. The novel opens, "From beyond the screen of bushes which surrounded the spring, Popeye watched the man drinking" (3), and only afterward does it become clear who Popeye is, whom he is watching, and what the man is drinking. When the lawyer, Horace Benbow, looks up to see the strange man staring at him as he drinks from the spring, he immediately assumes that he is about to be accosted by a bootlegger or gangster and says defensively, "If it's whiskey, I don't care how much you all make or sell or buy. I just stopped here for a drink of water. All I want to do is get to town, to Jefferson" (6). Benbow's assumption is basically correct; Popeye is, in fact, a bootlegger waiting for his truck to arrive from Memphis. He transports and sells the corn liquor made by a band of local moonshiners, and this plot detail immediately sets the stage for a story awash in sex, violence, and illegal alcohol.

Faulkner biographer Richard Gray asserts that much of *Sanctuary*'s narrative substance arose from the author's "own experience of the dark underbelly of Southern life: his acquaintance with local moonshiners, his visits to the bars and brothels of Clarksdale and Memphis, his knowledge of notorious gangsters like 'Popeye' [Neil Karens] Pumphrey—a wealthy bootlegger who was supposed to be cripplingly shy with women" (163). Indeed, Faulkner's intimate knowledge of the underground liquor economy informs many details of *Sanctuary,* especially those depicting the uneasy relationship between the so-called respectable townspeople, including Horace Benbow, Gowan Stevens, and even Temple Drake, and the outlaw moonshiners living in the remote, decaying mansion known as the Old Frenchman place. After their initial encounter at the spring, Popeye forces Benbow to return with him to the hideout, ostensibly to make sure that he is not a revenue agent. Through a number of details that surface during the conversations among the moonshiners, Faulkner reveals his own sophisticated understanding of the mechanics of the illegal liquor trade. For example, when the educated but naive Benbow asks the slow-witted Tommy why, as a part of Lee's operation, he allows Popeye and the "Memphis folks" to drive the truck full of moonshine back and forth to Tennessee, Tommy patiently explains to him, "Aint no money in these here piddlin little quarts and half-a-gallons. Lee just does that for a-commodation, to pick up a extry dollar or two. It's in makin a run and getting shut of it quick, where the money is" (21). Even the simple-minded Tommy understands the economics of bootlegging better than Benbow, and Faulkner's portrayal of the small-town lawyer ignorant in the ways of the country moonshiners suggests the profound disconnection between life within and beyond city limits.

The contradictory stance that the townspeople of Jefferson take toward Prohibition becomes particularly apparent through the trial of Lee Goodwin, who has been wrongly accused of Tommy's murder. For four years Goodwin had quietly made and sold liquor to local citizens with neither any interference from the law nor any complaints from the grateful buyers. But as soon as he finds himself in trouble, the townsfolk quickly change their minds and imagine him capable of corrupting the morals of their supposedly upstanding, law-abiding community. Because many of them equate lawlessness regarding Prohibition with lawlessness in general, they draw the simple but faulty conclusion that if Goodwin is willing to violate the Volstead Act, he must also be willing to commit murder. With disgust, Benbow tells Miss Jenny, his widowed sister's elderly great-aunt-in-law, the town gossip regarding Goodwin's situation:

> "[Goodwin's] business out there is finished now, even if the sheriff hadn't found his kettles and destroyed—"
> "Kettles?"
> "His still. After he surrendered, they hunted around until they found the still. They knew what he was doing, but they waited until he was down. Then they all jumped on him. The good customers, that had been buying whiskey from him and drinking all that he would give them free and maybe trying to make love to his wife behind his back. You should hear them down town. This morning the Baptist minister took him for a text. Not only as a murderer, but as an adulterer; a polluter of the free Democratico-Protestant atmosphere of Yoknapatawpha county." (127)

Benbow's ire may have reflected Faulkner's own feelings toward hypocritical drinkers who purchase illegal liquor and yet act as if they are beyond reproach. According to biographer David Minter, Faulkner himself had purchased liquor from local moonshiners for many years, and "he admired their courage and resourcefulness, and even shared some of their contempt for 'respectable' society" (108). Unfortunately, in this case, hypocrisy prevails. Goodwin's now unavoidably public reputation as an outlaw moonshiner dooms him from the start, and the townspeople's prejudice against him, coupled with Temple's perjured testimony, positions him as a scapegoat for the murder and, ultimately, the victim of a lynch mob.

Faulkner uses several characters in *Sanctuary* as mouthpieces for critical commentary regarding Prohibition; interestingly, all of them wish for a system—unlike the one in place—that could effectively outlaw liquor traffic in America. Ruby, Lee Goodwin's common-law wife and the mother of his sickly baby, indignantly declares to Benbow that moonshiners like her husband and his cronies "don't break the law just for a holiday," and that if she had her way, "I'd hang every man that makes it or buys it or drinks it, every one of them" (161). Ruby indirectly blames the ineffective Prohibition laws and all that they engender for the desperate situation in which she and Goodwin find themselves. Ruby is not alone in her frustration with the way that Prohibition culture forced the producers of illegal liquor to the very bottom rung of the social ladder. Benbow also blames Prohibition for the ills that befall men involved in the liquor trade. Taking Ruby's morbid wish one step further, he fantasizes to Miss Jenny, "I'm going to do what [Ruby] said; I'm going to have a law passed making it obligatory upon everyone to shoot any man less than fifty years old that makes, buys, sells, or thinks whiskey" (166). Even the brutal Popeye, when he sees the men congregated on the porch of the broken-down house one night, muses to himself in a moment of surprising dark humor, "Jesus Christ . . . I told [Goodwin] about letting them sit around all night, swilling that goddam stuff. There ought to be a law" (96). There *is* a law, obviously, but the ineffectual Volstead Act fails to satisfy these characters' desires for a world in which liquor, and its attendant problems, does not exist.

In fact, a surprising measure of anti-alcohol sentiment appears in the novel, as Faulkner reveals the extensive liquor-related corruption not just in small-town Mississippi, but also in the cities of Jackson and Memphis. At one point in the novel, Senator Clarence Snopes, Jefferson's state representative, endeavors to explain to Benbow the sordid goings-on surrounding the illegal liquor traffic in Jackson. When Benbow ingenuously asks him, "How are things going at the capital?" Senator Snopes paints for him "a picture of stupid chicanery and petty corruption for stupid and petty ends, conducted principally in hotel rooms into which bellboys whisked with bulging jackets upon discreet flicks of skirts in swift closet doors" (175). Thus, it is not particularly surprising that Senator Snopes locates the missing Temple Drake on one of his frequent trips to the whorehouses in Memphis, a city known in the 1920s as the murder capital of the United States and where the underworld culture of Prohibition flourished unchecked. In fact, a murder in a speakeasy called the Grotto foils Temple's one attempt to escape from Popeye's control. She covertly arranges to meet Red—a man she believes will rescue her—at the Grotto, but Popeye finds out about her plan, accompanies her to the speakeasy, and murders Red in cold blood. Red's funeral, also held at the Grotto, is hosted by a wealthy bootlegger named Gene who decants bottles of booze into a punchbowl while urging his heavy-drinking guests, "Come on, folks. It's all on Gene. I aint nothing but a bootlegger, but [Red] never had a better friend than me. Step up and drink, folks. There's more where that come from" (244). In this world, even funerals are held in speakeasies rife with violence and saturated with illegal liquor.

What Faulkner reveals throughout *Sanctuary* is not the gleeful, mischievous attitude of the patrons at urban cabarets who revel in their transgressions against the law and propriety. There are no scenes of exuberant partiers dancing the fox-trot or enjoying conversations over a pitcher of highballs, such as those in F. Scott Fitzgerald's *The Beautiful and Damned* (1922), Carl Van Vechten's *Nigger Heaven* (1926), or Wallace Thurman's *The Blacker the Berry . . .* (1929). Rather, Faulkner's transgressors are grim, desperate people. The moonshiners, epitomized by Lee Goodwin, are abused not only by the law enforcement agents whose job it is to prosecute them, but also by their collaborators in crime, the liquor buyers, who demonstrate no loyalty to or sympathy for them. The city bootleggers are callous criminals, mired in a violent world of murder and corruption without any real possibility for redemption. Politicians such as Senator Snopes drag their honorable positions through the mud by taking slugs off flasks of smuggled booze in out-of-town hotels and whorehouses. Temple Drake turns desperately to gin as a means of temporarily escaping her unendurable transformation from popular college student to sexual prisoner. Liquor even punishes Gowan Stevens, the recreational drinker; after all his insufferable bragging about how real men learn to drink at the University of Virginia, Stevens invariably vomits, passes out, or makes monumentally bad decisions (such as abandoning Temple at the Old Frenchman place) when he imbibes. Very little joy or pleasure comes from the bottle in this novel, but immeasurable suffering begins and ends there.

Sanctuary's bleak portrait of the ills of liquor and the culture that surrounds it comes as something of a surprise given that Faulkner himself had neither fondness nor respect for the Prohibition laws. He, like many other American writers of his generation, felt indignant that the government would attempt to improve the collective morality of the nation by intervening in the private affairs of its citizens. He further lamented the fact that so many Americans were in favor of such prohibitive legislation. In 1950 Faulkner, living in the still-dry county of Lafayette, Mississippi, nearly twenty years after the repeal of National Prohibition, wrote a letter to the editor of his hometown newspaper, the *Oxford Eagle,* proclaiming, tongue-in-cheek, how he resented being cast as a proponent of legal beer because he was "as much an enemy of liberty and enlightenment and progress as any voting or drinking dry" in town. He went on to assert the so-called "virtues" of keeping Oxford dry:

> Our town is already overcrowded. If we had legal beer and liquor here where you could buy it for only half of what we pay bootleggers . . . we would have such an influx of people, businesses and industries with thirty and forty thousand dollar payrolls, that we old inhabitants could hardly move on the streets; our merchants couldn't sleep in the afternoon for the clashing and jangling of cash registers, and we older citizens couldn't even get into the stores to read a free magazine or borrow the telephone.
>
> No; let us stick to the old ways. Our teen-age children have cars or their friends do; they can always drive up to Tennessee or to Quitman County for beer or whiskey, and us graybeards who don't like to travel can telephone for it, as we have always done. Of course, it costs twice as much when it is delivered to your door, and you usually drink too much of it, than if you had to get up and go to town to get it, but better [that] than to break up the long and happy marriage between dry voters and illicit sellers, for which our fair state supplies one of the last sanctuaries and strongholds.[5]

Faulkner's sarcasm is unmistakable, and his points are well taken. The era of moonshiners is not over even today; despite general repeal of Prohibition, home manufacturers still attempt to dodge licensing fees and taxes by secretly distilling their whiskey, and local newspapers in rural areas still chronicle the occasional raid on an outlaw still. But the heyday has passed. "The long and happy marriage between dry voters and illicit sellers" that Faulkner described in his 1950 letter was still on its riotous and sometimes violent honeymoon during the 1920s, and nowhere is that more evident than in the literature of the time.

Despite the common popular culture depictions of moonshiners as carefree country bumpkins, many Prohibition-era writers did indeed cast them as complicated, and sometimes miserable, characters. Moonshiners in American literature often occupy the unenviable role of social outcast; their illegal profession separates them from mainstream society, and their lack of wealth and power prevents them from attaining any significant level of social respectability. Bootleggers, on the other hand, appear to have had more social mobility than moonshiners, perhaps due to their more urban and suburban centers of operation and their greater income potential. While moonshiners in Prohibition-era fiction suffer the indignities of pursuit and arrest, and in some cases even death, bootleggers, for the most part, fare rather better in the novels and short stories of the period.

The Bootlegger

Don't Shoot, I'm Not a Bootlegger
—Automobile sticker popular in the 1920s

American writers of the Prohibition era embraced the outlaw character of the bootlegger, and the variety of works in which he—for bootleggers in literature were nearly always men—appears during this period testifies to his remarkable flexibility. Bootleggers in Prohibition-era fiction run the gamut from high-society tycoons like Jay Gatsby in F. Scott Fitzgerald's *The Great Gatsby* (1925), to sleazy lowlifes like Henry Patmore in Rudolph Fisher's *The Walls of Jericho* (1928). Bootlegging in the United States was a surprisingly egalitarian occupation, and Prohibition legislation made it possible for anyone with a little ambition and enough money to buy a few pints of booze to make money selling it on the black market. Thus, although Gatsby and Patmore had little else in common, they shared a "profession" that catapulted them into prominent positions in their respective social circles.

Although bootleggers often entered the illegal liquor trade as individual entrepreneurs, many of them soon became caught up in the world of organized crime. Powerful mob bosses such as Al "Scarface" Capone in Chicago and Salvatore "Lucky" Luciano in New York recognized the virtually unlimited amounts of cash to be made thanks to the Eighteenth Amendment, and they wasted no time creating their bootlegging networks, establishing their territories, and intimidating their competition. Bootlegging syndicates, like the legal business conglomerates that also emerged in the 1920s, understood that securing market shares and gobbling up rivals was the best way to ensure continued financial success. Liquor shipments were perpetually being hijacked; cases of booze stolen or smuggled from one source were often stolen again before reaching their final destination. Gangland bootleggers occasionally paid for their crimes with jail time and fines, but they lived to a great extent beyond the reach of the law. Protective and well-bankrolled gang leaders would simply "put the fix" on police, federal agents, and even judges, paying them regularly in exchange for protection from legal interference in their thriving "business."

Bootleggers boldly infiltrated virtually every corner of American life. Historian Herbert Asbury claims that "By the spring of 1920, [college] campuses swarmed with bootleggers, and most college towns supported a larger number of speakeasies than they ever had saloons" (*The Great Illusion* 162). A 1925 *New York Times* headline announced, "Harvard Warns Bootleggers To Keep Clear of Dormitories," and the article went on to quote a university policeman as commenting, "We are at last getting the situation [of on-campus bootlegging] under control, something we have been trying to accomplish ever since prohibition was supposed to come into force."[6] Even the government that crafted the Prohibition amendment and the Volstead Act was not innocent. Mabel Walker Willebrandt, the assistant U.S. attorney general, lamented in *The Inside of Prohibition* (1929) that "Bootleggers infest the halls and corridors of Congress and ply their trade there," and she alleged that members of Congress and other government officials considered themselves "above and beyond the inhibitions of the prohibition law" (113).

Despite their awareness of the close connection between organized crime and bootlegging rings, many Americans simply refused to believe that bootlegging was a serious crime. Unlike the shadowy mobsters who aroused fear in the general population, bootleggers were generally considered useful associates who could provide booze quickly and reliably, albeit at exorbitant prices. The citizenry's casual attitude toward bootlegging in the 1920s is affirmed by court records, which suggest that juries exercised tremendous leniency in Volstead violations cases. Historian Norman Clark cites one prosecuting attorney who notes in his annual report, "the few convictions for liquor violations were of visitors or those to whom no jury could have had sympathy. Our own bootleggers are small retailers who, if convicted at all, the juries seem to have a feeling that the possession of intoxicating liquor of such inferior quality, is enough punishment, in itself" (163). And in some instances wealthy bootleggers actually bankrolled important social welfare initiatives; the infamous Al Capone himself sponsored soup kitchens and charitable organizations in Chicago. While powerful bootlegging kingpins did intimidate the masses, many people felt rather sympathetic toward local bootleggers who provided them with the liquor they insisted on having.

The fine art of bootlegging took a number of forms in the 1920s. One common bootlegging tactic was to smuggle booze across the Canadian border into the United States, using whatever vehicles were available. Records indicate that smugglers transported liquor in every imaginable container, including pocket flasks, hot water bottles tucked inside their

Figure 3

A gentleman modeling a "vest" used for smuggling liquor under an overcoat, Detroit, ca. 1920. Courtesy of the Walter P. Reuther Library, Wayne State University.

clothes, hollow canes, toboggans (in the winter, of course), baby carriages, bicycles, rowboats, cars, and even armored trucks. One Works Progress Administration (WPA) oral history chronicles the adventures of a bootlegging gang from Barre, Vermont, whose members made their money crossing back and forth across "the Line" (the U.S.-Canadian border) with carloads of smuggled ale. The narrator recalls:

> My brothers, the older ones, had a gang bootlegging. They had a bunch of big old Packards and Caddies. I went in with 'em and we made plenty dough. There was dough in that racket all right, and it was fun to bring it in. Times was good then [i.e., during Prohibition], everybody had money, everybody was spending it . . .
>
> We ran mostly ale. We got it in Canada for five bucks a case and sold it here for fifteen or twenty. You could load a lot of ale into those big crates we had. We kept five or six cars on the road all the time. We sold [to] everybody in Barre and Montpelier from the poolroom crowd to the town bigshots. . . . We ran a lot of stuff 'cross that Line, I'm telling you. . . .
>
> We know the officers and they know us. You know, the same as

you know football players on another team, something like that. There was one French sonofabitch gave us plenty of trouble. We lost a few loads but we never lost a man. . . . When the patrol started chasing us I'd hold 'em up, block the road on 'em, to let the boys with the loads get away. We had a smoke-screen [a device that poured thick smoke out of the back of the car] on the pilot car. We'd come hell-roaring down over that Line and hit back roads all the way home. We had hideouts in barns and garages along the way. Some of the people we had to pay, some we just had to leave a case of beer.[7]

This perception of bootlegging as a game that pitted the clever bootleggers against the humorless police and federal agents frequently appears in oral histories and literary accounts of the Prohibition era. While this dichotomy certainly was true to some extent, it is important to remember that this so-called game cost many lives. The *Washington Herald* conducted a survey in 1929 that revealed at least 1,360 people had been fatally shot by federal agents or local law enforcement during the first decade of Prohibition, and at least one thousand more were wounded (Asbury, *The Great Illusion* 167). Untold numbers were killed in episodes of gangland violence. Thousands more died from drinking tainted liquor distributed through bootlegging operations. In 1923 the *Ladies' Home Journal* advertised its latest issue, featuring an article titled "Murdered by Bootleggers," with these allegations: "Twenty-nine government agents have been murdered by bootleggers and rum runners. Thousands of 'moderate drinkers' have been poisoned by deadly bootleg booze. Decent citizens, who shudder at the thought of murder, who have never committed robbery or arson or bigamy, break the Constitutional law without compunction. Defiance of the Prohibition is a national joke."[8] While dodging Prohibition laws may have seemed like a "joke" to many citizens, or may have been nothing more than a game to this Vermont bootlegger in his souped-up Cadillac, others felt less of a thrill living outside the law.

Stanley Walker, in his entertaining contemporary study of New York's nightlife during Prohibition, *The Night Club Era* (1933), offers a more sober look at the figure of the urban bootlegger. Because Prohibition made it possible to make a great deal of money through the unregulated underground liquor traffic, Walker explains, many people erroneously believed that bootleggers were automatically "friends of the prohibition law." To prove his point, Walker cites an acquaintance of his as an example of a bootlegger who felt victimized because his status as a liquor purveyor put him in close contact with the criminal underworld. This particular bootlegger, Walker notes, "made money, but he had his headaches. He was, like so many others, a law-abiding citizen at heart. He would no more have swindled anyone, or forged a check . . . than he would have shot down babies with a machine-gun or slipped a customer a Mickey Finn. He liked to run a place where gentlemen came to drink and talk and eat, and that was all there was to it. He would have much rather done it legally," but the law no longer allowed for such a place to exist unmolested (35).

Most bootleggers, however, apparently spent more time expanding their liquor business and spending their money than they did longing for the good old days of legal, pre-Prohibition saloonkeeping. To keep their business growing, some bootleggers moved into another common liquor racket that involved the distribution of medicinal whiskey through so-called pharmacies. During Prohibition, the Volstead Act permitted doctors to prescribe whiskey to their patients for medicinal purposes; this fact was greatly abused by almost everyone with access to a prescription pad. In 1920 tens of thousands of doctors (or alleged doctors) suddenly applied for licenses to dispense medicinal alcohol. In one WPA oral history, a former bootlegger describes the process of dodging the laws regarding medicinal alcohol:

> Listen, plenty goes on in a drug store. In prohibition they used to peddle booze. . . . Well, why not? A shot of good rye is the best medicine yet for whatever ails you. The counter man has the blanks, see, and if he's in cahoots with a doc who wants to pick up a little extra, he'll sell a book of blanks, signed by the doc, to a legger, who fills in for how many cases he wants to take out, and it goes under the prescriptions. On an R.X. [*sic*] you're covered, see, and if any questions asked, it's the doc takes the rap.[9]

Many drugstores became primarily concerned with dispensing whiskey rather than medicine, and crooked pharmacists, doctors, and bootleggers were able to launder vast amounts of money through these so-called pharmacies. By the end of the decade, huge drugstore syndicates had become some of the largest illegal liquor operations in the country.

The notorious Cincinnati bootlegger George Remus was primarily responsible for making pharmacies as important as speakeasies in terms of selling Prohibition-era liquor. Working exclusively with medicinal alcohol, Remus became a multi-millionaire largely because he had the foresight to purchase a government-authorized medicinal distillery in 1920. By 1924 he owned fourteen distilleries that were supported by a huge network of drugstores dispensing medicinal whiskey (Behr 95–97). The connection between pharmacies and bootlegging did not escape the hard-drinking F. Scott Fitzgerald, who was undoubtedly acquainted with the procedures involved in acquiring whiskey from a drugstore. In Fitzgerald's most

accomplished novel, *The Great Gatsby,* the specter of bootlegging and illegitimate drugstores, as well as stolen bonds, hovers in the background of
the luxurious lifestyle enjoyed by the mysterious Jay Gatsby.

Gatsby's shadowy personal history fascinates many of his hundreds of
party guests, most of whom have never met him and probably would not
recognize him in person. Guessing wildly at the nature of his business and
the source of his money provides amusement to those partygoers who
assume the worst of him yet are all too eager to visit his impressive mansion and drink his expensive liquor. At one of Gatsby's frequent social
events, a woman who clearly has never met her host asserts confidently
and casually to her friend, "He's a bootlegger . . . One time he killed a man
who had found out that he was the nephew to Von Hindenburg and second cousin to the devil" (61). Apparently the evils of liquor, Germans, and
Satan are inextricably linked in the mind of this drunken partygoer.
Others also speculate on Gatsby's links to the liquor black market; even
Nick Carraway, Gatsby's friend and the narrator of the novel, admits that
among Gatsby's acquaintances, "contemporary legends such as the 'underground pipe-line to Canada' attached themselves to him" (98). In fact,
large-scale bootlegging represented one of the few logical explanations as
to how anyone in the early 1920s from an unknown family could have
accumulated such an incredible fortune at such a young age.

Although he becomes Gatsby's close friend (primarily because he is
cousin to Gatsby's long-lost love, Daisy Buchanan), Nick remains aston-
ishingly oblivious to Gatsby's real line of work. When Daisy's husband
Tom accuses Gatsby of having criminal connections, the loyal Nick immediately dismisses these allegations, but without any justification or evidence to the contrary.

> "Who is this Gatsby anyhow?" demanded Tom suddenly. "Some big
> bootlegger?"
> "Where'd you hear that?" I inquired.
> "I didn't hear it. I imagined it. A lot of these newly rich people
> are just big bootleggers, you know."
> "Not Gatsby," I said shortly. (109)

Either Nick is in utter denial of Gatsby's profession or he is wholly faith-
ful to his idealistic vision of his neighbor, for Nick seems to possess
absolutely no curiosity regarding the source of Gatsby's considerable fortune. Even their vague conversation about Gatsby's "little business on the
side," during which Gatsby offers Nick a chance to "pick up a nice bit of
money" doing "a rather confidential sort of thing" (83), apparently fails to
arouse Nick's suspicions. Remarkably, neither does their odd meeting with

underworld boss Meyer Wolfsheim, who assumes that Nick is the man seeking "a business gonnegtion" about which he and Gatsby had spoken previously (71). Nick seems perfectly satisfied with Gatsby's facile explanation that he inherited his money from his deceased family.

Others, however, are not so easily pacified by Gatsby's unlikely explanation of his past. Tom Buchanan, in particular, feels driven to unmask Gatsby as a criminal and a bootlegger. After attending one of Gatsby's lavish parties, Tom fumes, "I'd like to know what he is and what he does . . . and I think I'll make a point of finding out." Daisy responds with what Gatsby himself had admitted to her: "He owned some drug-stores, a lot of drug-stores. He built them up himself" (110). Tom's deep distrust of Gatsby, coupled with his understanding of drugstores as bootlegging fronts, compels him to make further inquiries that actually reveal to the reader Tom's own connections with underworld figures. Tom learns through a friend of his named Walter Chase (who served jail time for his connections with Gatsby and Wolfsheim) that at least part of their racket involves the distribution of medicinal alcohol. When Gatsby informs Tom that Daisy wants to end their marriage and run away with him, Tom desperately goes on the attack, using the only ammunition he has at his disposal:

> "I found out what your 'drug-stores' were." He turned to us and spoke rapidly. "He and this Wolfsheim bought up a lot of side-street drug-stores here and in Chicago and sold grain alcohol over the counter. That's one of his little stunts. I picked him for a bootlegger the first time I saw him, and I wasn't far wrong." (134)

Tom's strategy works; Gatsby defends himself wildly against these accusations while Daisy retreats further and further into herself, finally realizing that whatever fantasy she had had of her reunion with Gatsby was now nothing but a "dead dream." At the end of the afternoon Tom sends Daisy and Gatsby home together, confident that Gatsby's "presumptuous little flirtation" has come to a quiet, if bitter, end (135).

Tom's friend Walter suggested that Gatsby's speakeasy-drugstores made up merely a small part of Gatsby's larger empire, and, later in the novel, more veiled references to Gatsby's underworld enterprises confirm this suspicion. While in Gatsby's house, attending to funeral details, Nick fields an unexpected long-distance call from Chicago. Thinking that it must be the phone call from Daisy that he has been expecting, Nick answers eagerly:

> "This is Slagle speaking . . ."
> "Yes?" The name was unfamiliar.

"Hell of a note, isn't it? Get my wire?"

"There haven't been any wires."

"Young Parke's in trouble," he said rapidly. "They picked him up when they handed the bonds over the counter. They got a circular from New York giving 'em the numbers just five minutes before. What d'you know about that, hey? You never can tell in these hick towns—"

"Hello!" I interrupted breathlessly. "Look here—this isn't Mr. Gatsby. Mr. Gatsby's dead."

There was a long silence on the other end of the wire, followed by an exclamation . . . then a quick squawk as the connection was broken. (167)

This brief, somewhat cryptic conversation confirms for the reader what Tom suspected all along—Jay Gatsby's involvement in not just bootlegging but an even bigger operation: stolen bonds. Yet, as critic Thomas Pauley has noted, Nick seems surprisingly unruffled by this piece of news. Indeed, this revelation does nothing to undermine what Pauley calls Nick's "startling conclusion that [Gatsby] is essentially an innocent victim of other people's heartlessness" (233). The textual evidence indicates, however, that quite the opposite is true. Gatsby's meteoric rise to the top of such a powerful syndicate of illicit alcohol and illegitimate bonds suggests he was an extremely clever criminal who was far more devious than anyone, especially Nick, could have imagined.

Thomas Pauley asserts that "Jay Gatsby effectively overturned the dated assumption that gangsters were lowlifes from the Bowery and replaced it with an upscale figure who was enviably wealthy and fashionably stylish" (225). Gatsby's posturing as a "gentleman," however, was not uncommon for prosperous bootleggers during the Prohibition era. Many bootleggers and gangsters accumulated so much money and power during the 1920s that the next logical step appeared to be breaking the only barricade left: entrance into the highest echelon of elite society. Gatsby's desire to redeem himself in Daisy's eyes by owning an extravagant home and material luxuries was consonant with many historical accounts of rich gangsters attempting to buy respectability with their fat bankroll of liquor money. For example, George Remus threw countless parties in his attempt to be accepted by the upper crust of Cincinnati; William Vincent "Big Bill" Dwyer entertained high society elites at his grand estate on Long Island; and Lucky Luciano bragged about his close relationships with the Bachs, the Whitneys, and other prominent New York families.

The practice of selling whiskey as a so-called druggist quickly became, in both black and white communities, a pseudo-respectable occupation.

Claude McKay mentions this phenomenon in *Harlem Glory* (1999), his brief, posthumously published portrayal of black life during the 1930s, in which he recalls, "Harlem was the paradise of bootleggers. . . . Prohibition had made the defiance of the laws general and racketeering respectable" (15). The tremendous profits available in liquor trafficking led men of varying races and socioeconomic classes to buy their way into decent society and thus become what was known as a "gentleman bootlegger." Such social maneuvers were not limited only to the very wealthy or even to whites. George Schuyler and Theophilus Lewis lampoon this phenomenon as it existed in Harlem in their "Shafts and Darts" column, published in the August 1925 issue of *The Messenger:*

> Someone must hustle the hooch from manufacturer—foreign or domestic—to the ultimate consumer, and someone must go through the motions of preventing them from doing so. So we have the bootlegger, and the enforcement officer; flowers of 20th century *syphilization.* The latter generally accepts his position because he is too cowardly or lazy to be a bootlegger, the former has with his usual audacity re-inforced [*sic*] by great wealth, begun to force an entrance into society. Of course the fact that he IS a bootlegger is not mentioned aloud in polite circles. We hear of him as a "druggist," a "perfumer" or some other innocuous name, and often he has such an establishment for a blind for his more lucrative business. The increase in the number of Negro druggists is positively amazing.[10]

Rudolph Fisher also takes up this idea of the "gentleman bootlegger" forcing his way into exclusive society in his novel *The Walls of Jericho.* Henry Patmore is a successful Harlem bootlegger who carefully cultivates his persona as a well-bred, well-dressed, highly cultured individual. Yet Fisher makes it painfully clear that "Pat" does not behave like a gentleman, and in the course of the novel he attempts to rape a young woman and deliberately sets fire to a man's home. Patmore may aspire to belong to uppercrust Harlem society, but his actions suggest he is little more than a common thug, quick to use violence to achieve his goals.

Both black and white critics of the late 1920s praised Fisher for his honest depiction of ordinary working-class Harlem residents in *The Walls of Jericho.* Fisher affectionately portrayed the rough camaraderie of life in the speakeasies and pool halls of Harlem, while at the same time focusing on a love story between a hard-working piano mover named Shine and a morally upstanding maid named Linda. But just as central to the plot are the crooked dealings of Henry Patmore, the neighborhood bootlegger and owner of Patmore's Pool Hall. Reminiscent of real-life Harlem underworld figures such as millionaires Barron Wilkins and Casper Holstein, Patmore looks and acts the part of the freewheeling, self-confident businessman. He also takes an aggressive interest in women, and the narrator explicitly describes how Pat was known in the neighborhood to be "a perfect ladies man":

> He had all the qualifications: money to burn, with a constant large supply of bank notes on his person—after the fashion of bootleggers—excellent taste in dress, as exemplified tonight by a sack suit of light greenish gray, a shirt of slate radium silk with collar to match, a bright green satin cravat caressing a diamond question mark, and a breast pocket polka dot handkerchief, whose crepe border matched the tie. He was large and self-assured with an engaging manner and a flashing smile. (40)

Despite these attractive but superficial qualities, Patmore is most assuredly the villain of the novel, and his sinister nature quickly bleeds through his carefully posed exterior and ostentatious wardrobe.

Like Jay Gatsby, Patmore carefully assesses his position in the community and then takes advantage of it to its fullest potential. Unlike Gatsby, though, his goal is not to recreate one perfect, magical love. Rather, Patmore attempts to conquer sexually as many women as he can—if not by attracting them with his charm then luring them with his considerable money. As a result,

> Patmore's conquests were many and his reputation enviable. Nor can it be denied that he made the most of this reputation among his fellow men, taking little pains to conceal either the nature of his activities or the identity of their object. He even allowed it to be suspected that there were dickty[11] homes where he made it convenient to deliver liquor only during the hours when the head of the house was absent. Of this he did not openly boast, of course, at least, when he was sober. That would have been bad business indeed. (41)

As a businessman, Patmore should know better than to do anything to jeopardize his liquor dealings. But, as Fisher intimates, unlike the light-drinking Gatsby, Patmore's judgment is sometimes clouded by his propensity to enjoy his own product just a little too much.

Patmore's Pool Hall is a primary setting of the novel, and the place where Shine and his cronies spend a great deal of their time drinking, gambling, and quarreling. As the owner of this establishment, Patmore is a high-profile member of the community, and his patrons accordingly pay him the respect he demands. He is far from merely a benevolent barkeeper, however, and his malevolent tendencies surface early in the novel. After he learns that Fred Merrit, a wealthy light-skinned attorney, has made plans to move to Court Avenue, an exclusive white street on the outskirts of Harlem, Patmore explains to Shine his own uncomfortable relationship with Merrit. Ten years earlier, when Patmore had run over and killed a pedestrian with his car, Merrit negotiated a ten-thousand-dollar fine that kept Patmore out of jail. The bootlegger still holds a grudge against Merrit but tells Shine that he has forgiven and forgotten Merrit's involvement in that payoff. Now Patmore claims that he wants to become Merrit's liquor supplier, but he fears their earlier dealings would make Merrit reluctant to trust him. So Pat pitches a business partnership to Shine, enticing him to act as the "agent" in a shady bootlegging scheme:

> "Listen. I'm handling a Canadian Club that'll sell itself, no stuff. If I can get him to sample it, he'll take it—order it for himself and recommend it to his friends. It's bound to go big, see? But here's the thing: if he knows I sent it he'll figure I'm trying to poison him and be scared to touch it, see? Now I got half a case on hand he can have and I got ten bucks you can have if you deliver it along with his things in the morning. . . . With your job, you could work up a wonderful delivery service for me no suspicion attached to it, see? Here's your chance, man—start out as my agent." (17–18)

Shine immediately recognizes that behind all this talk of Canadian Club whiskey and no hard feelings, Patmore actually plans to deliver poisoned liquor to his nemesis and then let Shine take the fall. Shine declines Pat's offer at once, but what neither Shine nor the reader understands is that Patmore's vengeful plans to destroy Merrit are not so easily squelched.

Unable to find a way to poison the attorney, Pat jeopardizes the safety of others in the Harlem community by burning Merrit's house to the ground. Patmore takes advantage of residents' predictable assumption that a black resident would not commit such a heinous act. Indeed, most onlookers immediately attribute this act of arson to angry whites seeking retribution for Merrit's unwelcome presence on an all-white street. Furthermore, although both Shine and Merrit know for certain that Patmore is the arsonist, nothing in the novel indicates that he will be tried or punished for his crime. Even Merrit, who has suffered the most for Patmore's crimes, grudgingly acknowledges his admiration for the devious bootlegger smart enough to execute such a perfect crime. And the other patrons of Patmore's seem only to admire him the more for his aggression toward Merrit, the "fay nigger" who endeavored to move out of Harlem proper onto the prestigious Court Avenue (144). At bottom, it seems that there is little Patmore can do to alienate his patrons. His status as a rich, powerful, and ruthless bootlegger ensures his reputation as an unassailable leader and neighborhood hero.

The bootlegger's frequent appearance in the literature of Prohibition-era America is often overlooked or underrated by today's readers. While bootleggers have essentially disappeared from our contemporary cultural experience, they were important figures during the 1920s, both experientially and symbolically. The bootlegger, to many, occupied an impressive and enviable position in society; he was perceived as brave enough to defy the U.S. Constitution for a living, smart enough to get very rich very fast, ambitious enough to ally himself with powerful protective forces, and clever enough to supply ordinary Americans with booze that they could not have acquired themselves. Evil bootleggers, in literature at least, are seldom portrayed as evil *because* they are bootleggers. Rather, malevolent figures such as Henry Patmore or even Popeye are evil in spite of their occupation. Jay Gatsby's casual comment "What about it?" when Tom first accuses him of selling liquor at his drugstores encapsulates an entire generation's collective response to the accepted role of the bootlegger in Prohibition-era America.

The Prohibition Agent

> The dry agent, not alone by the intrinsically unpopular nature of his calling, but by his duplicity, his bad manners, his cheapness, and his occasional brutality, made himself the symbol of all that was wrong with the law.
> —Stanley Walker, *The Night Club Era* (1933)

Few figures of the Prohibition era were more maligned than the federal agents hired to enforce the Volstead Act. Hated by the wets for trying to enforce an unpopular law, hated by the drys for wallowing in the corruption so endemic to Prohibition, federal agents had few friends and many enemies. Theirs was truly an impossible task: to dry up the supply of liquor that was illegally flowing into the country or being manufactured behind closed doors. They were charged with closing down all illicit watering holes, from grimy speakeasies to grand cabarets. A force ten times—or perhaps even a hundred times—the size of the force actually employed by the Bureau of Revenue could not have done the job. Historical accounts of the period suggest that most agents quickly wearied of trying to sweep back the tide of illegal alcohol with their pitiful little brooms. They made the occasional raid on a speakeasy for the sake of appearances and then spent the rest of their time drinking and loafing in their favorite blind pig.

Of course, exceptions did exist. Two of the most famous prohibition agents, Izzy Einstein and Moe Smith, were by far the most effective and well-known revenuers in the country. Although they were assigned primarily to New York City, Izzy and Moe actually traveled on numerous out-of-town assignments to make arrests in New Orleans, Hollywood, Cleveland, St. Louis, Atlanta, Pittsburgh, Chicago, and several other cities. Bootleggers and speakeasy proprietors from coast to coast feared Izzy and Moe for their uncanny ability to gain the trust of whoever was serving drinks in a particular joint. Often, the agents relied on clever disguises and phony accents to pull off their bust. They posed as everything from orchestra musicians to rabbis to pickle salesmen in their quest to wheedle drinks from unsuspecting barkeepers, and they made almost five thousand arrests in fewer than five years on the job. The Bureau of Revenue ultimately fired Izzy and Moe, allegedly for unprofessional behavior but actually because they made the rest of the force look so woefully inept.[12]

Stanley Walker described what he believed to be the more typical "swinish prohibition agent" in New York—a drastic contrast to the honest, hard-working Izzy and Moe. These ordinary agents' blatantly corrupt behavior elicited nothing but scorn from onlookers:

> In New York the agent could walk less than a block from his headquarters before setting out to dry up the town, and get a wonderful meal and all he could drink for nothing—at any one of several places. It became the custom of these indolent fellows to establish certain protected hang-outs all over the city, places where they forced the proprietor to pretend that they were welcome, and to use them as a base for operations. It was a common sight in certain New York speakeasies to see a group of agents enter a place at noon, remain until almost midnight, eating and drinking, and then leave without paying the bill. (51)

Despite their relatively small numbers, Prohibition agents were a fairly public presence. They might not have made very many arrests, but they were a visible part of the urban landscape.

In the literature of the Prohibition era, however, the federal agent occupies a much more shadowy position. He seldom appears as an actual character, even in works preoccupied with drinking culture, yet his presence is distinctly felt throughout a number of important Prohibition-related texts. In fact, like the bogeyman, the revenue agent seems to be a more effective literary device when he remains poorly defined. Perhaps this is because if an agent were to be portrayed as an actual character, he might be seen for what he is—an individual with a wife and children to support, albeit with the frequent assistance of ill-gotten graft and kickbacks. So instead of risking readers' sympathy for such a character by fleshing out his motives and intentions, most authors simply allow the dreaded Prohibition agent to skulk in the background. The reader does catch occasional glimpses of him—usually with his feet propped up on the bar, enjoying his fill of free drinks while the speakeasy proprietor helplessly refills his whiskey glass over and over again. The Prohibition agent appears briefly in *The Walls of Jericho,* hanging out in the gambling room of Patmore's Pool Hall and playing cards with the neighborhood regulars in much the spirit of Stanley Walker's description. Prohibition agents also make cameo appearances in Wallace Thurman's *The Blacker the Berry . . . ,* in which they attempt to bust some obviously inebriated cabaret-goers, and in Claude McKay's *Home to Harlem* (1928), in which they raid a popular buffet flat. But in none of these works does the enforcement agent warrant more than a derisive passing glance.

The revenue agent much more frequently makes "off-screen" appearances in the literature of the Prohibition era. He arrests Granpap Kirkland for moonshining in Grace Lumpkin's *To Make My Bread,* but the reader only hears of this incident secondhand. He also prowls in the backgrounds of Faulkner's *Sanctuary* and Anderson's "A Jury Case," finding and smashing stills only after the moonshiners have already been arrested or run off. Seldom is the agent the first on the scene, bravely combating the crime and corruption that pervaded Prohibition-era America. Rather, the revenue agent in literature is portrayed as a cowardly creature, living off graft when he can and arresting the powerless when he must. For most fiction writers, the compelling stories belonged to the violators of the Prohibition laws, not those to whom the law was entrusted.

Of course, exceptions to this rule do exist, and in most cases these exceptions are to be found in pro-Prohibition literature. Writers who position revenue agents as central figures in their stories tend to occupy an anti-liquor stance best achieved by making the crusader against alcohol the hero. One notable example of the heroic revenuer is Kip Tarleton, the earnest federal agent at the center of Upton Sinclair's *The Wet Parade* (1931), an unabashedly pro-Prohibition novel that advocated both increased government dedication to the problem of enforcement and enthusiastic grassroots political agitation by conscientious, reform-minded citizens. Sinclair himself was a lifelong teetotaler who was haunted by the memories of his alcoholic father and of his two dear friends, novelist Jack London and poet George Sterling, both heavy drinkers who ultimate-

Figure 4
Texas customs agents posing with confiscated Mexican liquor, 1928. Copyright by and courtesy of the Photography Collection, Harry Ransom Humanities Research Center, The University of Texas at Austin.

ly committed suicide. In *The Wet Parade,* Sinclair drew upon his own New York City childhood in the creation of his two central characters, Maggie May Chilcote and Kip Tarleton, both of whom turn radically against alcohol after witnessing their fathers' harrowing ordeals with alcoholism.

Critic William A. Bloodworth claims that the reform-minded Sinclair had been planning to write a pro-Prohibition novel since at least 1930, when he was scandalized by a poll published in *Literary Digest* alleging that a majority of Americans favored the repeal of the Eighteenth Amendment (128). Firm in his erroneous belief that most Americans supported Prohibition, and that the shortcomings of the liquor legislation were due to lax government enforcement and corrupt revenue agents, Sinclair embarked on a novel that was to demonstrate, beyond any reasonable doubt, the righteousness and viability of the Prohibition cause. Despite his personal enthusiasm for Prohibition, Sinclair himself acknowledged, in a 1931 letter, that he was in the process of writing a "very bad prohibition novel" (Harris 268). The avowedly "wet" H. L. Mencken, Sinclair's long-time friend, had little patience for his anti-alcohol stance and even less for his heavy-handed writing style. In his review published in *The Nation,* Mencken marveled that in *The Wet Parade,* "Mr. Sinclair undertakes a feat unprecedented in swell letters: he makes a Prohibition agent his hero." In doing so, Mencken continues sarcastically, Sinclair's "cunning as a literary artist does not diminish. His dialogue is highly polished. 'Please, please, Papa!' cries Maggie May to her wine-cursed father, Mr. Roger Chilcote. 'Please do not drink any more!' 'Oh, little girl, little girl,' he replies, 'what can Papa do? I cannot give it up! It is a fiend that has got me!'"[13] Stanley Walker concurred with Mencken's criticisms, noting in his review that sentimental passages of *The Wet Parade* "are hacked out as if with a meat-ax, and the writing is devoid of charm."[14]

Although the novel is plagued with many embarrassing attempts at dramatic dialogue, *The Wet Parade* actually received a number of positive reviews from conservative publications, including one from *Christian Century* that effused, "it is a whale of a book."[15] Several reviews likened the novel to Harriet Beecher Stowe's *Uncle Tom's Cabin* in that both novels offer highly sentimentalized stories of innocents who have suffered unjustly from a pervasive social ill—in Sinclair's case, excessive drinking by a loved one. *The Wet Parade* also sold better than many of Sinclair's previous novels, and in 1932 it was made into a successful feature film for MGM (also called *The Wet Parade*) starring Myrna Loy, Robert Montgomery, Jimmy Durante, Walter Huston, and Lewis Stone (Harris 268–69).

Despite Sinclair's obvious political agenda, *The Wet Parade* offers today's readers a great deal of insight into the ways in which Prohibition legislation affected both the urban residents of New York and the bayou dwellers of rural Louisiana, where Maggie May's family owns a sugar plantation. And Sinclair does attempt to portray both sides of the Prohibition debate, giving voice to the "wet" argument primarily through the characters of journalist Jerry Tyler and poet Roger Chilcote, Jr., who fervently believe that "it was every citizen's duty to break such a [repressive] law as much as possible, because the sooner it was discredited, the sooner it would be repealed" (259). But the darlings of Sinclair's novel are Maggie May Chilcote, the zealous temperance activist, and her husband Kip Tarleton, the revenue agent killed in the line of duty in the final chapter, which is predictably called "Sacrifice." Too honest to accept any of the considerable graft money offered to him, Kip spends his days and nights walking the streets of New York in his shabby clothes, collecting evidence against speakeasy owners and suffering the abuse heaped on him by friends and strangers alike. As the narrator notes near the end of the novel, "Yes, it was too bad that a decent fellow should have gone into such a disreputable business; making himself into a snooper and a sneak, lying to people, and taking advantage of their hospitality to betray them and send them to jail! So the public thought about a prohibition agent" (404). Sinclair's project, in part, is to disabuse the public of their uncharitable views toward revenuers, offering the example of a kind husband and gentle father who devotes his life to public service simply because, as he tells his supervisor, "I believe in prohibition" (328).

As Mencken points out in his review, Sinclair does make a radical departure from most Prohibition-era fiction by casting a teetotaling prohibition agent into the unlikely role of hero. Unfortunately, Kip himself is a rather unlikely character: loyal, brave, and almost nauseatingly honest. In a scene midway through the novel, Kip loses his comfortable position as assistant estate manager after he refuses to lie to the police about his wealthy and powerful employer's bootlegging operation. Later, he swallows his masculine pride in order to assist his wife in her successful career as a temperance lecturer. Kip would obediently "carry on Maggie May's correspondence, and keep track of dates, and collect her fees when there were any, and clip the comments in the newspapers, and mark the favorable passages. On the evening of the lecture he would put on his best clothes, and carry her wrap . . . [N]ow and then, behind his back, people would refer to him as Mister Maggie May Tarleton" (310). When serving as his wife's secretary and manager becomes too humiliating even for the slavishly devoted Kip, he joins the Prohibition service to further the cause in which he and his wife so fervently believe. The fact that after six years of toil he is martyred to this cause, shot to death by a bootlegger, only reinforces his wife's hatred of "the Demon Rum" that had "taken her father, her brother, and now her husband" (426). Maggie May channels her grief into activism, offering temperance supporters a slogan that also concludes the novel:

PROHIBITION HAS NOT FAILED!
PROHIBITION HAS NOT BEEN TRIED!
TRY IT! (431)

Sinclair's ultimate point, offered through Maggie May's public entreaties, is that Prohibition is a just cause that will ultimately succeed not through better law enforcement but through the active support of militant women who are not afraid to storm the doors of speakeasies everywhere and thus "break the power of John Barleycorn over our nation!" (430).

Upton Sinclair's *The Wet Parade* is not, of course, the only successful pro-Prohibition novel of the 1920s, though it is perhaps the only one penned by an American author widely recognized in the twenty-first century. Other popular writers of the Jazz Age did compose novels that exposed the systemic corruption that hindered enforcement of the liquor laws, including such now largely forgotten works as Ednah Aiken's *If Today Be Sweet* (1923), Charles Francis Coe's *Hooch!* (1929), Lawrance M.

Maynard's *The Pig Is Fat* (1930), and Royce Brier's *Crusade* (1931). Yet all these works highlight not the horrors of alcohol consumption but the impossibility of rigorously enforcing Prohibition given the inadequate financial resources appropriated by the government and the overwhelming determination of the drinking citizenry to have their booze, whatever the cost. Most authors of the era, regardless of their personal feelings about Prohibition, recognized that Prohibition agents, tainted by corruption and graft, were frequently part of the problem rather than part of the solution. Thus their demonization in the fiction of the age comes as no great surprise; it is only the occasional honest agent, such as Kip Tarleton, who surprises us.

When one tries to imagine the culture of Prohibition today, wily Appalachian moonshiners and indolent New York federal agents may not spring to mind as quickly as, say, the carefree flapper or the machine gun–toting gangster. Yet all varieties of liquor providers—the moonshiners who distilled it, the bootleggers who sold it, and the federal agents who usually allowed these activities to go on unmolested—played critical roles in the evolution of Prohibition culture. Many contemporary writers acknowledged the contributions these figures made to daily life by incorporating such characters into their panoramic vision of Jazz Age America, yet too often references to these individuals slip by unnoticed. To understand the cultural landscape of the 1920s and early 1930s portrayed in the literature of that era, readers must attend to the depictions of moonshiners, bootleggers, Prohibition agents, and other important figures in the underground liquor traffic. These representations resonate with significance specific to that chapter of our nation's history, and understanding the culture that spawned these figures adds to our appreciation of the literature produced during the "dry decade."

CHAPTER 3

These Wild Young People:

DRINKING AND YOUTH CULTURE

We have educated [youth] too well for them to respect our present goings-on.
—John Erskine, "The Prohibition Tangle" (1927)

People of all ages disobeyed the Prohibition laws, and they did so for innumerable reasons. Some drank because they felt no obligation to obey a law they found ridiculous, or because they enjoyed the taste of alcoholic beverages, or because they were alcoholics and couldn't stop drinking. Others drank for the social interactions that were provided by cocktail parties or evenings at a nightclub. Still others—particularly young people—drank because defying the Prohibition laws functioned much like bobbing one's hair, dancing the camel walk, smoking cigarettes, and tearing around town in automobiles; it signified one's embrace of a rebellious, modern lifestyle. Members of the "older generation" wrung their hands and wrote shrill letters to the editor decrying "these wild young people" and their bold disregard for traditional values and behaviors. But no amount of moralizing could keep many young people from carrying hip flasks, attending cocktail parties, and patronizing speakeasies with a brazen, defiant attitude that many of their elders believed typified, as Frederick Lewis Allen put it, the "Problem of the Younger Generation," a problem that quickly became "a topic of anxious discussion from coast to coast" (79).

National Prohibition certainly did not create a cultural "generation gap" in the United States, but it coincided with a remarkable reorientation in American popular culture that focused on youth and youthfulness. This evolution of a specifically youth-oriented culture, especially one that appeared to defy the moral authority of its elders and rebel against long-established social conventions, greatly alarmed many members of the older generation. Historian Paula Fass writes in *The Damned and the Beautiful* (1977) that after World War I, older people perceived that youth culture had appeared "suddenly, dramatically, even menacingly on the social scene" (6). They bewailed this youthful menace in countless articles and editorials citing the breakdown of traditional morality, and they blamed young people outright for upending the traditional social order. Naturally, the young resented being perpetually cast as scapegoats for all the ills of modern society; one exasperated young writer lamented in a 1920 *Atlantic Monthly* article, "hardly a week goes by that I do not read some indignant treatise depicting our extravagance, the corruption of our manners, the futility of our existence, poured out in stiff, scared, shocked sentences before a sympathetic and horrified audience of fathers, mothers, and maiden aunts—but particularly maiden aunts."[1] These fissures between the younger generation (broadly thought of as people between their middle teens and their middle twenties) and the older generation of their parents and grandparents emerged in the early moments of post–World War I America. Soon these fissures widened into a full-fledged generation gap, forever altering the relationships between young and old and permanently modifying commonly accepted standards of behavior.

Although American youth shouldered much of the responsibility for the dissipation of traditional social behaviors, these same youth simultaneously found themselves the focus of an intense cultural obsession. As immoral and disrespectful as they appeared to some older people, many perceived youth to be "smart," "frank," and otherwise appealing, even glamorous, figures who invented and enacted the latest fashions. Almost overnight, movies and advertising transformed youthfulness into a valuable commodity to be bought and sold in the marketplace. Thus, at the very same moment that young people were being reproached for their callous disregard for traditional conduct, they were also being lionized by people twice and three times their age, who slavishly imitated their clothing styles, haircuts, slang phrases, and dance moves. The young were at once America's cultural leaders and its social scapegoats for a single reason: they were seen as the embodiment of all that was new, radical, and "modern." Modernity, however, proved to be a dangerous, double-edged sword.

Youth culture of the 1920s garnered so much attention, from so many distinct perspectives, that looking back from our vantage point it appears that nearly all of America during that decade must have been white, well-off, and college-aged, full of confidence and power, craving liquor and cigarettes. Of course, this was far from the case. But because of the American media's obsession with the stereotypes of the daring flapper and the rugged collegiate man, Prohibition-era movies, music, literature, and advertisements featured their stories over and over again. In truth, the stereotypical images of the white, privileged flappers and sheiks had as little to do with the real-life experiences of most young people as Al Capone did with the average Prohibition-era bootlegger. Movies, advertisements, and periodical literature often exaggerated their depictions of outrageous young people to the point that they became mere caricatures—little more than symbolic repositories for the anxieties of an older generation. Whatever fears and insecurities the newly emerging modern life engendered, from the danger of cars to the immorality of contraception, it seemed that they could all be blamed on the irreverent, decadent, ill-mannered youth.

Countless discussions and examinations of youth culture, as represented by the figures of flappers and their beaux, appeared in newspapers and magazines around the country throughout the decade. "Flapper Jane," a descriptive article by Bruce Bliven, appeared in a 1925 issue of *The New Republic*—an unusual choice for a magazine generally devoted to politics and economics, but perhaps indicative that the flapper had by this time clearly invaded all realms of public life. The article primarily identifies the outward characteristics of a typical flapper and then probes very briefly into the attitudes that embody the flapper lifestyle. "Jane," the author's Every-Flapper, is "a very pretty girl" who is "heavily made up, not to imitate nature, but for an altogether artificial effect—pallor mortis, poisonously scarlet lips, richly ringed eyes—the latter looking not so much debauched (which is the intention) as diabetic." Bliven goes on to describe in some detail Jane's modern new wardrobe, which includes nothing more than shoes, stockings, a short dress, and "step-in" underwear.

> A step-in, if you are 99 and 44/100ths percent ignorant, is underwear—one piece, light, exceedingly brief but roomy. Her dress, as you can't possibly help knowing if you have even one good eye, and get around at all outside the Old People's Home, is also brief. It is cut low where it might be high, and vice versa. The skirt comes just an inch below her knees, overlapping by a faint fraction her rolled and twisted stockings . . . The corset is dead as the dodo's grandfather . . . The petticoat is even more defunct . . . The brassiere has been abandoned, since 1924. . . .
>
> These which I have described are Jane's clothes, but they are not merely a flapper uniform. They are The Style, Summer of 1925 Eastern Seaboard. These things and none other are being worn by all of Jane's sisters and her cousins and her aunts. They are being worn by ladies who are three times Jane's age, and look ten years older; [and] by those twice her age who look a hundred years older. (243)

This "flapper uniform" may not describe the clothing and hairstyle of every woman in the eastern United States, as the author alleges, but it does, to varying degrees, describe characters as different in lifestyle and background as Temple Drake in William Faulkner's *Sanctuary* (1931), Harriett

Williams in Langston Hughes's *Not Without Laughter* (1930), Cordelia Jones in Wallace Thurman's "Cordelia the Crude" (1926), and Gloria Patch and Daisy Buchanan in F. Scott Fitzgerald's *The Beautiful and Damned* (1922) and *The Great Gatsby* (1925), respectively, as well as countless other young women who populate the literature of the 1920s and early 1930s.

Regardless of whether members of the older generation approved or disapproved of youth culture as it existed in the 1920s, they had no choice but to deal with it. The "revolution in manners and morals," as writers frequently referred to the effect that the younger generation had on American culture of the time, was far too widespread and influential to be ignored. An advertisement in a 1925 issue of the *Saturday Evening Post*, addressing the older generation, recognizes the power that youth had on everyday life:

> You may regard the new generation as amusing or pathetic; as a bit tragic, or rather splendid. You may consider their manners crude, their ideals vague, their clothes absurd. Their cynical, humorous discussions of social conditions may stir you to admiration or fill you with helpless rage. But it is useless to deny that these youngsters have a definite bearing on the thought, literature, and customs of our day. (Stevenson 142)

Youth Culture of the 1920s

> . . . the most terrible of all the evils of prohibition is the affect [*sic*] on our children and our young people in teaching them disrespect for law. Aren't all the little children in the land growing up to hold the very Constitution of our country in disrespect and contempt?
> —Booth Tarkington, "The Neck, and Bush Thring" (1929)

American literature did a remarkable job of chronicling the lives of Jazz Age icons such as the flapper and her beau, the "sheik." These young characters often represented newly emerging standards of morality and expressed their commitment to behaving more freely than their parents' generation by engaging in what were considered, at the time, radical behaviors. Countless young women smoked cigarettes, wore makeup, rolled their stockings down below their knees, dressed in revealing outfits, and danced suggestively and sensually with young men to the popular new jazz music. Hemlines rose along with college enrollment—women as well as men flocked to university campuses to partake not just of higher education but also of the fast-paced social scene. And throughout all these transformations rumbled the constant tension between carefree lawlessness, best symbolized by the cocktail glass and hip flask, and the pressures of conforming to more traditional standards of behavior.

The beautiful young flapper has come to symbolize the flamboyant 1920s in our collective imagination, but the term itself predates the Jazz Age by at least a century. H. L. Mencken explains that in early nineteenth-century England, *flapper* denoted "a very immoral young girl in her early teens"; by the early twentieth century the term had migrated to America and had come to be used, in Mencken's words, as "one of a long series of jocular terms for a young and somewhat foolish girl, full of wild surmises and inclined to revolt against the precepts and admonitions of her elders" (314–15). Elizabeth Stevenson, in *Babbitts and Bohemians: From the Great War to the Great Depression* (1967), admiringly describes the flapper as "a new American girl, a new woman, a new arrangement of the elements of sex and love. She no longer exists; she existed for only a few years in the mid- and late twenties, but during that short epoch she was a completely defined and recognizable type" (139). The passage of time has indeed demonstrated that the flapper was an ephemeral, unadaptable creature. The Jazz Age was her only natural environment; after the Great Depression of the 1930s she virtually disappeared from the pages of literature and history.

The figure of the quintessential flapper embodies what many people today associate with post–World War I femininity: a young woman with short bobbed hair, a straight slim dress, and a long beaded necklace or feathered headpiece, drinking gin punch and dancing the Charleston to the wild syncopations of a jazz band. Subject to a set of social standards entirely different from those her mother had experienced as a young woman, this generic flapper smokes cigarettes in a long holder, wears fur-trimmed jackets and small cloche hats, drives an automobile, and kisses any boy she likes. She wears her stockings rolled down and her hemlines just below her powdered knees, and she lets her unlaced galoshes flap around her ankles. She may have read Freud—she has certainly heard of him—and bandies about words like "fixation" and "fetish" as she and her friends puzzle out the meanings of their dreams. She can legally vote, thanks to the Nineteenth Amendment, but she probably doesn't. She likes crossword puzzles, has earnestly chanted Émil Coué's revolutionary self-help mantra ("Every day in every way, I am getting better and better"), and can play a respectable game of mah-jongg. The current craze of dance marathons entertains her tremendously, and perhaps she has even participated in one (although she leaves the flagpole-sitting to the men). She has asked the Ouija board about her future on a number of occasions. The wonders of modern advertising influence her daily life, and she chooses her facial soap and breakfast cereal and party dresses based on what her favorite movie stars use and eat and wear. She loves the cinema and goes at least once a week, but she identifies more with the daring, sexy Clara Bow than with the girlish Mary Pickford, known throughout the 1920s as "America's Sweetheart." She adores movie idols Rudolph Valentino and Douglas Fairbanks. And she knows of at least one man who did not come home from World War I.

This generic female flapper's generic male counterpart is a young man with slicked-back hair parted down the middle, in the style of the fashionable "sheik"—a term that was popularized by matinee idol Rudolph Valentino's blockbuster 1921 movie of the same name. On a regular day he wears knickers and argyle socks and sweater vests and a peaked cap, or perhaps his "Oxford bags"—huge baggy pants not unlike those favored by many of today's teenagers. But to a party he would wear spats on his shoes, a bow tie, a double-breasted suit, a bowler hat, and a raccoon coat. If he attends a college that has a Greek system, he avidly cheers for the varsity football squad and has undoubtedly rushed a popular fraternity. He has a "line" that he uses on women he likes, which he has refined through months of use on dozens of girls. He loves the comedies of Charlie Chaplin and Buster Keaton, and although he would have seen Al Jolson in *The Jazz Singer* in 1927, he would not have bet money that "talkies" would last. He listens to the music of Paul Whiteman and Eddie Cantor, and he enthusiastically dances the Black Bottom and the fox-trot at the co-ed parties he frequently attends. He drives a semi-reliable flivver, drinks all manners of rotten Prohibition liquor, and is a great fan of the newfangled "cocktail parties." Prohibition does pose some slight inconveniences; along with the risk of being caught in a raid or being frisked by police, he also worries that the liquor he buys might be toxic.[2] He has become accustomed to his women friends drinking, smoking, and petting at parties; the ethics of his parents' generation seem to him infinitely outdated.

Now, perhaps a very few young, wealthy, white, urban men and women of the 1920s fit every broad stereotype mentioned above. However, numerous young people from a variety of backgrounds and circumstances did share at least a handful of these characteristics of youth culture, many of which evolved directly out of Prohibition legislation. Yet any investigation into the lasting effects of Prohibition culture must necessarily seek to avoid casting the "Roaring Twenties" into merely the standard, stereotypical molds that many people today associate with the era. Obviously, the decade "roared" very differently for white middle- or upper-class New Yorkers than it did for, say, northern black domestics, or white southern textile workers, or midwestern German immigrant farmers. Even though

F. Scott Fitzgerald's portrayal of 1920s culture is perhaps more familiar to us, believing that his depiction of Prohibition-era life is any more authentic or representative than Langston Hughes's or Sinclair Lewis's would be like believing that an account of the 1960s by Hugh Hefner or a history of the 1990s by Donald Trump would speak for and to all Americans.

Dozens of writers used young, ebullient figures of the flapper and the sheik to identify both the tenor of the times and the radical changes that transformed manners and morals during the years surrounding the Great War. One of the most common and visible ways that the youth of the 1920s demonstrated their celebration of the "modern" was to participate in the widespread culture of Prohibition. This participation involved a willingness not only to drink unpalatable liquor with unrestrained enthusiasm, but also to frequent the sites where Prohibition culture flourished. The "flapper set"—both men and women—raced their flivvers to roadhouses, speakeasies, parties, and dances, all the while belting back shots of whiskey or gin, or encouraging others to do so. Individual members of this social set may or may not have been drinkers, but overall, members of this younger generation seemed to approve of drinking despite the Prohibition laws; to obey the law and one's parents in quiet acquiescence was decidedly "old-fashioned." Elizabeth Stevenson explains that the goal of the flapper was to appear at odds with the beliefs of old fogeys by "[taking] the breath of staid observers with her flip spontaneity, her short-lived likes and dislikes, her way of skating gaily over thin ice" (141).

The flapper's enthusiasm for living just a hair outside the law, "skating on thin ice," reveals in part the evolution of women's social roles during the 1920s. Suffragists and reformers of the nineteenth century had led the campaigns for not just women's right to vote and an increase in women's political and economic opportunities, but specifically the passage of anti-liquor laws. The ratification of the controversial Eighteenth Amendment was believed to be a great victory for women, primarily because, in many cases, women and children suffered from violence and poverty due to the excessive drinking habits of their husbands and fathers. Unexpectedly, however, the gender-inclusive speakeasy almost immediately replaced the male-dominated saloon, and cocktail parties brought drinking into the home for both men and women. Gender equality in venues such as the speakeasy was surely not what women's rights supporters had in mind when they cleared the way to the voting booth, and many of these reformers interpreted the social conduct of the "new woman" not as liberated but rather as self-indulgent and irresponsible. Although in hindsight the initiation of women into the culture of drinking appears to have been inevitable, few Prohibition supporters at the time, male or female, anticipated the full-fledged integration of young women into the world of hip flasks and bathtub gin.

Figure 5
A young flapper Charlestons with a lively old geezer in John Held, Jr.'s famous cover illustration for *Life* magazine, February 18, 1926. Courtesy of the Library of Congress.

Some members of the younger generation recognized, even at the time, that the existence of the Prohibition laws had induced them to drink perhaps more than they might have otherwise. A student-written editorial published in a 1926 issue of the *Wisconsin Daily Cardinal*, the University of Wisconsin's student newspaper, asserts that "Without doubt, prohibition has been an incentive for young folks to learn to drink." The writer concludes that this tendency of young people to drink alcohol despite the new legislation has led to "a general breaking down of respect for national law in the minds of the people who are law abiding citizens at heart. . . . [T]he Eighteenth Amendment has accomplished nothing but the ruination of our gastronomic organs, our taste, and our one time respect for federal law. The Volstead law has been an ineffective weapon to stop drinking. Its failure shows that it is impossible to legislate morals" (Fass 321). Historian Paula Fass concurs, stating that "Prohibition got in youth's way because it was . . . an anachronism that made the young law-breakers in spite of themselves" (323–24).

Perhaps the attitude of many young people toward alcohol resulted directly from the examples set by their elders, as historian Herbert Asbury claims. Because the young were, Asbury suggests, "imitative as monkeys," they invariably copied their parents' behaviors regarding illegal drinking: "They helped their elders handle the distilling and brewing apparatus in their homes, saw them guzzling liquor, making drunken passes at one another's wives and husbands, and nursing hangovers. They heard little conversation that didn't deal with the high cost of booze, the difficulty of controlling fermentation, the proper quantity of yeast, and the sterling qualities of 'my bootlegger.'" Teenagers raised in this environment inevitably came to believe that drinking was "the correct thing for all up-to-date young folks to do" (*The Great Illusion* 160).

Contrary to many portrayals of youth as hedonistic, immoral creatures, much reliable evidence suggests that young people of the 1920s, while not necessarily law-abiding, were actually quite a bit more innocent than their elders believed them to be. Although the young collectively indulged in drinking, smoking, dancing, and petting to an extent that far exceeded the behaviors of the previous generation, there is little evidence to suggest that they succumbed to higher levels of alcoholism or teen pregnancy than their elders had at their age. That is, much of the wild behavior of the "flaming youth" of the 1920s was a show, put on for each other's benefit and for the benefit of their exasperated elders. For example, many anecdotal sources suggest that it was often desirable for popular young women to play the part of a "speed." So although they might enjoy being kissed by a number of boys, that did not always mean that they "went the distance" with any of them. Likewise, visible drunkenness at parties was considered quite smart among some young crowds, and so partiers may have played up their intoxication for the appreciation of their peers. As Asbury recounts, "In the younger set it became smart to drink, and smarter still to get drunk, while the boy who passed out was looked upon as a he-man of parts and something of a hero" (*The Great Illusion* 160). It is impossible to estimate, however, how many of these dead-drunk boy heroes were just playing along for the prestige that accompanied wholesale indulgence in illegal drinking.[3]

But for many young people, participating in Prohibition-era drinking was, in other words, an example of braggadocio, of appearing to live on the cutting edge of fashion while simultaneously maintaining one's personal values. This youthful innocence, in direct contrast with their outwardly sophisticated appearance, marks a number of the decade's most memorable literary youths.

In William Faulkner's *Sanctuary,* the novel's central female character, Temple Drake, a popular and attractive Ole Miss undergraduate from a wealthy and respectable Mississippi family, appears to embody virtually every imaginable stereotype of the Prohibition-era flapper. In brief, *Sanctuary* follows the story of Temple as she and Gowan Stevens, one of her boyfriends, become stranded at a rural moonshiners' hideout. After Stevens abandons Temple, a malevolent and sexually impotent bootlegger, Popeye, murders a moonshiner named Tommy, brutally rapes Temple with a corncob, and then sequesters her in a Memphis brothel where he forces her to have sex with other men while he watches. The rest of the novel traces Temple's life in Memphis until her eventual rescue, as well as Tommy's murder trial, at which the wrong man is convicted and subsequently lynched.

At the beginning of the novel, Temple's most serious transgressions appear to involve sneaking out of her dormitory to meet her boyfriends, actions that have landed her on disciplinary probation. She spends much of her time socializing with the town boys during the week and with the college boys on the weekends, and the narrator notes that on any given evening one could catch a glimpse of Temple

> in speeding silhouette against the lighted windows of the Coop, as the women's dormitory was known, vanishing into the shadow beside the library wall, and perhaps a final squatting swirl of knickers or whatnot as she sprang into the car waiting there with engine running on that particular night. The cars belonged to town boys. Students in the University were not permitted to keep cars, and the men—hatless, in knickers and bright pull-overs—looked down upon the town boys who wore hats cupped rigidly upon pomaded heads, and coats a little too tight and trousers a little too full, with superiority and rage.
>
> This was on week nights. On alternate Saturday evenings, at the Letter Club dances, or on the occasion of the three formal yearly balls, the town boys, lounging in attitudes of belligerent casualness, with their identical hats and upturned collars, watched her enter the gymnasium upon black collegiate arms and vanish in a swirling glitter upon a glittering swirl of music, with her high delicate head and

her bold painted mouth and soft chin, her eyes blankly right and left looking, cool, predatory and discreet. (28–29)

Temple's "predatory" look, at least as it appears to the jealous town boys, may in fact be just a pose; she, like most flappers, is far more innocent than she appears. Although Temple "pets" with boys to the extent that she gets her name scrawled on the men's room wall in the train depot, she has evidently managed to preserve her virginity until the time that Popeye first rapes her. Her protective mantra "My father's a judge," uttered whenever a boy gets too aggressive or passionate, has kept her sheltered from the more forbidden and dangerous aspects of life.

Temple reveals the surprising extent of her innocence in her first exchange with Ruby, the only woman living with the moonshiners at their hideout, the Old Frenchman place. Feeling safer with another woman than with the gang of male outlaws in the other room, Temple sits in the kitchen and pours out her story while Ruby prepares supper. When Temple broaches the topic of escaping from this frightening house of frightening men, her naïveté surfaces. "I'm not afraid," Temple tells Ruby bravely. "Things like that don't happen. Do they? They're just like other people. You're just like other people. With a little baby. And besides, my father's a ju-judge . . ." (56). Temple refuses to acknowledge that she could be a target for "bad things"; although she rebels against her father's authority in small ways, such as stealing out of her dormitory, at the same time she genuinely believes in his ability to protect her. Shortly after this exchange, however, Temple comes to realize that nobody, not even her father, will save her. Popeye destroys Temple's sexual innocence, precipitating her descent into alcoholism and sexual debasement, and thus permanently ends her days as a flapper.

Faulkner characterizes the second part of Temple's story, in which Popeye keeps her in Reba's whorehouse in Memphis, in part through her relationship with alcohol. Her sexual subjugation is understood through veiled, sometimes cryptic comments scattered throughout the section, but her alcoholic debasement floats on the surface of the story. At first Temple refuses the glasses of raw gin that Reba brings to her to calm her down, but soon she changes her mind and drinks eagerly—hoarding her tumblers of liquor and demanding more. It is easy to understand, of course, how Temple might turn to alcohol to provide relief from her traumatic situation, but we should also remember the symbolic power of Prohibition-era drinking. The endless supply of gin helps to establish for the reader both the depravity of the Memphis brothel and Temple's own increasing moral dissipation.

Popeye's treatment of Temple is shockingly cruel, yet many conservative readers may have been inclined to blame Temple's reckless social life, at least in part, for her ultimate undoing. Certainly a more level-headed, "old-fashioned" girl would not have jumped off the Starkville train and risked expulsion to be with the insufferable Gowan Stevens in the first place and thus would never have encountered Popeye, who would never have been able to make her his sex slave. In a similar vein, conservative readers may also have interpreted the wild, sexual behavior of Cordelia in Wallace Thurman's short story "Cordelia the Crude" (1926) to have inevitably precipitated her life as a prostitute. In fact, the title subtly suggests this interpretation; the word *crude* was commonly employed by members of the older generation to describe the alarming manners and morals of young Jazz Age women. Ironically, though, at the beginning of the story Cordelia is not portrayed as crude, although, the narrator explains, she was "widely known among a certain group of young men and girls on the avenue as a fus' class chippie" (6). Although *chippie* often refers to a female prostitute, in Thurman's story the term appears only to mean a fast, fun, popular girl; it becomes apparent at the end of the story that Cordelia, before her encounter with the narrator, was not in fact a prostitute.

Rather, Cordelia Jones is a sexually experienced but emotionally innocent sixteen-year-old girl whose family has forced her to leave her small South Carolina hometown and accompany them to Harlem. She quickly finds that survival in Harlem requires a shrewd adaptability that her parents, determined to live decent and hard-working lives, struggle to acquire. Cordelia, however, feels no desire to get a job or an education, and instead she embraces the carefree life of drinking, carousing, and picking up men in "the foul-smelling depths of her favorite cinema shrine" (5). It is there that she first meets the narrator of the story; he follows her into the theater and they spend the duration of the performance "petting." She notes that he is "different from mos' of dese sheiks" (6) because he refrains from trying to grope her thighs; he soon proves that he is indeed markedly "different." The couple becomes more amorous on their way back to Cordelia's apartment, but before they get to her door, the flustered and embarrassed narrator unexpectedly shoves two one-dollar bills into her hands and flees. Later in the story, we gather, this awkward and basically innocent encounter signals Cordelia's entrance into a life of prostitution.

Despite her status as a Harlem prostitute, Cordelia does embody many of the stereotypical attributes of a Jazz Age flapper. She wears short dresses and open galoshes that flap about her ankles, keeps her hair in a short bob underneath her stylish hat, and attends rent parties where she drinks bathtub gin and dances the Charleston. More importantly, her entire story is one of open rebellion against her parents and their plans for her life.

Although her parents manage to prevent her marriage to a South Carolina pig farmer by dragging her to New York, "the mere moving to Harlem had not doused [her] rebellious flame" (5). Rejecting school and work, Cordelia "victoriously defied her harassed parents so frequently when it came to matters of discipline that she soon found herself with a mesmerizing lack of home restraint" (5–6). Cordelia uses this freedom to invent her own identity separate from that of her family, and while her chosen path may compare poorly to her parents' sober, hard-working lives, the point is that Cordelia exercises her ability to choose her own destiny. Interestingly, the narrator does not condemn her for her choices. Thurman's biographer, Eleonore van Notten, observes "a notable absence of a centralized moral conscience in [the] story and a refusal on the part of the narrator to pronounce judgment upon either Cordelia or upon the potentially corrupting influence of urban life" (139–40). This may be attributable in part to Thurman's own personal enthusiasm for the rebelliousness of youth culture, in all its colorful, "crude," and often inebriated manifestations.

The final scene, the briefest in the story, is also the most revealing both in terms of the flapper's relationship to Prohibition-era culture and to Cordelia's ultimate loss of innocence. The narrator encounters Cordelia at a rent party, six months after their first meeting in the Roosevelt Theatre when he paid her two dollars for letting him kiss her. The entire party is awash in illicit alcohol, and at the center of it all is Cordelia, "savagely careening in a drunken abortion of the Charleston and surrounded by a perspiring circle of handclapping enthusiasts" (6). The "cauterizing liquor" (6) she has drunk has evidently dulled her wits, for she cannot immediately place the face of the man who changed her life by showing her that her sexual favors had a corresponding dollar value. Transformed from a more typical flapper type—a nice girl, but fast and bold and independent—into a more degraded figure, Cordelia becomes for the reader a lesson in the effects of Prohibition culture upon the innocent and the unwary.

These two examples of Temple and Cordelia should not suggest that every literary depiction of flappers ends inevitably with their sexual debasement, although it is interesting to note that a significant number of flappers do seem to end up as prostitutes in 1920s American fiction. Nevertheless, a number of flappers succeed in life despite, or perhaps because of, their wild youth. One example of a flapper whose youthful unruliness leads first to prostitution but, eventually, to success is Harriett Williams, the African American heroine of Langston Hughes's *Not Without Laughter*. Despite her relative poverty and geographic isolation, Harriett clearly has her finger on the pulse of all that is new and modern in American culture. Although she, like Temple and Cordelia, spends part of her youth as a prostitute, Hughes portrays Harriett and her peer group as a lively and refreshing change from the staid conservatism of the older generation.

Not Without Laughter, the largely autobiographical novel of Hughes's early life, relates the story of the Williams family. Ostensibly revolving around Sandy, the young Hughes figure who comes of age during the course of the novel, the narrative actually devotes nearly as much attention to the family members who surround Sandy during these formative years. His mother, Annjee, and his grandmother, Hager, represent highly traditional, conservative religious and social conventions and epitomize the old-fashioned morals of the "older generation." Sandy's Aunt Tempy represents the African American social climber—she regularly attends the Episcopal church, avidly reads W. E. B. Du Bois's *The Crisis,* and tries to instill in Sandy the goal of upward mobility and economic advancement. But it is Sandy's young Aunt Harriett, the rural African American flapper, who represents the pervasiveness of the rebellious youth culture even in the rural, deeply religious Midwest.

Harriett's character demonstrates how widespread and influential national forces such as advertising, music, and fashion had become by the 1920s. She lives in small-town Kansas, hundreds of miles from any major metropolitan center, and her country life bears practically no resemblance to the lives of urban trendsetters. Harriett is certainly no white, wealthy, country-clubbing Fitzgerald-style flapper, and yet she does manage to stay abreast of the latest trends in fashion and in behavior. Her clothes are not purchased at Macy's or Gimbel's, but her short colorful dress and silk stockings are exactly in keeping with what stylish urban women were wearing at the time. The narrator describes how Harriett pulls on her "red silk stockings, bright and shimmering to her hips," in preparation for a party at the local roadhouse. Then she "powdered her face and neck, pink on ebony, dashed white talcum powder at each arm-pit, and rubbed her ears with perfume from a thin bottle. Then she slid a light blue dress of many ruffles over her head. The skirt ended midway between the ankle and the knee, and she looked very cute, delicate, and straight, like a black porcelain doll in a Vienna toy shop" (43–44). Like the privileged flappers in Fitzgerald's stories, Harriett also smokes cigarettes, drinks liquor, rides in automobiles with boys, sneaks out to be with her boyfriends, and dances all the fashionable dances. Fitzgerald's women might dance at the country club and drink scotch, while Harriett and her friends congregate at the country roadhouse and drink gin, but except for these minor details their social lives are remarkably parallel. Modern advances in advertising, magazines, movies, and radio, which nationalized popular culture in the 1920s and established standards in fashion and conduct, overcome

Figure 6
Scott and Zelda Fitzgerald on their honeymoon, 1920. Courtesy of the Library of Congress.

Harriett's geographic isolation by offering her access to the latest in youthful trends.

Dozens of other writers of the 1920s likewise chronicled the complicated and fascinating elements of Jazz Age youth culture. Through their fiction, they demonstrate how the young tried to make sense of a world that juxtaposed the disillusionment caused by the Great War and the repression of the Prohibition laws with the optimistic promises of a modern future. Other, now largely forgotten works of the 1920s, including Percy Marks's *The Plastic Age* (1924), Warner Fabian's *Flaming Youth* (1923), and Michael Arlen's *The Green Hat* (1924)—highly successful best-sellers in their day—also contributed to Americans' acquaintance with the new morality of the flamboyant youth culture and perpetuated crazes in both fashion and taste. But the American writer that readers today most closely associate with youth culture of the 1920s is undoubtedly F. Scott Fitzgerald, the self-appointed spokesperson for the flapper set.

Fitzgerald's stories and novels of the 1920s offer image after image of attractive, wealthy young people, their flirtations, their scandals, and their tragedies. Young people looked to his books to validate their rapidly evolving culture; older people looked to his books to find out what was really going on in the lives of their teenaged children. Fitzgerald occupied an unusual position by representing himself as not merely an outside observer of youth culture, but as an experienced and enthusiastic participant. Indeed, biographical accounts suggest that the alcoholic, perpetually broke

Fitzgerald was one of the wildest youths of them all, and in the past few decades stories of him and his wife Zelda touring through speakeasies and jumping into public fountains in grand inebriated style have taken on the flavor of American legend. Because of his close acquaintance with and affection for youth culture, Fitzgerald's renderings have become important historical as well as literary documents.

In his portrayals of the younger generation of the 1920s, Fitzgerald reveals a sense of determination that is notably absent from more flighty depictions of the flapper class. The young, popular people in his stories work very hard to stay popular—they strategize, they manipulate, they try to read the subtle but important signs emanating from their peer group. In "Bernice Bobs Her Hair" (1920), for example, Marjorie Harvey, the popular flapper figure, summarizes the ruthlessness of female competition by admitting, "these days it's every girl for herself."[4] This sentiment precipitates Bernice's fateful haircut and her subsequent "scalping" of her selfish cousin Marjorie. Nancy Lamar, the self-proclaimed "famous dark haired beauty" of "The Jelly-Bean" (1920) and one of the "most popular members of the younger set," plays the beautiful and ruthless flapper who drinks her whiskey straight from the bottle and tantalizes every young man at the dance until, in her drunken state, she marries the wrong man.[5] In "Winter Dreams" (1922), Judy Jones is the dazzling and wealthy flapper figure who, according to one jealous onlooker, "always looks as if she wanted to be kissed."[6] But in all of these cases and dozens more, the flapper and her boyfriends are not blithe, light-hearted young playmates. Instead, they dance and drink and joyride and pet with a grim sense of determination to be happy and have fun, regardless of the cost. A sense of awful desperation exists just beneath their joyous exteriors, as if occupying this position of wealth, privilege, and beauty is a tremendous chore that will be relieved only by the separate but equally heavy burden of marriage.

The burden of marriage falls particularly heavily on Gloria Gilbert Patch, the flapper at the center of Fitzgerald's 1922 novel *The Beautiful and Damned*. The unmarried Gloria Gilbert, daughter of a reasonably prosperous family from Kansas City, Missouri, is considered "the most celebrated and sought-after young beauty in the country" (65). Highly attuned to the trends of the day, Gloria prides herself on staying a step ahead of the latest fashions in hairstyles and clothing and knowing all the latest slang, dances, and songs. She drinks excessively, drives recklessly, and kisses any number of love-struck men; when anyone challenges her behavior she declares brazenly, "I detest reformers, especially the sort that try to reform me" (49). She is the perfect example of the privileged flapper—the beautiful young girl with neither cares nor responsibilities—and the inevitable result is that the people she encounters treat her not as an individual but as a gorgeous object, "a thing of exquisite and unbelievable beauty" to be possessed and worshiped (242). Like Fitzgerald's other flapper heroines, though, Gloria also works extremely hard to keep up with this life and its expectations, and so it comes as no great surprise when she decides to marry Anthony Patch, the handsome young heir to the thirty-million-dollar Patch fortune, and forego the exhilarating but exhausting life of the desirable single girl.

As shining examples of hedonistic youth culture, Gloria and Anthony drink socially—to have fun and entertain themselves and their friends. They host countless cocktail parties for their society set in the early days of their marriage, and they frequently go out for drinks at various hotels and restaurants. But as their marriage becomes increasingly unhappy, the role that alcohol plays in their lives changes dramatically. Instead of drinking to be smart and fun and daring, they find themselves drinking to escape both the relentless boredom of their situation and their frustrations with each other. Even when their funds run dangerously low, Anthony somehow manages to scrounge up seventy-five dollars for a case of bootleg whiskey that the two of them consume grimly, in desperate self-pity. Anthony's uncontrollable alcoholism soon comes to dominate their home life, and Gloria's habitual drinking, although perhaps not as blatantly self-destructive as his, contributes to her dramatic transformation from the toast of New York society to a hollow, miserable matron.

The luminous Daisy Fay Buchanan in Fitzgerald's *The Great Gatsby* provides another example of a flapper figure occupying that slippery transitional state between the recklessness of youth and the steadiness of marriage. But unlike Gloria Patch, who refuses to relinquish her irresponsible and selfish ways, Daisy matures after her marriage into a woman far more accepting of the older generation's conservatism. Although only in her mid-twenties, she is nevertheless a wife and a mother—two important responsibilities that society demands she take seriously. Unlike Gatsby, who wholeheartedly believes that one can recreate the past and return to simpler days, Daisy understands that certain life decisions cannot be unmade. Gatsby's offer of love and escape tempts her, but in the end she proves unwilling to renounce either her husband or her daughter to pursue Gatsby's romantic ideals and her own fading youth.

Fitzgerald reminds us, however, that Daisy has not given up all vestiges of her younger self. In particular, parties and cocktails remain prominent on her agenda, and she eagerly drinks highballs and juleps whenever they are offered. In this way, Daisy resembles other married people in 1920s literature who, while dissociated from youth culture in most ways, share with them a taste for illegal alcohol. However, Daisy's drinking may resemble Gloria Patch's in that cocktails offer a means for her to escape, temporarily, the pain of her troubled marriage and the ghost of her past love. Like Gloria, married life for Daisy has become a dreary mess, and perhaps the giddy high that comes with consuming bootleg whiskey conjures fleeting images of long-ago happiness. The sad truth about flapper characters such as Daisy Buchanan and Gloria Patch, who seem to hold the world in their hands before they turn twenty, is that from that glorious pinnacle of beauty and popularity that they reach at such a young age, the quality of their lives can do nothing but diminish.

The Older Generation

. . . most everybody of my generation feels that the worst of the whole prohibition evil is the way the older people seem to be showing more and more disrespect for the law and the Constitution, the older they get.
—Booth Tarkington, "The Neck, and Bush Thring" (1929)

Looking back on the tumultuous 1920s, F. Scott Fitzgerald recalled, "May one offer in exhibit the year 1922! That was the peak of the younger generation, for though the Jazz Age continued, it became less and less an affair of youth. The sequel was a children's party taken over by elders" (qtd. in Leuchtenberg 174). Indeed, while the young girl may have invented the revolutionary figure of the flapper, "it was her mother who kept it going" (Leuchtenberg 174). It seemed that virtually everybody wanted to be young in the 1920s and would undergo everything from starvation diets to dancing lessons to glandular operations to revisit the idealized days of frivolous youth. In fact, marketing and advertising techniques had become so sophisticated that youth was presented to consumers as a purchasable commodity. Soaps could wash away wrinkles, shampoos could brighten hair, and of course rouge, lipstick, and face powder could recreate the outer markings of youthful beauty, advertisers assured the nation's women. Daring, trendy behaviors such as dancing the Charleston and drinking gin punch provided, or so it seemed to many middle-aged folks, something akin to the actual experiences of youth.

Historian Paula Fass offers a dichotomous model to illustrate an important ideological split within the older generation of the 1920s. She describes two distinct camps: the progressives and the traditionalists. To progressives, the "flaming youth" of the 1920s embodied all the most attractive and stimulating elements of American popular culture. Progressives modeled themselves on the fashions and manners of this younger crowd, agreeing with youth that Victorian mores were neither useful nor relevant in the modern age. In particular, breaking Prohibition laws by drinking illegal booze provided these liberated members of the older generation a convenient and socially acceptable way to demonstrate their daring. It was a relatively safe, easy, and popular way to appear transgressive and up to date. Of course, the specific reasons why so many middle-aged and older Americans rejected the authority of Prohibition legislation vary widely. Some were merely unwilling to sacrifice a personal habit that provided them a certain amount of pleasure, even when it meant they would have to break the law to continue to imbibe. But many so-called progressives were primarily attracted to the glamour that youth culture associated with drinking.

The traditionalists, on the other hand, believed the youth culture that flourished after the Great War seriously threatened America's future. The shocking new behaviors, particularly of young women, undermined long-cherished systems of morality and offended conservative images of propriety. Alternately perplexed and enraged by the values of youth culture, traditionalists drew upon deep stores of religious faith and sober patriotism to denounce the wild behavior of the younger generation. Short dresses, close dancing, and whiskey flasks were surely the work of the devil, went one common argument; good Americans obey the law, went another. To most traditionalists, Prohibition was a positive, reasonable move by a government seeking to improve the lives of all Americans by controlling the behavior of its most reckless and dangerous citizens.

Traditionalist members of the older generation counted among their ranks many of the most devoted guardians of conventional morality and propriety. Prohibition-era literature is sprinkled with these characters—devout, well-meaning, and firmly convinced that their beloved America was quickly going straight to hell. Perhaps not surprisingly, authors seldom portrayed these characters in positive ways; in fact, Prohibition supporters are commonly seen as either dour sticks-in-the-mud or excessive evangelicals—sometimes both at the same time. Editorial cartoons of the 1920s continually poked fun at these terribly earnest characters—the elderly spinster schoolmarm who demands abstinence from all forms of celebration, the gaunt-faced, high-collared preacher who thunders about the hellfires that await the drinker in the next life, the insufferable reformed drinker who exhorts listeners to follow his lead. Even in Upton Sinclair's passionately pro-Prohibition novel *The Wet Parade* (1931), the various stereotypes of temperance reformers are encapsulated in an inebriated anti-Prohibition street oration during which the speaker warns: "The hordes of Methodism are on the march, about to descend upon you. I see them advancing, an army of schoolma'ams, hatched-faced old maids in spectacles and poke-bonnets, mounted upon camels; Puritan preachers in tall hats, with green umbrellas under their arms, sitting proudly upon the front seats of a battery of water wagons!" (65). Although Sinclair's novel ultimately attempts to dismantle these derogatory stereotypes, in most fiction of the Prohibition era, society's teetotaling moral guardians appear lifeless or hopelessly out of touch alongside their fashionable, hard-drinking companions.

F. Scott Fitzgerald paints an immortal picture of the stereotypical Prohibitionist of the older generation in *The Beautiful and Damned*. An ardent teetotaler, the elderly Adam "Cross" Patch is the hard-nosed, reform-minded, fantastically wealthy grandfather of the irresponsible but charming Anthony Comstock Patch. After he had reached middle age and amassed a considerable fortune, Cross Patch decides "to consecrate the remainder of his life to the moral regeneration of the world. He became a reformer among reformers. Emulating the magnificent efforts of Anthony Comstock, after whom his grandson was named, he leveled a varied assortment of uppercuts and body-blows at liquor, literature, vice, art, patent medicines, and Sunday theatres" (4). The ill-named Anthony, who cannot understand Cross Patch's zeal for social reform, looks down upon his efforts to rid the world of its most enjoyable pleasures. In fact, Anthony spends nearly his whole life waiting eagerly for his grandfather to die and leave him a huge inheritance, with which he can then live out his dissolute life in aristocratic idleness.

Understandably, Anthony tries to keep his great fondness for liquor a secret from his grandfather, who does not tolerate drinking under any circumstance. But Anthony and his wife Gloria epitomize all the wildness and impracticality of the stereotypical Roaring Twenties; even the promise of a multi-million dollar inheritance does not inspire them to rein in their alcoholic lifestyle. When Cross Patch surprises Anthony and Gloria at their home during a particularly drunken cocktail party, on the very same day that he donates fifty thousand dollars to the Prohibition cause, the furious patriarch cuts his grandson out of his will. When the elder Patch dies a few months later, some thirty million dollars winds up in a charitable trust instead of in Anthony's empty pockets—a high price for the younger man to pay for throwing a cocktail party.

Fitzgerald portrays Cross Patch not as a noble philanthropist or shrewd businessman, or even as a wealthy old man entitled to dispose of his estate as he wishes, but instead as a narrow-minded, petty old fool. Cross Patch epitomizes popular 1920s conceptions of the hard-core Prohibitionist— old, ornery, and unwilling to condone any aspect of youth culture that is not as sober and devout as he is himself. Anthony describes his famous grandfather to his friends as "a pious ass—a chicken-brain" who appears, at least from Anthony's youthful perspective, "a prig, a bore, and something of a hypocrite" (71). Anthony may be the wrong person to cast aspersions on another's character—he is no saint himself. But the reader (and the author) can almost manage to forgive him his narcissism and self-indulgence, at least in part, for he is young, handsome, and charismatic. Most authors of the 1920s, including Fitzgerald, zealously linked the faults of the decade's older moral guardians to their relentless, futile striving to return America to its prewar codes of behavior.

The traditionalists who haunted the literature of the 1920s were not always as unappealing as Cross Patch, though they were often just as vig-orous in their condemnation of youth culture. In Langston Hughes's *Not Without Laughter,* the narrative foil for young Harriett, the wild flapper, is Hager Williams, her pious Christian mother. Hager agonizes helplessly over Harriett's decisions about clothes, friends, and parties, and she cannot understand how her daughter could act so shamelessly un-Christian. In frustration and anger at Harriett's lack of remorse, she wails, "Lawd knows I don't know what I's gonna do with you. I works fo' you an' I prays fo' you, an' if you don't mind, I's sho gonna whip you, even if you is goin' on seventeen years old!" (80). In fact, when scolding proves ineffective, Hager does not hesitate to beat Harriett—she will employ any method to instill in her "terribly alive young daughter" some sense of modesty, sobriety, and godliness. Hager's greatest fear is that illegal liquor will be served wherev-er Harriett goes with her friends, and of course she is right. Gin and whiskey flow freely at the rural roadhouses that draw the young crowds, along with jazz music, dancing, and other manifestations of what Hager believes to be lewd and immoral conduct.

Hager's Christian values and traditionalist outlook set her up to be the killjoy in this scenario, even though all her bluster is merely an honest attempt to keep her daughter safe from the influences of her fast crowd. But Harriett is not interested in being safe—she only wants to have fun drinking, dancing, singing, and, in her words, "trying to be happy." Hager's speech, peppered with phrases like "dear Jesus" and "Lawd a mercy," only demeans her further in Harriett's eyes—after a particularly vicious fight Harriett flings at her mother the worst insult she can muster: "You old Christian fool!" (45). Hager grew up in a world in which chil-dren listened to their elders and obeyed the laws of the church and the gov-ernment. Understandably, the fast-paced youth culture of flivvers, road-houses, jazz music, and gin is not just foreign to her but frightening as well. Yet Hughes portrays Hager—not the volatile Harriett—as the unreason-able one, for believing that old rules could possibly apply to a new generation.

Of course, Cross Patch and Hager Williams are extreme representations of older people who believe Prohibition to be a necessary, righteous measure to restrain the frivolity of the young. Each of them falls squarely into the traditionalist camp, as outlined in Paula Fass's study. But not everyone fits so neatly into the category of traditionalist or progressive—many members of the older generation were simultaneously attracted to and repelled by the new morality of youth culture and their ardent championing of the modern life. Perhaps the most memorable such literary character to fall between these two categories is the maddeningly conformist George F. Babbitt of Sinclair Lewis's 1922 best-seller, *Babbitt*.

No one would regard George Babbitt, a middle-aged businessman with a wife and two children, as a member of the younger generation. In fact, he represents all that youth culture decried as hypocritical and old-fashioned: he has a steady job, a solid income, and a respectable place in the community. He attends church, donates money to worthy causes, takes some mild interest in his teenaged children's lives, and otherwise embodies all aspects of a boring middle-class life in a middle-sized midwestern city where many citizens take seriously the Don't Make Prohibition a Joke Association. Yet he also feels an undeniable attraction to youth culture—one that makes him uncomfortable around his children's friends and leads him to pursue an embarrassing affair with a younger woman and an inappropriate friendship with a fast young crowd. At the same time that he feels most proud of his respectable life, he longs for the adventures and romance of a lost youth.

Babbitt maintains a fascinating, and probably common, philosophical position regarding Prohibition and drinking. The narrator tells us mockingly that "Babbitt was virtuous. He advocated, though he did not practise [*sic*], the prohibition of alcohol" in the same way that "he praised, though he did not obey, the laws against motor-speeding" (41). Babbitt believed in Prohibition exclusively for the benefit of other people—"it's a mighty beneficial thing for the poor zob that hasn't got any will-power," for example, but for upstanding fellows like himself and his close friends, Prohibition is nothing more than an annoying "infringement of personal liberty" (125). Yet the outward show of propriety and sobriety means everything to Babbitt—he highly disapproves of a younger neighborhood couple, the Doppelbraus, whom he dismisses as "Bohemian" and whose obviously German surname likely suggests to him (as well as to many readers of the 1920s) a predisposition for strong drink. Local gossip supports this assumption. "From [the Doppelbraus'] house came midnight music and obscene laughter; there were neighborhood rumors of bootlegged whisky and fast motor rides" (21) that George Babbitt, family man and community pillar *par excellence*, simply cannot condone, at least not outwardly.

Although Babbitt himself indulges in the intermittent drinking spree, the appearance of being a law-abiding citizen means a great deal to him. He carefully cultivates a respectable persona that reflects his status as a successful businessman and enthusiastic town booster. His self-righteous sense of morality and entitlement manifests itself in small distinctions that Babbitt makes between himself and the nameless inferiors who also happen to inhabit his world. For example, although he occasionally procures an illegal and highly prized bottle of hooch, as a matter of principle Babbitt "did not possess a cocktail-shaker. A shaker was proof of dissipation, the symbol of a Drinker, and Babbitt disliked being known as a Drinker even more than he liked a Drink" (98). For a middle-aged conservative like Babbitt, concern for reputation far exceeds the relatively unimportant matter of one's personal ideology.

Babbitt's fondness for drinking, coupled with his undeniable attraction to youth culture, leads him to cultivate a kind of friendship with a group of fashionable but obnoxious young men and women collectively referred to as "the Bunch." Although he clearly does not belong in this crowd, the Bunch humors him and lets him tag along, pathetically out of place, to their parties and dances. On one occasion, Babbitt sneaks away from home to accompany some of the "young gallants" of the Bunch on a drinking spree with some "bouncing young women whom they picked up in department stores and hotel coatrooms." An awkward, humiliated, and painfully hung-over Babbitt later remembers with shame:

> There was a motor car, a bottle of whisky, and for him a grubby shrieking cash-girl from Parcher and Stein's. He sat beside her and worried. He was apparently expected to "jolly her along," but when she sang out, "Hey, leggo, quit crushing the cootie garage,"[7] he did not quite know how to go on. They sat in the back room of a saloon, and Babbitt had a headache, was confused by their new slang, looked at them benevolently, wanted to go home, and had a drink—a good many drinks. (304)

Clearly an outsider in this gang of young socialites, still Babbitt cannot overcome his attraction to the gaiety of the swinging single life and do the sensible, obvious thing: act his age and go home to his family.

Along with his anxieties about his advancing age and his increasingly noticeable disconnection from youth culture, Babbitt is deeply disconcerted by the transformations he witnesses in his own teenaged daughter, Verona, and his son Ted's girlfriend, Eunice Littlefield. Eunice in particular baffles him—he has watched her grow up from the time she was a little girl, and now that she is seventeen, dreaming of being a movie star and smoking cigarettes, she barely resembles the youngster in Babbitt's memory. After one encounter with the disarmingly attractive Eunice, the narrator reveals some of Babbitt's fretfulness: "the agreeable child dismayed him. Her thin and charming face was sharpened by bobbed hair; her skirts were short, her stockings were rolled, and, as she flew after Ted, above the caressing silk were glimpses of soft knees which made Babbitt uneasy, and wretched that she should consider him old" (201). The middle-aged Babbitt is simultaneously unnerved by and attracted to Eunice, discomfited by her observable sexuality and unsure what his role is in relation to this young neighbor. Most of all, he is crushed by the knowledge that she and her flapper friends could never think of him as a peer or a partner, but only as Ted's father, an old man, forever a member of the "older generation."

The chasm between the generations never appears larger to Babbitt than it does when his son Ted throws a co-ed party in their home. Although he and his wife chaperone the event, Babbitt is not at all certain that his presence prevents any of the well-known immoral behaviors so often associated with crowds of teenagers from occurring:

> Babbitt had heard stories of what the Athletic Club called "goings-on" at young parties; of girls "parking" their corsets in the dressing-room, of "cuddling" and "petting," and a presumable increase in what was known as Immorality. To-night he believed these stories. These children seemed bold to him, and cold. The girls wore misty chiffon, coral velvet, or cloth of gold, and around their dipping bobbed hair were shining wreaths. He had it, upon urgent and secret inquiry, that no corsets were known to be parked upstairs; but certainly these eager bodies were not still with steel. Their stockings were of lustrous silk, their slippers costly and unnatural, their lips carmined and their eyebrows penciled. They danced cheek to cheek with the boys, and Babbitt sickened with apprehension and unconscious envy. (203)

These beautiful, worldly young women were living lives far removed from Babbitt's own experiences, and he mourns that his time for such irresponsibility and frivolity has already passed.

His parental instincts overcome his self-indulgent sentimentalizing, however, when Babbitt suddenly notices that the party guests have been periodically retreating to their cars to smoke and drink. His personal affinity for liquor has nothing to do with his role as the responsible chaperone for a teenager's party, and he feels obliged to prevent these youth from boozing while he is in charge. Covertly spying the glowing tips of their cigarettes in the dark and hearing the boys and girls giggling together in their cars, the ambivalent Babbitt "wanted to denounce them but . . . did not dare." So he tries tactfully to redirect their attention, which proves wholly ineffective:

> When he had returned to the front hall he coaxed the boys, "Say, if any of you fellows are thirsty, there's some dandy ginger ale."
>
> "Oh! Thanks!" they condescended.
>
> He sought his wife, in the pantry, and exploded, "I'd like to go in there and throw some of those young pups out of the house! They talk down to me like I was the butler! I'd like to—"
>
> "I know," she sighed; "only everybody says, all the mothers tell me, unless you stand for them, if you get angry because they go out to their cars to have a drink, they won't come to your house any more, and we wouldn't want Ted left out of things, would we?"
>
> He announced that he would be enchanted to have Ted left out of things, and hurried in to be polite, lest Ted be left out of things. (203–4)

Babbitt simply cannot grope his way through the maze of new cultural norms that he himself did nothing to create. Although he could smell whiskey on the breath of several boys, including his son, Babbitt feels emasculated in the presence of these bewitching young sheiks. No longer a confident occupant of the parent role, he becomes a sycophant who tries to preserve whatever social status and popularity his son might currently possess. All the while he longs for the time when he could pass for a party guest instead of the party host.

According to H. L. Mencken, who wrote approvingly of *Babbitt* in his 1922 essay "Portrait of an American Citizen," George Babbitt "is no worse than most, and no better; he is the average American of the ruling minority in this hundred and forty-sixth year of the Republic. He is America incarnate, exuberant and exquisite." If Mencken is correct, then "America incarnate" occupied a remarkable dual position. Required by age and parental obligations to denounce the behaviors of the younger generation, yet unable to deny their genuine attraction for youth culture, Babbitt and hundreds of thousands of people like him made an uneasy peace with the lifestyles of their children. Babbitt is not alone in his understanding that to be thought old or old-fashioned was to be deemed worthless by the younger, ruling classes of the Jazz Age. His wistful encounters, alongside those of countless other middle-aged figures of the decade, reveal that there exists no more painful theme in the literature of the 1920s than the yearning of the old to be young once again.

Our collective national imagination makes it easy for us to picture the young, liberated men and women of the Jazz Age laughing in the face of Senator Volstead and his toothless Prohibition laws. Modern youth participated in the Prohibition-era drinking culture to an extent that politicians and reformers could never have anticipated. It surely never occurred to Volstead and his fellow congressmen that anti-liquor laws would make drinking even more attractive to rebellious, disillusioned postwar youth searching for a modern identity to match their modern world. They never guessed that young partiers, self-consciously defining themselves in dramatic contrast to their elders, took pleasure in rebelling against both the legal strictures of the Prohibition laws as well as the moral strictures against alcohol in general. It should come as no surprise, then, that much of this era's literature characterizes flappers and sheiks for the reader via their relationships to the culture of Prohibition. A flask in the pocket or a cocktail in the hand of a character could tell readers as much about them as would a page of labored description about politics and ideologies. Examining how and why youth culture rebelled against their Victorian influences with whiskey and gin offers us a glimpse into the world of the trendy, "younger set" of 1920s America—a crowd long extinct, but without whom such memorable literary figures as Daisy Buchanan, Temple Drake, and even the venerable George F. Babbitt would not exist.

CHAPTER 4

Hidden in Plain Sight:
THE DRINKING JOINTS

Smash! Smash! For Jesus' sake, Smash!
—Carry A. Nation

Armed with a hatchet, a Bible, and an uncompromising hatred of alcohol, temperance reformer Carry Nation's infamous demolition of saloons in turn-of-the-twentieth-century Kansas foreshadowed later prohibitionists' zealous dismantling of thousands of drinking establishments in cities and towns across the country. Concerned far more with banning the drink than reforming the drinker, Nation and her legion of temperance workers believed that eliminating saloons would lead directly to clean living, responsible parenting, and renewed religious faith. The "Cold Water Pledge" and the "Lincoln Legion Pledge," pre-Prohibition documents that teetotalers signed to signify their personal rejection of alcohol, were promises of economic sanction against saloons as well as, for former drinkers, vows of self-reformation. But what the temperance supporters did not realize was that banning the saloon would in no way guarantee the end of public drinking in America. In fact, Prohibition laws backfired in ways that Carry Nation and other temperance leaders never imagined: the death of the saloon gave birth to a thriving industry of illegal drinking establishments far more varied than had ever before existed.

By the late nineteenth century, most small towns that had not enacted local dry laws boasted at least one commercial saloon, usually run by a brewery, where men could congregate and drink. In cities, public drinking generally took place in saloons and hotel bars, often characterized by the long mahogany, brass-railed bars for which they were named. These urban drinking establishments usually attracted a fairly homogeneous clientele, based on the neighborhood, ethnicity, occupation, or some other commonality among the men who drank there. While most saloons and bars did not officially prohibit women, public drinking in the nineteenth century was chiefly a male pastime. Working-class women's drinking was usually limited to their purchase of ten-cent pails of beer (called "growlers") from the side entrances of the saloons, to be carried away and consumed in the privacy of their own homes or in the company of other women on neighborhood stoops. Purchasing these pails of beer was called "rushing the growler" (Murdock 54) and children were frequently enlisted to perform this common household chore.

By the beginning of the twentieth century, the spaces for upper- and middle-class public drinking expanded to include more heterosocial venues. The rising popularity of partner dancing in the 1890s spawned public dance halls, which historian Catherine Murdock describes as "brightly lit and festive spaces" that were "often located in the back room or second floor of a saloon" (76). Public dance halls were considered by many middle-class observers to be dens of iniquity, largely because individuals and single-sex groups were admitted, and so much mingling, drinking, and dancing among strangers made it difficult to distinguish "respectable working-class girls from prostitutes soliciting clients" (Murdock 77). More reputable were the afternoon dances in cabarets and hotel ballrooms, often called "tango teas" or "tea dances," which, by 1912, served tea and booze to the married and unmarried couples who came to drink, socialize, and dance. Sleazy basement cabarets that served liquor primarily to men had existed in cities such as New York since the turn of the twentieth century, but when public social dancing became popular, Murdock explains, "entrepreneurs moved cabarets to street level, cleaned them up, and began catering to respectable audiences" of both men and women drinkers (74).

The Eighteenth Amendment drove much of this public drinking into the home, but many Americans refused to relinquish completely their favorite public venues. As a nationwide black-market liquor economy sprang up, the urban saloon transformed into the popular speakeasy that hid in plain sight among more legitimate businesses in practically every city and town. Wealthy urban dwellers and curious tourists continued their love affairs with those cabarets and nightclubs that changed as a result of Prohibition into high-class, well-protected, and extremely expensive saloons and, at times, drug emporiums for dealers and users of cocaine, heroin, and marijuana. Rural drinking spaces also underwent a radical change during Prohibition; country taverns, which had often been attached to the general store or some other central location, moved to more discreet sites in order to discourage inquisitive revenuers. Thus an old barn or abandoned building by day took on by night the role of riotous roadhouse or "jook joint," complete with music, dancing, and plenty of moonshine liquor.

American writers of the Prohibition era often set their fiction against the backdrop of these public drinking spaces for a variety of reasons and effects. The simplest explanation for the countless appearances of speakeasies, roadhouses, and cabarets in the literature of the 1920s is that these places, illicit or not, were an undeniable part of the American landscape. If literary realism demands attention to the details of everyday life, then such places cannot be excised from the ordinary experiences of Prohibition-era Americans. These scenes, however, are not ideologically neutral. A woman enters a speakeasy and orders a highball in Dorothy Parker's "Big Blonde" (1930); couples dance and drink gin at a roadhouse in Langston Hughes's *Not Without Laughter* (1930); a man and woman eager to drink descend into a raucous Harlem cabaret in Carl Van Vechten's *Nigger Heaven* (1926); none of these moments is accompanied by overt political rhetoric condemning—or even mentioning— Prohibition. Yet all of these scenes tacitly identify the characters as transgressors who willingly—even enthusiastically—defy the U.S. Constitution to pursue their own gratification. These individual scenes, small as they are, contribute to a much larger theme in American literature that pits the virtues of obeying the law against the rewards of achieving personal pleasure. In many of these instances, the rewards of drinking easily justify the lawbreaking that accompanies it.

Speakeasies

Let me in, please, Charlie, no one here but me,
I'm speakin' easy, gimme a pint of Tan-que-ree.
—Barbecue Bob, "Blind Pig Blues," 1928

It is important to remember that in the years immediately preceding Prohibition, public drinking was relatively affordable. As historian Madelon Powers explains in *Faces Along the Bar: Lore and Order in the Workingman's Saloon, 1870–1920* (1998), a glass of beer in a typical working-class saloon cost five cents and came with a free lunch that usually depended on the ethnicity of the saloon's clientele and might range from sandwiches to bratwurst to spaghetti to Irish stew (59, 128). But with the advent of Prohibition, liquor prices climbed considerably. Of course, some low-class urban dives sold noxious slugs of "smoke"—a combination of alcohol and water—for as little as ten cents a drink. But drinkers who wanted somewhat better liquor had to come up with substantial cash. In Chicago speakeasies, for example, the average price of a whiskey highball shot from 15 cents to 75 cents after Prohibition went into effect (Barr 238). In fancier places, a cocktail might sell for $1.50 or even more. And in urban "clip joints," which specialized in taking advantage of unsuspecting, out-of-town "suckers" by getting them hopelessly drunk and robbing them blind, each drink might cost upwards of two dollars (Asbury, *The Great Illusion* 198–99; 214). Not surprisingly, Americans found it increasingly difficult to afford to buy liquor. As a result, many of them either curtailed their drinking or turned to thriftier home-made concoctions: cider, beer, wine, and occasionally moonshine liquor. The exorbitant rise in retail liquor prices affected wealthier drinkers very little; indeed, while one study indicated that the consumption of beer (the traditional drink of the working classes) declined during Prohibition by as much as two-thirds, during the same period the consumption of distilled spirits increased by 10 percent and wine by more than 60 percent. This and other studies concluded that people who were fairly well off appeared to be drinking as much as, if not more than, they did before Prohibition went into effect.[1]

Drinkers who did have a bit of disposable cash jingling in their pockets generally purchased their illegal liquor at their neighborhood speakeasy. The etymology of the term *speakeasy* cannot be traced with absolute certainty, but H. L. Mencken believed it to be an Americanized form of "speak softly shop," an ancient Irish term denoting any illegal drinking spot, especially one that catered to the working class (*American Language* 265). Customers were requested to "speak softly" when ordering liquor, to prevent law enforcement agents from overhearing. American speakeasies during Prohibition were also commonly called "blind pigs" or "blind tigers." The origin of the nineteenth-century term *blind pig* is usually attributed to a clever saloonkeeper in Maine (where statewide prohibition legislation was passed in 1851). This saloonkeeper, knowing that the sale of liquor violated the law, instead sold his patrons tickets to view a blind pig he kept in a back room. Along with admission, every viewing customer was treated to a free glass of rum (Clark 48). "Blind tiger" may have come about in a similar way. Speakeasies acquired dozens of other nicknames during Prohibition, most of which have fallen out of use in the years since repeal, including "gin mill," "jimmy," and "shoe polish shop," which makes rather more sense if one knows that in the 1920s whiskey was sometimes referred to as "shoe polish" (Mason 170–71).

In states and counties that had, by local option, gone dry long before National Prohibition took effect, speakeasies already dotted the landscape, selling liquor acquired from local moonshiners, neighboring counties, and nearby states that remained wet. But with the official nationwide closing of the saloons at midnight on January 16, 1920, the speakeasy industry exploded. "Speaks" operated behind locked doors in apartments, in out-of-the-way commercial properties, or in the back rooms and cellars of more legitimate businesses such as candy stores, beauty parlors, and funeral homes—sometimes as literally underground operations. Many of them

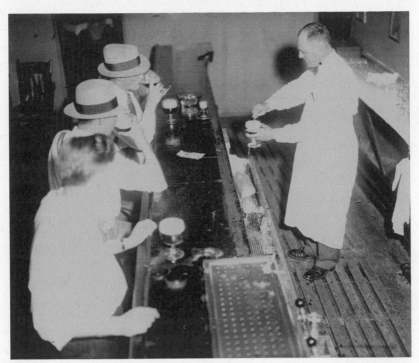

Figure 7
Interior of a Detroit speakeasy, 1931. Courtesy of the Walter P. Reuther Library, Wayne State University.

existed under the guise of a pool hall, drugstore, soda fountain, or sweet shop, with a back room bar that was inaccessible from the street. Speakeasies sometimes had music and dancing, but because these establishments were usually quite small, they often employed only a single piano player or a small musical ensemble. Business did not pick up in many urban speakeasies until after 3:00 A.M., when most cabarets were legally required to close. All-night partiers often stopped by a speakeasy (which, given its unlawful existence, was unbound by city curfews) on their way to breakfast.

Security at speakeasies was, of course, critical. Sometimes bouncers unlocked the door for patrons only after scrutinizing them through a peephole and demanding to hear a password. To streamline this process, some speakeasies actually gave regular customers official membership cards to present to the bouncer (Mason 97). Complete strangers were admitted only if they knew the proprietor, knew the password, could produce the card of a trusted reference, or could otherwise convince the bouncer or bartender that opening the door would not lead to a raid or an arrest.

These precautions were important to the proprietor, for if federal agents raided the speakeasy, bartenders could be arrested for selling liquor in violation of the law and patrons could be arrested and fined for illegal possession of alcohol or for public drunkenness—an embarrassing and sometimes expensive proposition that was also, obviously, bad for business. Furthermore, the speakeasy could be declared "a common nuisance," padlocked for up to a year, and designated "closed" by virtue of a sign placed on the door (Clark 140–41). In many cases, the proprietor would respond to this padlocking by promptly reopening in a different location, sometimes even in the same building. Speakeasies were so common in urban neighborhoods that there are accounts of residents posting signs on their front doors that read, "This is a private residence. Please do not ring" in the same way that city dwellers today try to keep thieves out of their cars by putting up signs in the window that say "No Stereo." In 1926, famous New York prohibition agent Izzy Einstein estimated that there were as many as a hundred thousand speakeasies in the greater New York City area; in 1930 New York Representative William Sirovich concurred with this estimate. The New York City police believed there were far fewer— about 32,000—but of course it was impossible to determine with any real accuracy how many speakeasies existed at any given time in any given city. As New York police commissioner Grover Whalen commented, "All you need is two bottles and a room and you have a speakeasy" (Asbury, *The Great Illusion* 210).

Except for certain security measures, many speakeasies were practically indistinguishable from the saloons that preceded them. Some such establishments, however, found ways to accommodate not only drinking but also the more sexual behavior that was being practiced in public, particularly among the young. One 1930 *New York Times* article reported,

> In many of the speakeasy saloons of today are large rear rooms honeycombed with private stalls, each a distinct unit and each designed to screen from public view the couples who occupy them. . . . These stalls are very popular with young people, and speakeasies have been observed in the West Forties where, on Saturday nights, there is a line of young couples waiting their turn for a vacant stall. The privacy thus afforded, together with the sale of intoxicants, invites and fosters disorderly conditions.[2]

The euphemism "disorderly conditions" clearly indicates some degree of sexual activity taking place in these stalls; thus certain speakeasies fostered not just defiance of the Prohibition laws but also defiance of traditionally conservative courtship and sexual practices.

Speakeasies were ubiquitous, especially in urban areas, and even the most naive Prohibition supporter could not deny their existence. As the 1920s wore on and enforcement became even less effective, security measures relaxed considerably. One 1920s Detroit journalist sarcastically lamented the effect of Prohibition when he wrote, "It was absolutely impossible to get a drink in Detroit unless you walked at least ten feet and told the busy bartender what you wanted in a voice loud enough for him to hear you above the uproar" (Mason 77). In fact, speakeasies became such a prominent element of social life in urban areas that, despite their supposed invisibility, they took on very visible roles in many movies from the Prohibition era. Dozens of blues, jazz, and novelty songs were also published about speakeasies, including Barbecue Bob's "Blind Pig Blues" (1928) and Bessie Smith's famous "Gimme a Pigfoot" (1933).

Speakeasies invaded popular culture not just through music and cinema but also through literature. Writers as diverse as Sinclair Lewis, Dorothy Parker, Jean Toomer, Rudolph Fisher, Grace Lumpkin, and Claude McKay all use speakeasies as places where their characters willingly make themselves vulnerable to the consequences of law enforcement. Speakeasies in literature offer characters important spaces in which they can act outside the law, demonstrate their disdain for outdated behavioral codes, boost their social status in certain circles, and, of course, satisfy their desire to drink. With the exception of Lewis's *Babbitt* (1922), whose title character, George Babbitt, feels anything but nonchalant about his illegal errand at a speakeasy, the rest of these authors demonstrate how characters who defy Prohibition by patronizing speakeasies come to see lawbreaking itself as casual—even insignificant—behavior.

Two years after the tremendous success of *Main Street* (1920), Sinclair Lewis published *Babbitt,* a satiric story of middle-class conformist George F. Babbitt—moderately successful realtor, enthusiastic Zenith city booster, proud automobile owner, bored husband, and bewildered father. The recently enacted Prohibition laws annoy Babbitt and his friends, who firmly believe that such laws are fine for intemperate laborers and immigrants but who also feel strongly that such laws ought not disturb their own respectable middle-class lives. Babbitt considers himself to be an upstanding, law-abiding, patriotic person, and he is proud of his respectable social standing in Zenith. Yet the lawlessness engendered by Prohibition also appeals to him, and he longs to surprise his friends by playing the part—only temporarily, of course—of a reckless lawbreaker. He also believes that acquiring a bottle of liquor would seem, to his friends, like such a bold, transgressive act that their admiration for Babbitt would necessarily increase significantly. Thus he determines to disregard the liquor laws in order to boost his standing among his middle-aged, middle-class, conservative social set.

On the day that he and his wife are to host a dinner party for several couples, Babbitt ventures into a rough area of Zenith in search of a quart of bootleg gin to serve to his guests that evening. Feeling simultaneously guilty and exhilarated by his illicit foray, the uneasy Babbitt "looked at every policeman with intense innocence, as one who loved the law, and admired the Force, and longed to stop and play with them" (94). Convincing himself that he would be taken as a businessman on a legitimate visit if he were to be seen by anyone he knew, Babbitt steps cautiously into the forbidden yet compelling world of Healey Hanson's speakeasy:

> He entered a place curiously like the saloons of ante-prohibition days, with a long greasy bar with sawdust in front and streaky mirror behind, a pine table at which a dirty old man dreamed over a glass of something which resembled whisky, and with two men at the bar, drinking something which resembled beer, and giving that impression of forming a large crowd which two men always give in a saloon. The bartender, a tall pale Swede with a diamond in his lilac scarf, stared at Babbitt as he stalked plumply up to the bar and whispered, "I'd, uh—Friend of Hanson's sent me here. Like to get some gin."
>
> The bartender gazed down on him in the manner of an outraged bishop. "I guess you got the wrong place, my friend. We sell nothing but soft drinks here." He cleaned the bar with a rag which would itself have done with a little cleaning, and glared across his mechanically moving elbow. (95)

Lewis offers a glimpse of speakeasy culture through the naive eyes of George Babbitt, and in the process he reveals to his readers his own familiarity with the 1920s liquor scene. His use of the term "resembled" to describe the actual whiskey and beer in the speakeasy would have resonated with Prohibition-era readers; since only soft drinks were sold in such an establishment, according to the bartender, the drinks merely *looked* like whiskey and beer. Unfortunately for the customers, their drinks probably only resembled whiskey and beer in taste, as well.

The diamond pin in the bartender's lilac scarf is another instructive detail that would not have gone unnoticed by a 1920s readership. A clear indication of the prosperity of the underground liquor economy, the bartender's diamond and showy ascot stand out in sharp relief against the backdrop of the "greasy bar," "streaky mirror," and seedy neighborhood. The squalid atmosphere of the speakeasy belies its affluence; individual customers such as the "dirty old man" drinking whiskey may not have had very much money, but even speakeasies in poor areas often made their owners relatively wealthy and consequently made the risk of arrest and imprisonment seem less intimidating. The bartender's response to Babbitt's appeal would have also been familiar to any speakeasy patron who had ever tried to wheedle a drink in an unfamiliar establishment. While it seems patently obvious that booze was available, the bartender's affected indignation, "in the manner of an outraged bishop," when the uncomfortable Babbitt stammers his request for gin, is both humorous and realistic. Americans attuned to Prohibition culture would have understood that the bartender had very good reasons to distrust Babbitt, so obviously a stranger in this environment.

The anxious Babbitt, intimidated by both the illegality of his quest and the obstinacy of the bartender, nevertheless remains firm in his resolve to treat his party guests to some cocktails. After managing to gain an audience with the speakeasy's proprietor, Babbitt awkwardly blurts out his mission: "Say, uh, I'm going to have a party, and Jake told me you'd be able to fix me up with a little gin" (96). After withdrawing into the back room for an inordinately long time, Hanson emerges with a bottle and snaps at Babbitt, "Twelve bucks." Babbitt protests:

> "Say, uh, but say, cap'n, Jake thought you'd be able to fix me up for eight or nine a bottle."
>
> "Nup. Twelve. This is the real stuff, smuggled from Canada. This is none o' your neutral spirits with a drop of juniper extract," the honest merchant said virtuously. "Twelve bones—if you want it. Course y' understand I'm just doing this anyway as a friend of Jake's."
>
> "Sure! Sure! I understand!" Babbitt gratefully held out twelve dollars. He felt honored by contact with greatness as Hanson yawned, stuffed the bills, uncounted, into his radiant vest, and swaggered away. (96)

Like the bartender in his employ, the well-dressed Hanson is cautious about selling his liquor—a practice that ensures his continuing economic success as a black-market merchant. He does not need to push a sale, because liquor of any quality, at virtually any price, found customers during Prohibition, and Hanson knew perfectly well that if Babbitt would not pay the outrageous price of twelve dollars for the gin, some other fool most certainly would. Lewis's ironic jab at the "honest merchant" who "virtuously" defended the quality of his product as he soaked his nervous

customer for twelve bucks is compounded by Babbitt's unmistakable
naïveté; handing over the money to the wily Hanson makes him feel
"honored by contact with greatness."

Babbitt himself feels anything but cheated after his daring foray into
the underworld of the speakeasy. Acquiring the gin ensures the success of
his party, and its extravagant price only adds to the prestige that Babbitt
intends to gain from sharing it with his guests. Almost as appealing to him
is his thrill at concealing the illicit and expensive bottle under his coat and
then in his desk until he returns home, and "all afternoon he snorted and
chuckled and gurgled over his ability to 'give the Boys a real shot in the
arm to-night'" (97). And, just as he suspected, Babbitt's friends are eager
to partake of the forbidden fruit. After Babbitt asks his guests coyly, "Well,
folks, do you think you could stand breaking the law a little?" (100), he
proudly serves his carefully mixed pitcher of cocktails to his eager friends
who, predictably, shower their host with praise as they guzzle their drinks.[3]

Healey Hanson's speakeasy offers a good example of a typical early Jazz
Age underground drinking establishment, in which security was relatively
tight and liquor was sold at exorbitant prices. But as the decade pro-
gressed, security in many such joints relaxed considerably. By the mid-
1920s, efficient enforcement of the laws had proved altogether impossible,
and many cities and towns less sympathetic to the Prohibition cause,
including New York City, left the problem of enforcement entirely to the
understaffed federal agencies empowered by the Volstead Act. By 1925
thirsty customers were less likely to feel at risk of arrest in urban
speakeasies such as Barney's, the combination poolroom, tobacco shop,
and blind pig that Martin Arrowsmith frequents in Lewis's novel
Arrowsmith (1925). While Barney's front room "was an impressionistic
painting in which a pool-table, piles of cigarettes, chocolate bars, playing
cards, and pink sporting papers were jumbled in chaos," Lewis writes, "the
back room was simpler: cases of sweet and thinly flavored soda, a large ice-
box, and two small tables with broken chairs. Barney poured, from a bottle plainly marked Ginger Ale, two glasses of powerful and appalling raw
whiskey" (62–63). Even as security loosened in the late 1920s, certain
minor precautions remained in place, and relabeling bottles to conceal
their actual contents was standard practice in speakeasies throughout the
years of Prohibition.

One important component of speakeasy culture that is not immediately apparent in these two descriptions from Lewis's novels is how common
the presence of women in these joints had become. Unlike pre-1920 public drinking culture, in which women played a far less conspicuous role,
many Prohibition-era watering holes attracted women in great numbers to
their smoky, pungent interiors. Stanley Walker comments hyperbolically,

in his 1933 informal history, *The Night Club Era,* that "soon after 1920 great, ravening hordes of women began to discover what their less respectable sisters had known for years—that it was a lot of fun, if you liked it, to get soused. All over New York these up and coming females piled out of their hideaways, rang the bells of speakeasies, wheedled drugstores into selling them gin and rye, and even in establishments of great decorum begged their escorts for a nip from a hip flask. It was all," Walker concludes, "very embarrassing" (30–31). Presumably, Walker believes that drinking men long accustomed to single-sex saloons were the ones most embarrassed by women who embraced public drinking. Nevertheless, women did patronize speakeasies in great numbers, and many Prohibition-era fiction writers chronicled their enthusiastic public drinking.

Dorothy Parker, herself an avid Prohibition violator, sets a number of stories in *Laments for the Living* (1930) in midtown Manhattan speakeasies. "Big Blonde," "Just a Little One," and "You Were Perfectly Fine," as well as several others, include female characters fully immersed in Prohibition-era drinking culture. Parker's vision of women drinkers, though, often rises above the stereotypes of the carefree flapper to investigate the more damaging consequences of Prohibition culture. In one of Parker's best-known stories, "Big Blonde," the sordid world of speakeasies deals a devastating blow to the protagonist, Hazel Morse, who, eager to assume the role of the perpetual "good sport" by palling around with men at local watering holes, spends inordinate amounts of time in those "small, recent restaurants occupying the floors of shabby brownstone houses, places where, upon mentioning the name of an habitué friend, might be obtained strange whiskey and fresh gin in many of their ramifications" (114). Deeming Prohibition to be only "a basis for jokes," because she and her friends "could always get all [they] wanted" (114), Hazel embraces the life of the gregarious barfly in the constant company of attentive men. While drinking more than her share of bad liquor and laughing at all the appropriate times, Hazel gradually succumbs to alcoholism and a growing understanding that the life of a freewheeling flapper does not necessarily lead to either freedom or joy. Rather, the trendy imbibing of gallons of liquor ensures the demise of her marriage, her friendships, and her happiness. When her suicide attempt fails, she is left with only her whiskey bottle to comfort her. In the story's final, bleak scene, Hazel's heartbreaking prayer, oddly rendered in the third person, is: "Oh, please, please, let her be able to get drunk, please keep her always drunk" (210).

Prohibition-era drinking in Parker's "Just a Little One" has far less tragic results for the female protagonist. In this short, humorous story set in a speakeasy, the narrator, an experienced and enthusiastic imbiber, requests each of her many drinks to be "just a little one." The story opens with an overt comment on the increasing laxity of Prohibition enforcement; the narrator sarcastically remarks to Fred, her companion: "I think you're perfectly marvelous, discovering a speakeasy in the year 1928. And they let you right in, without asking you a single question. I bet you could get into the subway without using anybody's name. Couldn't you, Fred?" (92). While she feigns a demure attitude toward drinking, she lets slip a few details that indicate she knows her way around a speakeasy, such as warning Fred explicitly that after a few drinks she always wants to adopt stray animals, and suggesting that real scotch would be a lovely switch after drinking the awful stuff she keeps at home.

Throughout the course of the story, the narrator gets progressively more inebriated as she tries to keep pace with her date's drinking. "I shouldn't like to see you drinking by yourself, Fred," she justifies. "Solitary drinking is what causes half the crime in this country. That's what's responsible for the failure of Prohibition" (92). During the span of a relatively brief conversation, she orders no fewer than six scotch highballs, all the while pleading with the bartender for them to be "just little ones." As she drinks, she becomes more and more belligerent toward her date and accuses him of caring for another woman. The story ends with the narrator, reassured of Fred's devotion, eagerly ordering one more "little" highball. This story is a revealing chronicle of Prohibition culture because the author and, presumably, the reader completely accept the notion of a respectable woman who drinks heavily in public. The speakeasy setting is merely a vehicle for spinning the tale—while the narrator's drunkenness provides comedy, the story itself focuses much more on her relationship with Fred than on the fact that she is getting publicly drunk. "Just a Little One" could not have been imagined before Prohibition, when respectable middle- or upper-class women would rarely, if ever drink, in a public place, let alone get noticeably inebriated.

In neither of these stories does Parker condemn her protagonists for their excessive intemperance; indeed, she seems decidedly sympathetic toward their weakness for the bottle. Parker recognizes that the Prohibition-era speakeasy offered women a socially significant space in which they could test the limits of female propriety in public.[4] No longer bound by the traditional tenets of womanhood, the modern American woman of Parker's stories feels free to experiment with a variety of such "fashionable" heterosocial behaviors as smoking, petting, and, of course, drinking. Parker does not seem the least bit alarmed by this shift in women's conduct, but the enormous outpouring of Prohibition-era stories and newspaper accounts of women ruined by their newfound freedoms (written by both men and women) indicated a common fear that if women succumb to strong drink and other traditionally unladylike behaviors, the "family values" of the nation would be forever compromised.

At the same time that speakeasies were supposedly threatening the foundations of American femininity, they were also offering working-class patrons, both black and white, important spaces in which to make political connections. Late nineteenth-century and early twentieth-century saloons offered venues for working men to organize and discuss politics; Prohibition-era speakeasies sustained this role. Countless deals regarding elections and labor disputes were hammered out over glasses of illegal liquor in blind pigs across the country, and agitators set up shop in local speakeasies to prevail upon workers to join a wide range of political organizations. For example, in Grace Lumpkin's heartbreaking proletarian novel *To Make My Bread* (1932), protagonist John McClure is approached one day by Robert, an older colleague, who invites him to have a drink at Carpenter's place, a popular blind tiger among the factory hands. During their conversation Robert entreats John to join the "town lodge," a euphemism in this case for the Ku Klux Klan, which "stood for the protection of the flag, and the motto was 'Keep out the foreigner and the nigger. Neither belongs'" (Lumpkin 293). Impressed by Robert's initiative and passion, John decides to join the lodge in order to promote the best interests of his struggling family. The blind tiger in *To Make My Bread* provides a relatively public venue in which mill workers congregate to drink and discuss the social and political issues most relevant to their lives.

Speakeasies often served as sites where people of very different economic and racial backgrounds mixed socially; as Milton "Mezz" Mezzrow, a well-known white jazz clarinetist of the 1920s, recalled, "It struck me funny how the top and bottom crusts in society were always getting together during the Prohibition era" (Leonard 50). Although speakeasies in white neighborhoods across the nation during the 1920s usually adhered fairly stringently to the common Jim Crow conventions, and many speakeasies in black neighborhoods catered to a black-only clientele, some "speaks" in black neighborhoods, referred to as "black and tan" joints, accommodated both black and white drinkers. Other speakeasies in black neighborhoods deliberately targeted white customers who hoped to imbibe both an illegal drink and a bit of "exotic" black culture at the same time. Regardless of their clientele, however, speakeasy proprietors conscientiously courted police officers and Prohibition agents who could at any time padlock their establishment and cart them off to jail for violating the liquor laws.

In Harlem, the nation's capital of African American culture during the Prohibition era, enforcement of liquor laws seems to have been as spotty and erratic as anyplace else. Some Harlem residents demanded increased police presence and stricter law enforcement, believing that white New Yorkers were flouting the liquor laws in their neighborhood in order to turn Harlem into a circumscribed vice district. In fact, in a front-page *New York Times* article on February 26, 1924, New York City police commissioner Richard Enright acknowledged reports that "men assigned to suppress 'speakeasies' and vice and gambling resorts in Harlem had been particularly lax," and he suspected that "some of them were accepting bribes to permit such places to exist." He had received more than one thousand complaints "indicating that the Federal prohibition law was being flagrantly violated in Harlem" and that a number of Prohibition enforcement agents "were 'on the payroll' of the proprietors of certain 'speak-easies' in Harlem." He promised to respond to these allegations with "dramatic action," but it remains unclear what action Enright and his police force took to curb these offenses.[5]

Irish, Italian, Jewish, and other white businessmen owned a disproportionate number of the successful speakeasies in Harlem; one 1929 survey of eighty-five Harlem speakeasies found that "about 90 per cent of these were owned and managed by whites, 5 per cent were owned by whites but managed by negroes and the other 5 per cent were owned and managed by negroes." The article went on to note, "in every case the customers were both white and negro."[6] According to David Levering Lewis, examples of actual Harlem speakeasies owned by African Americans include the Coal Bed, the Air Raid Shelter, and the suggestively named Glory Hole (242). The names of these establishments reflect both their small, dark quarters and their sense of the underground, both physically and psychologically. In his 1927 essay "Negro Life in New York's Harlem," Wallace Thurman describes the Glory Hole speakeasy in some detail:

> One particular place known as the Glory Hole is hidden in a musty, damp basement behind an express and trucking office. It is a single room about ten feet square and remains an unembellished basement except for a planed down plank floor, a piano, three chairs and a library table. The Glory Hole is typical of its class. It is a social club, commonly called a dive, convenient for the high times of a certain group. The men are unskilled laborers during the day, and in the evenings they round up their girls or else meet them at the rendezvous in order to have what they consider and enjoy as a good time. The women, like the men, swear, drink and dance as much and as vulgarly as they please. . . . Such places as the Glory Hole can be found all over the so-called "bad lands" of Harlem. They are not always confined to basement rooms. They can be found in apart-

ment flats, in the rear of barber shops, lunch counters, pool halls, and other such conveniently blind places. (*Collected Writings* 48)

Many of these dives functioned as pre-1920 saloons did, serving drinks for a relatively reasonable price—albeit far higher than before Prohibition—to working-class men and women who lived in the neighborhood. These hole-in-the-wall speakeasies were tremendously common; one 1929 article in *Variety* estimated that there were more than five hundred in Harlem alone (Schoener 80). And, just as in white neighborhoods, they often disguised themselves as drugstores, cigar stores, barbershops, candy stores, soda fountains, or delicatessens. "Harlem can boast of more drugstores than any similar area in the world, [and] a plethora of delicatessen stores may be found in the Negro sections of New York, most of which are simply disguised bootlegging stores," one Harlemite concluded in 1924. "And so many confectioners! One never dreamed the Negroes were so much in need of sugar" (Osofsky 147). Although customers probably could have bought candy in these confectioners' shops, it is likely that they would have been far more interested in "white mule" than in gumdrops.

Like the saloons of earlier days, working-class speakeasies in Harlem provided important sites for men to socialize and gamble, as well as to drink. Usually unwelcome at white fraternal organizations and often unable to afford more lavish entertainment, thousands of black working men frequented local blind pigs with regularity, wholly disregarding the laws aimed at dismantling such places. One Prohibition-era observer recounted:

> The speakeasies are the hang-outs for Negroes of meagre means. They seem to constitute the club rooms of the neighborhood. Over small glasses of cheap gin and steins of beer, half-drunk Negroes tell of their past experiences. Conversations centering around "numbers," baseball, boxing, liquor, and "sky-larkin'" may be heard. (Kiser 46)

Judging from a number of literary and anecdotal accounts of black working-class speakeasies, such establishments also served as places where customers discussed and argued about the important social and political issues of the day. For many, the benefits of having a place to drink and socialize far outweighed the relatively minor risks involved in patronizing an illegal speakeasy.

While the existence of black-owned or black-run speakeasies in urban areas hardly constituted "news," society reporters for white newspapers often published stories about them, fueling their white readers' fascination with African American culture. For example, the *New York Sunday News*

ran a story on November 3, 1929, called "'Speaks' Whoop After Clubs
Pipe Down." While nothing in the article ranks as particularly newswor-
thy, the story serves as a powerful advertisement for the entertainment
scene in Harlem. It begins:

> An important and interesting phase of the after-dark revelry that is
> rapidly transforming Harlem into the favorite midnight playground
> of the downtown spenders is the speakeasies. Peeping from nooks
> and crannies of 100 blocks, these little nests of revelry offer a type of
> entertainment that is found neither within the precincts of the night
> clubs or before the bars of the downtown booze joints. Scattered
> throughout the district at least ten to the square block, the "lap
> joints," as they are called by the neighbors' children, cure the thirsts
> of thousands, white and colored, nightly. (Schoener 84–85)

The article goes on to describe the process by which a white customer
might be admitted, the music he might hear once inside, the availability
of prostitutes, and the terrible quality of the liquor—all of which evidently served to recommend these places to white revelers looking for excitement in Harlem. Drawn by their assumption that African American musicians possessed native talent for performance, white "slummers" traveled
to black neighborhoods to sample the nightlife; the same newspaper article goes on to explain:

> With the instinct for entertainment that is inherent in the race, the
> colored speakeasy proprietor provides a show for those of his cus-
> tomers who can stay awake and listen, or watch. In the main, the
> speakies are patronized solely by colored men and women, but in the
> last year the so-called "better places" have made a strong bid for the
> white trade, the patronage of the man who becomes bored with the
> prancing of the cabaret revues. (Schoener 84–85)

Prohibition encouraged many upper- and middle-class white people to
treat black neighborhoods as their own personal vice playground and to
travel shamelessly to Harlem and other black districts to drink, gamble,
and solicit prostitutes. For their part, many African American residents
raged against the influx of white partiers whose presence in the clubs, they
believed, contributed to the ghettoization of the neighborhood. In a 1929
editorial entitled "Is This Really Harlem?" published in the black newspaper *The Amsterdam News,* the writer berates the magazine *Variety* for publishing a sordid "exposé" of Harlem's nightlife. The *Variety* article reads, in
part:

> Harlem has attained pre-eminence in the past few years as an amuse-
> ment center. Its night life now surpasses that of Broadway itself. From
> midnight until after dawn it is a seething cauldron of Nubian mirth
> and hilarity. Never has it been more popular. One sees as many lim-
> ousines from Park and upper Fifth Avenue parked outside its sizzling
> cafes, "speaks," night clubs and spiritual séances as in any other high-
> grade white locale in the country. . . . When it comes to pep, pulchri-
> tude, punch and presentation, the Harlem places have Broadway's
> night clubs distanced. Celebrities in all walks of life "make" the
> Harlem joints every night. (Schoener 79–80)

First excoriating this *Variety* article, the editorial writer then angrily accuses his Harlem readership of standing passively by while spoiled white New
Yorkers turn Harlem into a "raging hell" after dark. Articles like this one
in *Variety* contributed to the heavy white traffic in Harlem by emphasizing
not just the high quality of entertainment available there but also the like-
lihood of seeing and being seen by members of New York's high society.

Although the leaders of Harlem's churches and civic groups railed
against the speakeasies, many Harlem Renaissance writers avidly patronized these illicit drinking establishments. While certain members of the
intellectual elite, such as W. E. B. Du Bois and James Weldon Johnson,
generally confined their socializing to the refined gatherings hosted in
black and white middle- and upper-middle-class homes, according to historian Cary Wintz in *Black Culture and the Harlem Renaissance* (1988),
"young black writers," including Langston Hughes, Wallace Thurman, and
Rudolph Fisher, "submerged themselves in the primitive black culture that
flourished in the ghetto's speakeasies, gin houses, and jazzrooms" (93).
Wintz explains that it was in these speakeasies that "all of Harlem con-
verged: the prostitute, the washwoman, the petty gangster, the poet, and
the intellectual shared the blues and swayed to the beat of the jazz musicians" (93). Given the ubiquity of Harlem speakeasies and their roles as a
refuge of the working class, a haven for many black artists, and a popular
destination for middle-class whites, it comes as no surprise that speakeasies
appear in a significant number of Harlem Renaissance works, including
Rudolph Fisher's *The Walls of Jericho* (1928), Jean Toomer's *Cane* (1923),
Wallace Thurman's *Infants of the Spring* (1932), and several of Langston
Hughes's short stories.

Hailed by African American critic and writer Walter White as "the first
light novel of Negro life,"[7] Rudolph Fisher's *The Walls of Jericho* tells the
story of Shine, a black piano mover in Harlem, and his courtship of Linda,
a maid who works first for a rich white woman and then for Merrit, a light-
skinned African American man. Shine's rival for Linda's affections is

Patmore, the owner of the speakeasy where Shine hangs out and where many of the novel's scenes take place. Patmore's speakeasy, located on the ground floor of a Harlem tenement, is divided into three rooms. The narrator explains:

> In the saloon you could get any drink you had courage and cash enough to order; in the pool room you could play for any stake and use any language you had the ingenuity to devise. The third room was off the pool room and behind the saloon; this gave itself over to that triad of swift exchange, poker, black-jack, and dice. Such was Pat's standing in the community that you might at any time find in this little rear room a policeman sitting in a card game, his coat on the back of his chair, his cap on the back of his head. For men, Pat's was supremely the neighborhood's social center, where you met real regular guys and rubbed elbows with authority. (2)

Despite the frequent outsider presence of the police officer (who almost certainly never paid for his own drinks), Patmore's place is where the men discuss issues important to their community. For example, the working men who gather there talk at length about the possibility of a race riot prompted by black families moving into white neighborhoods—a possibility with which much of the novel is concerned. The centrality of Patmore's speakeasy suggests how such places served as important crucibles for working-class people to connect, socially and politically, with their neighbors.

Fisher also captures an element of Prohibition culture in his portrayal of Patmore's speakeasy that is often forgotten today. During Prohibition, one of the few ways to acquire alcohol legally was through a doctor's prescription. If a doctor prescribed whiskey for medicinal use, the patient could purchase the specified quantity (usually a pint) of genuine, unadulterated liquor at any local drugstore. Many young doctors got their start by selling prescriptions, or "scrips," to so-called patients, but established doctors were also known to make a great deal of money from the illegal prescription trade (Mason 78). Some druggists even operated without involving any doctors at all and would sell prewritten prescriptions to customers, along with the prescribed pint of "medicinal" whiskey. In *The Walls of Jericho*, Shine produces a pint bottle of prescription whiskey from his pocket and proceeds to drink it in front of Patmore. In disbelief, Patmore asks Shine, "You buy licker somewhere else and bring it to my establishment to drink?" The burly piano mover shoots back, "You hear me say it's 'scription. You ain' runnin' no drugstore, are y'? Yea, I bought it. Yea, I brought it here. Yea, I'm drinkin' it. Now what the hell about it?"

The intimidated proprietor stammers and slinks away, leaving Shine to drink from his drugstore bottle in peace (Fisher 9–10). This scene not only suggests the latent tensions between Patmore and Shine, which become much more pronounced later in the story, but also reveals the commonplace nature of drinking prescription whiskey recreationally during Prohibition.

While Fisher's novel uses the speakeasy as a site for fostering social connections among African Americans, Jean Toomer's groundbreaking *Cane* illustrates how speakeasies could also demarcate social categories and keep certain groups of people separated. For example, in the story "Esther," it is very clear to the residents of the southern town in which the story is set just who may patronize the speakeasy and who may not. Esther leads a lonely existence confined to her father's house and his store—the only spaces identified as socially acceptable for her. She languishes in both locations, dreaming for years of King Barlo, a hard-drinking gambler and rounder who, to the sheltered girl, represents all the adventurous and exciting possibilities of life. But the rough, masculine culture of Barlo and the other men on the street corner, drinking moonshine from soda bottles, is no more available to Esther than is the culture of Nat Bowle's speakeasy, which she finally enters in hopeless pursuit of the man about whom she has fantasized for so long:

> A turn into a side street brings her abruptly to Nat Bowle's place. The house is squat and dark. It is always dark. Barlo is within. Quietly she opens the outside door and steps in. She passes through a small room. Pauses before a flight of stairs down which people's voices, muffled, come. The air is heavy with fresh tobacco smoke. It makes her sick. She wants to turn back. She goes up the steps. She is violently dizzy. Blackness rushes to her eyes. And then she finds that she is in a large room. . . . She sees a smile, ugly and repulsive to her, working upward through thick licker fumes. Barlo seems hideous. The thought comes suddenly, that conception with a drunken man must be a mighty sin. She draws away frozen. Like a somnambulist she wheels around and walks stiffly to the stairs. Down them. Jeers and hoots pelter bluntly upon her back. She steps out. There is no air, no street, and the town has completely disappeared. (26–27)

Esther's pursuit of a fantasy lover, one who would love her and whisk her away from her lonesome, circumscribed life, leads her into a place where social convention forbids her to go. While men and women frequently drank together in public places during Prohibition, certain male-only "saloons" remained off-limits to women. Although the men in Nat Bowle's joint were certainly transgressing against the liquor laws, Esther's socially inappropriate appearance at the speakeasy was by far the more significant transgression of the scene—one that both surprises the men and completely unbalances Esther herself.

Toomer's scene takes place in a southern town far smaller and more provincial than New York's Harlem or Chicago's South Side, with a longer and deeper history of Prohibition. As a whole, the southeastern portion of the United States, more evangelical and conservative than much of the rest of the country, embraced the idea of legally prohibiting the liquor traffic well before the Eighteenth Amendment was ratified. During the Progressive era, many southern states and counties passed local option laws banning, in varying degrees, the manufacture, transportation, and sale of alcoholic beverages. According to historian Madelon Powers, before such prohibitive laws were passed, public drinking in the rural South had taken place mostly at country stores, which sold liquor and also doubled as taverns (62). In the evenings, particularly on weekends, drinks would be bought and shared by local residents, and musicians would often accompany the dancing of the patrons. These informal storefront "saloons," some catering to white and others to black clienteles, prefigured the country roadhouses that would spring to life throughout the rural South and Midwest, as well as other sparsely populated regions, after the passage of National Prohibition.

Roadhouses

> Jook is the word for a Negro pleasure house.
> —Zora Neale Hurston, "Characteristics of Negro Expression," 1934

The popularity of drinking houses in the nation's small towns and rural countryside during the 1920s indicates that the illegal drinking culture of Prohibition was in no way confined to the urban speakeasy. Usually referred to as roadhouses, barrelhouses, or jook (or juke) joints, these rural watering holes not only quenched their patrons' thirst for illegal booze but also served as popular sites for music making, dancing, gambling, prostitution, and drug use. Music historians Stephen Calt and Gayle Wardlow describe the typical country roadhouse as "a commercially operated recreation spot that contained several rooms and served as an all-purpose gambling den, dance hall, bar, brothel, and even boarding house" (59). Such places were usually open Friday to Sunday and welcomed both male and female customers. It was common during Prohibition for rural southerners to travel as far as thirty miles to socialize at a popular barrelhouse, which preserved its continued existence by paying off local law enforcement agents and occasionally accommodating phony liquor raids by the sheriff. Roadhouses were often located in out-of-the-way places, beyond town limits, parental vision, and inquisitive law enforcement officials, although they were sometimes situated near a small-town train depot, thus catering to travelers who might be passing through overnight. Often, the exteriors or the front doors of these roadhouses were painted green so that strangers could easily ascertain where they might be able to find a drink, a poker game, a prostitute, or whatever else they desired. A number of songs from the 1920s and early 1930s include references to these green country roadhouses, including Mississippi guitarist Charlie Patton's blues classic "Moon Going Down," which he recorded for Paramount in 1930 (Calt & Wardlow 60).

Most rural roadhouses catered to either a black or a white crowd—they generally did not serve an integrated clientele. Zora Neale Hurston's "Characteristics of Negro Expression" (1934) explains this popular site of rural Prohibition-era socializing in southern black communities:

> Jook is the word for a Negro pleasure house. It may mean a bawdy house. It may mean the house set apart on public works where the men and women dance, drink and gamble. Often it is a combination of all these. In past generations the music was furnished by "boxes," another word for guitars. . . . Pianos soon came to take the place of the boxes, and now player-pianos and victrolas are in all of the Jooks. Musically speaking, the Jook is the most important place in America. For in its smelly, shoddy confines has been born the secular music known as blues, and on blues has been founded jazz. The singing and playing in true Negro style is called "jooking."[8]

Hurston justifiably identifies the African American jook joint as the wellspring of a great deal of American musical culture, including such dance crazes as the Charleston and the Black Bottom, both of which swept through white middle-class America during the Roaring Twenties. Blues historian Paul Oliver, in *Blues Fell This Morning: Meaning in the Blues* (1990), maintains that many of the popular dances that reached Chicago, Detroit, Cincinnati, New York, and other northern urban centers had roots in the black folk culture of the South. Those dances that emulated animal movements, such as the Grizzly Bear, the Turkey Trot, the Bunny Hug, and Walking the Dog, which were popular before World War I, all originated in southern rural jooks (148–50).

Beyond musical entertainment, jook joints also provided patrons with access to plentiful liquor. Given the proximity of these roadhouses to rural stills, the drink most widely and cheaply available in such establishments was typically homemade moonshine—sometimes called "white mule," "white lightning," "panther sweat," "rookus juice," "squirrel dew," or any of several dozen other euphemisms (Hardin 87). But jooks were also popular for dispensing the commercial varieties of liquor more often available in urban speakeasies.[9] Of course, like liquor sold in the cities, it was usually adulterated by bootleggers who diluted it with water and then added coloring and flavoring to mimic, loosely, the taste of real whiskey. Even so, rural patrons were sometimes willing to pay twice the price of crude homemade corn liquor in order to drink this supposedly superior whiskey. One could also buy food at roadhouses and often even rent a room; thus roadhouses provided an important service for those African American travelers passing through communities that lacked a hotel willing to accommodate them (Calt & Wardlow 59–60).

In his autobiographical novel *Not Without Laughter* (1930), Langston Hughes describes such a roadhouse located in "the Bottoms," the black area of Stanton, a small Kansas town. Despite the poverty its residents suffered, Hughes describes the Bottoms as "a gay place" located literally across the railroad tracks from the white churches and the YMCA, a place where "folks ceased to struggle against the boundaries between good and bad, or white and black, and surrendered amiably to immorality" (216). The rollicking life in the Bottoms attracts the rebellious teenaged flapper Harriett and her friends and repels their conservative elders, who view this neighborhood with fear and disapproval. Hughes writes:

> To those who lived on the other side of the railroad and never realized the utter stupidity of the word "sin," the Bottoms was vile and wicked. But to the girls who lived there, and the boys who pimped and fought and sold licker there, "sin" was a silly word that did not enter their heads. They had never looked at life through the spectacles of the Sunday School. The glasses good people wore wouldn't have fitted their eyes, for they hung no curtain of words between themselves and reality. To them, things were—what they were. (216–17)

Hughes's obvious admiration for what he sees as the honesty of life in the Bottoms, untainted by pretension or phoniness, is echoed in the behavior of Harriett, the young black girl who dreams of escaping her strict Christian family and becoming a successful blues singer.

One night Harriett takes her young nephew, Sandy (whom she is supposed to be babysitting), to a dance at Chaver's Hall, a roadhouse in the Bottoms. This popular roadhouse is the social center for the town's young people—the place where they drink and dance and court and fight and learn to live in their world. The dozens of young, unsupervised couples get carried away with jazz music and gin drinking, but while Hughes acknowledges the chaotic nature of the evening, the dance scene actually contains little of the evil that Harriett's mother, Hager, fears. Instead, the older partygoers look after Sandy—even giving him money to buy food and sodas—and while some violence does occur (a man strikes his girl-friend at the very end of the scene), the roadhouse is portrayed in a gen-erally positive light.

Hager, however, worried about the safety and reputation of her rebel-lious daughter, scolds Harriett and severely whips both her and Sandy for attending the dance. Hager represents many members of her generation, both black and white, who feared that illegal drinking was increasing among both young men and young women. A number of polls from the late 1920s indicated that college-age drinking was rising, and "lurid reports of roadhouses, joy rides, rural 'beer farms' with rooms for rent upstairs," historian Catherine Murdock explains, "increased public suspicion that America was producing a generation of salacious alcoholics" (111). Unable to convince her daughter of the virtues of living a modest Christian life, Hager resorts to physical violence in a futile attempt to curb Harriett, the very model of the modern flapper in spite of her rural environment and limited financial resources.

Despite the numerous literary examples of members of the older gener-ation (like Hager) condemning the younger generation for their rowdy and rebellious ways, in many cases older drinkers actually followed the lead of the younger drinkers by finding their own way to watering holes full of late-night revelry. For example, in one scene in Sinclair Lewis's *Babbitt,* the middle-aged protagonist finds himself at a whites-only roadhouse in an old converted stable where "whisky was served openly, in glasses" (156) and people of various social classes mingled amiably. Babbitt pathetically tries to keep up with the antics of his young mistress and her friends, but pro-ceeds only to get embarrassingly drunk. Lewis describes how, at the road-house, Babbitt and his fellow drinkers get caught up in the frenzy of dance music and strong whiskey:

> Two or three clerks, who on pay-day longed to be taken for million-
> aires, sheepishly danced with telephone-girls and manicure-girls in
> the narrow space between the tables. Fantastically whirled the profes-
> sionals, a young man in sleek evening-clothes and a slim mad girl in
> emerald silk, with amber hair flung up as jaggedly as flames. Babbitt
> tried to dance with her. He shuffled along the floor, too bulky to be
> guided, his steps unrelated to the rhythm of the jungle music, and in

his staggering he would have fallen, had she not held him with sup-
ple kindly strength. He was blind and deaf from prohibition-era
alcohol; he could not see the tables, the faces. But he was overwhelmed by the girl and her young pliant warmth. (156)

Contrasting the fun-loving young people with the out-of-place, middle-
aged Babbitt, Lewis highlights the generation gap caused by Prohibition
culture—a gap that bewildered many adults who never anticipated that
their children would respond so transgressively to the new liquor laws.

Roadhouses and speakeasies not only highlighted generational differences but also provided a site where individual allegiances to the government's attempts to legislate morality were measured. Babbitt's entrances
into Healey Hanson's speakeasy and the out-of-the-way roadhouse indicate both a moral and a political decision that privileges the desires of the
individual over the perceived "common good." But this is not to argue
that Babbitt or any other transgressor necessarily denied the fundamental
tenets of Prohibition, or even the spirit behind the law. Rather, Babbitt
simply did not believe that these tenets applied to *him*. He and his hundreds of thousands of partners in crime chose their own individual prior-
ities over the law of the land, and the countless speakeasies and roadhouses that dotted the American landscape during Prohibition testify to this
wholesale refusal of the people to allow the government to dictate to them
what many considered to be a matter of personal choice.

Cabarets

Cabarets are peculiar, mind you. They're not like theatres and con-
cert halls. You don't just go to a cabaret and sit back and wait to be
entertained. You get out on the floor and join the pow-wow and help
entertain yourself.
—Rudolph Fisher, "The Caucasian Storms Harlem" (1927)

Along with the speakeasies and roadhouses, another critical site of
Prohibition culture, especially in larger metropolitan areas, was the cabaret
or nightclub. According to a New York Department of Licenses Report of
1927, a cabaret "shall mean any room, place or space in the city in which
any musical entertainment, singing, dancing or other amusement is permitted in connection with the restaurant business or the business of directly or
indirectly selling the public food or drink" (Erenberg xi–xii). Cabarets established few barriers between the entertainment and the crowd; no elevated
stage existed, and tables were crowded around the center floor so patrons

were in close proximity to the performers. The band usually set up off to one side of the floor or in a balcony, to keep from taking up valuable space for dancing. The patrons were right in the middle of the action, and during intermissions they were welcome to take to the floor to dance a few numbers.

The cabaret business in the United States began around the turn of the twentieth century; most of these early cabarets operated as combination saloons and dance halls in red-light districts and in the basements of city buildings. Around 1912 public dancing became a craze that endured in popularity until about World War I; during these years, many cabarets began targeting more "respectable" middle-class patrons (Murdock 73–74). Before Prohibition, drinking was the cornerstone of most cabaret experiences. A 1918 *Variety* article asserted, "Everything in and about the cabaret commences and stops with liquor. It starts the eating, it starts the buying, and even with the awful liquor prices, it starts everything else connected with the nightlife of Broadway" (Erenberg 130). With the advent of Prohibition in 1920, cabarets transformed themselves once again into establishments that ostensibly functioned only to provide entertainment, but in reality they served as fashionable places to buy and drink alcohol. Some cabarets remained in their underground locations as a security measure, while others operated in plain sight of police and enforcement officials, keeping their doors open through an expensive system of bribery and the strong-arm protection of organized crime.

Cabarets (also called nightclubs) differed from speakeasies in their focus on musical entertainment. Speakeasies and roadhouses usually reflected more of a pre-Prohibition, saloon-like atmosphere; while music and dancing were sometimes available, customers generally occupied themselves with talking, drinking, and gambling. However, cabarets drew customers primarily with their lavish entertainment; orchestra musicians, chorus girls, jazz singers, and comedy acts combined to create shows that sometimes lasted several hours. One 1932 description of a Harlem cabaret explains:

> Until about eleven o'clock the Negro orchestra plays while the patrons eat, drink and dance. Then the floor is cleared and the show begins. Brown-skinned girls and smiling, chocolate-colored, light-footed boys entertain the patrons. During an intermission at midnight the patrons use the floor for half an hour. By three or four o'clock the whites—the "dickeys," as the Negroes call them—who have "done Harlem," disperse as the entertainment ends. (Kiser 43)

While some working-class cabarets did exist, many nightclubs tried to attract more "exclusive" clientele by charging prohibitively high prices, including an admission price that usually went toward protection money paid to police and racketeers. Once inside, patrons could usually buy pints of bootleg liquor or bottles of champagne from their waiter at a premium price, or else they just ordered "set-ups" (cracked ice and water, club soda, or ginger ale) into which they poured the liquor they brought with them. Customers carefully kept flasks and bottles in their pockets—no liquor was displayed on tables in case of an unanticipated raid.

One of the reasons that cabarets in black neighborhoods were so popular was that they attracted diverse crowds of both black and white party-goers. As more and more wealthy white downtowners crowded into black neighborhoods for a few hours of entertainment, however, entrepreneurial Harlem cabaret owners either segregated their clientele or prohibited black customers altogether. Certain popular Harlem nightspots blatantly drew the color line, much to the dismay of local black residents. Although probably apocryphal, one well-known anecdote recalls the great blues composer W. C. Handy being turned away from the doors of the famous Cotton Club, though he could hear his own music wafting into the street from inside (Lewis 209). Claude McKay ruefully remembers in his auto-biography *A Long Way from Home* (1937) that during Prohibition, Harlem became "an all-white picnic ground and with no apparent gain to the blacks. The competition of white-owned cabarets has driven the colored out of business, and blacks are barred from the best of them in Harlem now" (133). Other upscale cabarets catered to white customers by simply pricing themselves out of most African Americans' financial reach; in 1929 the *New York Daily News* reported that the average price, per person, for an evening at the famous Connie's Inn came to more than fifteen dollars (in contrast, the nightly tab at an average cabaret might total two to four dollars per person) (Schoener 83).

Still, many cabarets catered to both black and white partiers. In *Black Culture and the Harlem Renaissance* (1988), historian Cary Wintz claims that Harlem cabarets "provided the most attractive feature of its night life and . . . for a time served as a melting pot for all classes of New Yorkers. Blacks of all types gathered in these nightspots to debate politics, religion, sex, and the 'race problem'; black writers entertained their white friends as well as their patrons and sponsors there" (92). This influx of white partiers into Harlem dismayed many in the black community. One of their major complaints about Prohibition-era cabaret life was that the incessant attention paid by the media to the night life of Harlem elided the many serious social problems that plagued ordinary black residents. In 1932 sociologist Clyde Kiser reported that the white "slumming parties" who traveled to Harlem for a taste of the exotic "usually see only what they expect to see. The night-club guests participate in the hilarity but seldom realize that while they sit until the wee hours of the morning in a Harlem cabaret

Figure 8
Interior of Connie's Inn, Harlem, New York, ca. 1920s. Courtesy of the Photographs and Prints Division, Schomburg Center for Research in Black Culture, The New York Public Library, Astor, Lenox and Tilden Foundations.

or night club, enjoying the entertainment furnished by Negro performers, there are thousands of black folk slumbering within a few blocks, ready the next day to begin another day of toil" (27).

White interest in African American culture was nothing new during Prohibition. Ever since antebellum minstrel shows traveled the country and then later, when the first black entertainers broke into vaudeville and Broadway, white cosmopolites had been fascinated by what they perceived to be the exotic primitivism of African Americans. Minstrel shows and other comedy acts reinforced the popular stereotype that black people were natural buffoons whose performances were closer to life than to art. *The Emperor Jones* (1920), *Shuffle Along* (1921), and other Broadway sensations featuring black casts and racial themes were extremely well received by white theatergoers during the Jazz Age. White audiences flocked to blues and jazz performances by such celebrities as Ethel Waters, Paul Robeson, Duke Ellington, and Louis Armstrong. This white preoccupation with Harlem culture and entertainment reached its apex in part due to the 1926 publication of Carl Van Vechten's best-selling novel, *Nigger Heaven.* In fact, one 1927 *New York Times* article specifically cited Van Vechten's novel as one important reason why Harlem was becoming an increasingly popular destination, claiming that "White people are beginning to discover this section, moved by the witnessing of such plays as 'Miss Lulu Belle' [*Lulu Belle* was a 1926 play about a black prostitute], and the influence of novels such as 'Nigger Heaven.'" The article went on to note, disapprovingly, "The interest aroused is not a healthy constructive interest, but more in the nature of a morbid curiosity."[10]

Despite, or perhaps because of, its controversial title, *Nigger Heaven* was an immediate commercial success. Initially banned in Boston, the novel ran through nine printings in four months, and Van Vechten was heralded as the consummate Harlem tour guide for white revelers. Van Vechten, in fact, was acquainted with only a small sliver of black Manhattan—his educated and talented friends were hardly representative of the working-class African Americans who made up most of Harlem's population. Yet his white readership, eager to see and know about Harlem, made Van Vechten the toast of New York. Historian Cary Wintz claims that "more than any other single individual," Van Vechten actually "created the Negro vogue" (94). Soon after the release of *Nigger Heaven,* "white middle-class America eagerly devoured anything with a black flavor to it. Black writers and poets suddenly found themselves pursued by publishers, exhibitions of African art brought crowds to museums and galleries, Amos 'n' Andy became a hit radio show, and slumming in Harlem became a favorite pastime for those looking for a sensual, exotic, and primitive thrill" (Wintz 94–95).

Nigger Heaven received a mixed reception from black intellectuals. A number of literary luminaries and leaders in the African American community, particularly Countee Cullen and W. E. B. Du Bois, sharply criticized the novel; in his 1926 review in *The Crisis,* Du Bois made the oft-cited comment that the crass portrayals of African American life in *Nigger Heaven* amounted to nothing less than "a blow to the face" of black hospitality.[11] Going a step further, in 1931 he announced the establishment of the annual Du Bois Literary Prize, a one-thousand-dollar award to be given to black writers for the purpose of "draw[ing] the thought and genius of our young writers away from the school of Van Vechten and the later McKay to a more human and truthful portraiture of the American Negro in the 20th Century."[12] Such important Harlem Renaissance figures as sociologist and Urban League founder Charles Johnson and writers Walter White, James Weldon Johnson, Wallace Thurman, and Rudolph Fisher, however, defended Van Vechten's novel. They claimed that many hostile critics of *Nigger Heaven* had never bothered to read beyond its inflammatory title, and that these so-called readers wrongly assumed that its white author harbored racist intentions. African American author Eric Walrond showed his support for the novel by sending Van Vechten a congratulatory telegram that commended him for portraying a vision of Harlem life that was "accurately creditably glamorously enshrined" (Pfeiffer xxx).

Despite the controversy that swirled around it for so many years, *Nigger Heaven* is in fact a simple, at times saccharine, story of the tumultuous love affair between two African Americans: Mary Love, a nauseatingly sweet librarian in Harlem, and Byron Kasson, a narcissistic would-be author. As Kathleen Pfeiffer notes in her introduction to the 2000 University of Illinois Press edition, Van Vechten devotes only a fraction of *Nigger Heaven* to the sordid Harlem nightlife for which it is largely remembered (xv). Indeed, Van Vechten's intentions appear to have been far broader than merely to depict the goings-on in the speakeasies and cabarets of Jazz Age Harlem, for his story addresses such important issues as white racism, race loyalty, and intraracial color prejudice. Nevertheless, although the seamy sides of Van Vechten's novel have perhaps been overemphasized over the years by its detractors, those compelling scenes that take place in the night-clubs and cabarets offer a revealing glimpse into this aspect of Harlem life during Prohibition.

In one early scene in *Nigger Heaven,* a black character named Anatole Longfellow (also called the "Scarlet Creeper")[13] and his female companion prowl the streets of Harlem in search of a desirable cabaret. Finally settling on the Black Venus on Lenox Avenue, the two of them "descended the stairs to the basement. As they walked down the long hallway which led to the dance-floor, the sensual blare of jazz, slow, wailing jazz, stroked their ears. . . . Couples were dancing in such close proximity that their bodies melted together as they swayed and rocked to the tormented howling of the brass, the barbaric beating of the drum." Anatole orders a pint of gin from a Charleston-dancing waiter, who quickly returns with a flask and two ginger-ale set-ups. "From his hip-pocket [the waiter] extracted a bot-tle containing a transparent liquid. He poured out the ginger ale. Anatole poured out the gin" (12–13). Customers at the Black Venus and other cabarets drink to excess, highlighting the side of Harlem life that consis-tently defied government-mandated temperance.

Many of the details of this scene and several others likely arose out of Van Vechten's personal experiences in Harlem cabarets; he was perhaps the most widely welcomed and recognized white person at upscale black cabarets dur-ing the 1920s. A regular at the famous Small's Paradise, an expensive cabaret on Seventh Avenue whose big-name blues acts and Charleston-dancing wait-ers catered to affluent white patrons, Van Vechten aligned himself with many well-known African American writers and artists. As a result he was able to make his way into a number of black clubs that few white men entered. In fact, Van Vechten became such a well-known authority on Harlem nightlife that his name appeared in the lyrics to a popular Andy Razaf song, "Go Harlem," published in 1930. Several different versions of the song lyrics exist; one set follows:

> Harlem, you are the playground
> For people downtown
> Harlem, they can't resist your spell.
> Harlem, the world is after
> Your magic laughter,
> One trip to that happy land
> And you will understand
> So, like Van Vechten,
> Start inspectin',
> Go Harlem, go Harlem, go.[14]

As these lyrics indicate, many white New Yorkers viewed Harlem as merely a place to visit, carouse, and then leave—a kind of debauched tourist attraction. The commercialization of black nightlife permeated Harlem, yet the average black resident reaped few benefits from these voyeuristic white "slummers." Rather, as Langston Hughes wrote in *The Big Sea* (1940), many hard-working black people deeply resented the rich white interlopers who drove up to Harlem in their taxis and limousines, "flooding the little cabarets and bars where formerly only colored people laughed and sang, and where now the strangers were given the best ringside tables to sit and stare at the Negro customers—like amusing animals in a zoo" (225).

Harlem Renaissance writers were among the first to articulate how the growing white interest in black life adulterated the representation of African Americans in the arts and perpetuated pernicious racial stereotypes. In a letter dated September 20, 1928, Zora Neale Hurston complained to Hughes, "It makes me sick to see how these cheap white folks are grabbing our stuff and ruining it. . . . My only consolation being that they never do it right and so there is still a chance for us" (van Notten 182–83). According to Hughes, though, many African Americans were complicit in what he considered to be a wholesale sellout of black culture, and they willingly commodified themselves and their art for white approval and white dollars. He reports in *The Big Sea* that after the Harlem cabarets began devoting themselves to wealthy white customers, "the lindy-hoppers at the Savoy even began to practise [*sic*] acrobatic routines, and to do absurd things for the entertainment of the whites, that probably never would have entered their heads to attempt merely for their own effortless amusements. . . . Some critics," Hughes admitted, "say that that is what happened to certain Negro writers, too" (226).

Ironically, Van Vechten himself recognized the frustration that many black Harlemites felt toward the white slummers who took advantage of the neighborhood's many entertainment venues. This recognition, however, did nothing to prevent him from enjoying his evenings at Small's Paradise and other fashionable Harlem joints. Yet Van Vechten raises this issue in *Nigger Heaven,* when two fairly minor characters, Olive and Howard, discuss how the colonization of the black cabarets by white patrons has made black residents feel like outsiders in their own neighborhood. Olive expresses outrage that since "so many white people come up here now to the cabarets," several places in Harlem have begun drawing the color line. Her fiancé responds, perhaps understatedly, that "it is a bore to have them [i.e., whites] all over our places while we are excluded from their theatres and restaurants merely on account of our colour, theatres and restaurants which admit Chinese and Hindus . . . and prostitutes of any nationality." Howard concludes, rightly, that in New York City "a white prostitute can go places where a coloured preacher would be refused admittance" and that, essentially, black residents are powerless to stop the cultural poaching taking place in Prohibition-era Harlem (45–46).

W. E. B. Du Bois echoed this despair, condemning the effects of white voyeurs on black Harlem in a short piece called "Harlem," which appeared in the September 1927 issue of *The Crisis.* Despite their many differences of opinion and his loathing for *Nigger Heaven,* Du Bois and Van Vechten did agree that white desire for the black exotic damaged both the self-esteem and the economic self-sufficiency of Harlem. Du Bois opened his article by commenting, "To none is it more difficult to steer between the Scylla of prudery and the Charybdis of unbounded license than to the present American Negro." The selfishness and carelessness of white New Yorkers, Du Bois argued, made a complicated situation even worse for black New Yorkers. Tempted by the seductions of drinking, gambling, and other forms of decadent behavior, the decision of black Harlemites to live a righteous life

> is made doubly difficult by the white onlookers—the writer and visitor from Broadway. They must be made to remember that Harlem is not merely exotic; it is human; it is not a spectacle and an entertainment; it is life; it is not chiefly cabarets, it is chiefly homes; it is not all color, song and dance, it is work, thrift and sacrifice. Left to itself with reasonable policing and sound public opinion, it will become a city of human hearts with more good for the world than bad. But bribed and bought by white wastrels, distorted by unfair novelists, and lied about by sensationalists, it will lose sight of its own soul and wander bewildered in a scoffing world.[15]

Du Bois's pointed reference to the "unfair novelists" who distort Harlem life at the expense of its residents targeted Carl Van Vechten, but it also likely included members of the young coterie of black writers who attempted to represent the spectacle of Harlem in their fiction.

At least one black writer, caring little about the reasons why white people visited Harlem, was quick to see that the trend Carl Van Vechten launched was a surefire moneymaker. Eagerly jumping on the bandwagon of white interest in black cabarets, Wallace Thurman wrote an article for the November 1928 issue of *Harlem: A Forum of Negro Life* called "Harlem Directory: Where to Go and What to Do When In Harlem." In this short piece, Thurman describes the best gin mills, restaurants, and cabarets in the district, gives their addresses (except for the speakeasies, of course), and even offers his services to white partygoers as their personal tour guide. "If you really desire a good time," Thurman writes, "make friends with some member on the staff of *Harlem* and have him take you to Mexico's or to Pod and Jerry's or to the Paper Mill" (Singh 64). For an evening's worth of hooch, the alcoholic and chronically broke Thurman willingly introduced his white Greenwich Village acquaintances to the best that Harlem nightlife had to offer, much to the dismay of Dorothy West and many of his other black friends. A number of times, according to West's biographical sketch of him, "Thurman would bring white guests to black establishments, get roaring drunk, make a terrible fool of himself, and infuriate many of his close friends." But despite this propensity for exploiting Harlem for personal gain, Thurman was in fact acutely aware of the racial schisms that were widening as a result of white tourism in Harlem (West 77–85).

In Thurman's *The Blacker the Berry . . .* (1929), the author takes a witty and satiric swipe at the sometimes awkward multiracial cabaret scene that permeated Prohibition-era Harlem. The novel's black protagonist, Emma Lou, works for Arline, a white stage actress who plays the part of a black showgirl in a popular Broadway show called *Cabaret Gal.* Many of the characters in the show are black, though the actors who play them are all white or very light-skinned African Americans. As Arline's personal maid and assistant, Emma Lou realizes that her employer knows virtually nothing of black culture and that *Cabaret Gal,* a show put on by white people for white audiences, offers the shallowest and most stereotypical portrayals of African American life. (Interestingly, when Emma Lou expresses interest in joining the show as a chorus girl, the manager rejects her because her skin is too dark and would therefore throw off his "color scheme.") When Arline's brother comes to town and wants a taste of authentic Harlem nightlife, she invites Emma Lou to act as their personal guide. Arline chooses the swanky Small's Paradise (Van Vechten's real-

life hangout) as their destination and is shocked to learn that Emma Lou
has never attended a cabaret.

> "What?" Arline was genuinely surprised. "You in Harlem and never
> been to a cabaret? Why I thought all colored people went."
>   Emma Lou bristled. White people were so stupid. "No," she said
> firmly. "All colored people don't go. Fact is, I've heard that most of
> the places are patronized almost solely by whites."
>   "Oh, yes, I knew that, I've been to Small's and Barron's and the
> Cotton Club, but I thought there were other places. . . . For God's
> sake, don't let on to my brother you ain't been to Small's before. Act
> like you know all about it. I'll see that he gives you a big tip."(104–5)

Unable to reconcile herself to the idea that some black people actually
refrain from the illicit cabaret culture, Arline willingly pays her employee
to keep up the appearance of being a typical black cabaret-goer and thus
preserve her and her brother's prejudices.

Once they arrive at the cabaret, Arline's brother orders set-ups of White
Rock and ice, casually mixing highballs with gin he pours from a hip
flask.[16] Their experience at Small's Paradise that night reveals how completely Harlem cabaret-goers assimilated the idiosyncrasies of Prohibition
culture. "Most of the tables around [Emma Lou] were deserted," the narrator notes, "their tops littered with liquid-filled glasses, and bottles of ginger ale and White Rock. There was no liquor in sight, yet [she] was aware
of pungent alcoholic odors. Then she noticed a heavy-jowled white man
with a flashlight walking among the empty tables and looking beneath
them. He didn't seem to be finding anything" (107). The Prohibition
agent's presence garners no attention from anyone except the naive Emma
Lou; the patrons all know that with their flasks and bottles hidden in their
pockets, they are in little danger of arrest.

Emma Lou's overall impression of the Harlem cabaret scene highlights
the phony and contrived gaiety of the patrons. She realizes that Arline's
brother's attempt to experience Harlem culture by attending an expensive,
white-dominated cabaret is not only futile but foolish as well. He, like his
sister, knows nothing of black culture and makes no effort to learn. Rather,
he prefers to join in the forced hilarity of the crowd, pretending to be an
insider in the Harlem cabaret scene. As he enthusiastically mixes his party
another round of highballs, the narrator astutely notes:

> All around, people were laughing. There was much more laughter
> than there was talk, much more gesticulating and ogling than the

usual means of expression called for. Everything seemed unrestrained, abandoned. Yet, Emma Lou was conscious of a note of arti-
ficiality, the same as she felt when she watched Arline and her fellow
performers cavorting on the stage in "Cabaret Gal." This entire scene
seemed staged, they were in a theater, only the proscenium arch had
been obliterated. At last the audience and the actors were as one.
(109–10)

Although Small's Paradise is a Harlem cabaret, Emma Lou, the dark-
skinned local resident, occupies outsider status in this club filled primarily with drunken white people. Thus, she can clearly perceive the pathetic
desperation of these white downtowners who try to experience the exotic
African American culture so widely touted in the press, literature, movies,
and songs, but who achieve nothing more than a hollow imitation of
revelry.

   Wallace Thurman was not the only black writer of the Prohibition era
to recognize the important social differences between cabarets where black
people congregate and cabarets where white people come to "experience"
black culture. For example, in the second section of *Cane,* Jean Toomer
makes numerous references to the pervasiveness of Prohibition culture and
illustrates how bootleggers and bathtub gin color the experiences of black
city dwellers. In "Bona and Paul," a short story set in Chicago, the two
main characters go to a racially mixed nightclub called the Crimson
Gardens. The black couple drink some cocktails, and then they decide to
dance. But out on the floor they are suddenly overwhelmed with self-
consciousness, feeling the white patrons staring at them as if they were the
main attraction. Then, in a moment of composure and control, "the dance
takes blood from their minds and packs it, tingling, in the torsos of their
swaying bodies. Passionate blood leaps back into their eyes. They are a
dizzying blood clot on a gyrating floor. They know that the pink-faced
people have no part in what they feel" (79). Bona and Paul's determination to separate themselves from the experience of being merely a part of
the white people's exotic entertainment salvages the evening; they know
implicitly that the "pink-faced people" cannot understand what they came
to the Crimson Gardens to see.

   The few Harlem cabarets that retained their all-black clientele during
Prohibition became a refuge for local residents seeking to escape white
voyeurs. In his 1937 autobiography *A Long Way from Home,* Claude
McKay recalls an incident in which he brought his white editor, Max
Eastman, to a cabaret called Ned's. "Ned's was one place of amusement in
Harlem," McKay recalls, "in which white people were not allowed. . . .
[But] I was such a good and regular customer of Ned's that I thought he

would waive his rule for me. But I thought wrong that time." The black bouncer bars the pair at the door, and when McKay catches the proprietor's eye, Ned's "jovial black face turned ugly as an aard-vark's and he acted as if I was his worst enemy. He waved his fist in my face and roared: 'Ride back! Ride back, or I'll sick mah bouncers on you-all!'" (131–33). Eastman took the rejection with understanding and grace, and in later years McKay thought of the incident not as painful or embarrassing, but instead as a positive, defiant moment in the history of a black cabaret during an era awash with money-hungry African Americans willingly participating in their own exploitation.

In his 1928 novel *Home to Harlem,* McKay may have based his portrayal of the Congo, an exclusively black cabaret, in part on his experiences at Ned's. Despite the tremendous success of Harlem cabarets that sought the white trade, the Congo, as its name suggests, remained true to its origins and to its neighbors: "a real throbbing little Africa in New York." McKay describes the Congo as a destination "entirely for the unwashed of the Black Belt. Or, if they were washed, smells lingered telling the nature of their occupation. Pot-wrestlers, third cooks, W.C. attendants, scrub maids, dish-washers, stevedores." He continues:

> Girls coming from the South to try their future in New York always reached the Congo first. The Congo was African in spirit and color. No white persons were admitted there. The proprietor knew his market. He did not cater to the fast trade. "High yallers" were scarce there. Except for such sweetmen that lived off the low-down dark trade.
>
> When you were fed up with the veneer of Seventh Avenue, and Goldgraben's Afro-Oriental garishness, you would go to the Congo and turn rioting loose in all the tenacious odors of service and the warm indigenous smells of Harlem, fooping or jig-jagging the night away. You would if you were a black kid hunting for joy in New York. (29–30)

McKay clearly privileges the Congo above other cabarets in Harlem—the low-down nature of the club and the absence of white customers appeal to many working-class black patrons. More importantly, the black revelry that white New York voyeurs fruitlessly seek occurs in the Congo without the benefit of famous bandleaders and Charleston-dancing waiters. The experience of dancing at the Congo in no way resembles the experiences of patrons at such expensive, segregated cabarets as the Cotton Club, Barron's, or Connie's Inn, and McKay and his characters exult in the difference.

While cabarets operate somewhat differently in black and white fiction of the Prohibition era, certain important similarities do exist. In both literatures, cabarets serve as sites of important social and moral transgressions, where people place the satisfaction of their own desires above the restrictions of the law. And, despite the friction between black residents and white tourists in certain African American neighborhoods, cabarets provided an environment in which a great deal of interracial cultural exchange took place. In a 1925 issue of *The Messenger,* columnist Chandler Owen describes the "black and tan cabaret" (a cabaret with a mixed-race clientele) as "America's most democratic institution." He argues that "the cabaret is a place where people abandon their cant and hypocrisy . . . the prison bars of prejudice are temporarily at least torn down, and people act like natural, plain human beings."[17] Cabaret-goers—at least those who patronized establishments in black neighborhoods—seemed to demonstrate a certain degree of racial tolerance at the same time that, through their drinking, they expressed their intolerance for government interference in their private lives.

Given the widespread proliferation of illegal public drinking spaces, some of which opened their doors just days after Prohibition went into effect, their frequent appearance in American literature of the 1920s and early 1930s seems only fitting. These sites, however glamorous or squalid, should not be casually overlooked by today's readers as places that carry little moral meaning in a text, for the circumstances that surrounded speakeasies, jook joints, roadhouses, and cabarets were far from casual. Not only were they places for revelry and celebration, but they also fostered gang violence, police interference, and, particularly in the case of African Americans, social and cultural alienation. And although they were actual, physical locations, they also occupied important places in the American imagination. Temperate, law-abiding citizens and reformers may have believed blind tigers and cabarets to be evil dens of vice and iniquity, but others considered them important gathering places that provided opportunities to demonstrate, publicly and collectively, disdain for the Prohibition laws and the social forces that fueled them. Ultimately, it was within the walls of these public drinking joints that so many Americans protested their government's attempt to modify their behaviors and improve their morals.

CHAPTER 5

"Let's Stay In":

THE PROHIBITION-ERA HOUSE PARTY

I like large parties. They're so intimate. At small parties there isn't any
privacy.
—F. Scott Fitzgerald, *The Great Gatsby* (1925)

People who enjoyed drinking alcoholic beverages in their own homes prior
to the passage of National Prohibition generally continued to do so after
1920. Under the provisions of the National Prohibition Act, individuals
were permitted to drink alcohol and to offer alcoholic beverages to guests
in their home as long as that liquor had been acquired legally (usually this
meant that the liquor had been lawfully purchased before Prohibition took
effect). Thus, house parties were permissible under the law, and much
social drinking during Prohibition took place at private parties that ranged
in size and scope from two couples playing bridge and drinking cocktails
in a modest apartment to hundreds of people dancing and drinking in the
opulent surroundings of a millionaire's mansion. Although countless private house parties featured illegally obtained liquor, Prohibition officials
seldom interfered in these noncommercial gatherings.

After the government revoked the license of the wealthy to enjoy
evenings of drunken revelry in large public places, those who owned lavish
mansions and huge bank accounts sometimes compensated by opening
their homes as if they were function halls or hotels. In American literature,
certain Prohibition-era house parties on this grand scale have achieved
almost mythic status; the revelry at Jay Gatsby's West Egg mansion in F.
Scott Fitzgerald's *The Great Gatsby* (1925), for example, may be unrivalled
in its splendid excessiveness. Some notable similarities exist between
Gatsby's parties and those thrown by George Remus, one of the wealthiest
bootleggers in Prohibition-era America, who rose from a relatively modest
career as a criminal lawyer to amass, through his medicinal liquor distribution schemes, more than forty million dollars' worth of assets by 1924.
Remus threw legendary parties at his Cincinnati mansion at which guests

would receive as favors engraved gold watches, diamond jewelry, hundred-dollar bills, and on one notable occasion, brand-new automobiles. Like Gatsby, Remus was known to retreat into his library to read even while his parties raged (Kobler 315–18). Critic Thomas Pauley suggests, however, that Gatsby may in fact be based more closely on Arnold Rothstein, a well-dressed, socially sophisticated gangster and gambler (226–28), and Fitzgerald biographer and scholar Matthew Bruccoli identifies Max Gerlach, a "gentleman bootlegger" and neighbor of Fitzgerald's in 1923, as another important model for Gatsby's character (33–36).

More significantly, the house parties in *The Great Gatsby* seem to reflect a level of socializing that upper-middle-class partygoers expected from the rich and the well connected during Prohibition, even if their wealth and connections arose from trafficking in illegal liquor. Fitzgerald's narrator, Nick Carraway, recalled the frequency and the excess of his wealthy friend's house parties:

> There was music from my neighbor's house through the summer nights. In his blue gardens men and girls came and went like moths among the whisperings and the champagne and the stars. . . . At least once a fortnight a corps of caterers came down with several hundred feet of canvas and enough colored lights to make a Christmas tree of Gatsby's enormous garden. On buffet tables, garnished with glistening hors d'oeuvre, spiced baked hams crowded against salads of harlequin designs and pastry pigs and turkeys bewitched to a dark gold. In the main hall a bar with a real brass rail was set up, and stocked with gins and liquors and with cordials so long forgotten that most of his female guests were too young to know one from another. (39–40)

Hundreds of guests carelessly exploited Gatsby's generosity, uninhibitedly downing his liquor as he, the underworld pretender to the upper class, sought in their company the social respectability he craved.

With an enormous sense of entitlement to their fun, coupled with an equally enormous disregard for other people's property, guests at Gatsby's house parties exhibited the selfishness and self-involvement of the privileged classes. "People were not invited—they went there," observed Nick. "They got into automobiles which bore them out to Long Island, and somehow they ended up at Gatsby's door. Once there they were introduced by somebody who knew Gatsby, and after that they conducted themselves according to the rules of behavior associated with amusement parks" (41). Even while attending his parties, guests would regularly gossip about their host's life, spreading rumors about his being everything

Summer Shack of a Struggling Young Bootlegger

Figure 9

This satiric cartoon, titled "Summer shack of a struggling young bootlegger," appeared in the August 3, 1922, issue of *Life* magazine. Just a few short years into National Prohibition, the phenomenon of the fantastically wealthy bootlegger had already infiltrated the national consciousness.

from a bootlegger to a murderer. Of course, Gatsby's preoccupation with Daisy likely prevented him from noticing how he was treated or thought of by his guests, most of whom he neither knew nor cared to know. But Prohibition culture brought these rich, cultured, and well-established people together to enjoy the illicit offerings of a man generally believed to be a criminal. Such a social mix would have hardly been likely, let alone common, in the years preceding Prohibition. However, the passage of the Eighteenth Amendment caused social and economic worlds to collide that, in other circumstances, would have never met, and among many of the young rich socialites of the time, the acquaintanceship of gangsters, bootleggers, and racketeers was something to brag about, not to hide.

Cocktail Parties

Cocktail parties have become the line of least resistance in entertaining. All you need is a case of synthetic gin and a tin of anchovy paste. The greater the number of guests, the smaller and more airless the room, the stronger the gin, the more successful the party.
—Alice-Leone Moats, *No Nice Girl Swears* (1933)

Most parties of the 1920s, in both real life and literature, could not compare in scale to the ones at Remus's or Gatsby's mansions. Rather, most people who liked to drink socially would throw and attend smaller, less ostentatious parties held in smaller, less ostentatious homes. Many of these house parties during Prohibition might best be described as "cocktail parties," for the mixing and drinking of cocktails frequently served as the primary purpose of the gathering. The etymology of the word *cocktail* cannot be established with certainty, but it first appeared in print in an 1806 New York newspaper and described a drink made of spirits, water, sugar, and bitters. By the mid-1800s the term "cocktail" was used in the United States primarily to describe a before-dinner liqueur (*apéritif*), and by the end of the nineteenth century it had also come to be associated with food served as an appetizer (hence our contemporary familiarity with fruit, shrimp, and oyster cocktails). By the advent of Prohibition, though, a cocktail was generally understood to be an alcoholic beverage.

Mixed drinks had been a part of American drinking culture since colonial times, but with the passage of National Prohibition and the subsequent preponderance of vile-tasting homemade gin and adulterated wood alcohol, cocktails offered drinkers of both sexes a particularly welcome opportunity to disguise the wretched taste of available spirits. Not surprisingly, certain cocktails quickly took on gendered associations. As historian Catherine Murdock explains in *Domesticating Drink: Women, Men, and Alcohol in America, 1870–1940* (1998), men drank martinis and

Manhattans, while women often chose sweeter drinks such as gin fizzes, lime rickeys, and "Mamie Taylors" (gin mixed with ginger ale and served with a lime or a cherry) (107–9). Both sexes drank generic "highballs"—liquor diluted with club soda, tonic water, or ginger ale, and served in tall glasses over ice. Although alcoholic beverages themselves were prohibited, the widespread proliferation of perfectly legal cocktail paraphernalia, including shakers, trays, glasses, napkins, and other bar accoutrements, fueled enthusiasm for these parties. In a list of ideas for fashionable Christmas gifts, the December 14, 1929, issue of the *New Yorker* even suggests a twenty-dollar novelty cocktail shaker in the form of Charles Lindbergh's plane, "for lawbreakers who can still be patriotic and proud of their native land."[1]

Prohibition-era cocktail parties were inherently entangled with issues of money and class. High-quality bonded whiskey, for example, became a luxury that only the wealthy could afford, so inviting friends to partake of such expensive liquor became in itself a gesture useful to highlight one's own social status. As a result, many wealthy non-drinkers or light drinkers suddenly grew enamored of costly whiskeys and liqueurs for their value as prestige commodities. Cocktail parties in the 1920s likewise were not merely social gatherings. They were also symbolic affairs at which the upper class could at once flaunt their economic privilege, connections to the underground liquor traffic, willingness to defy the law, and remarkable generosity, all through the gesture of offering genuine Canadian whiskey or single-malt scotch to their guests. An article in the March 1923 issue of the *Ladies' Home Journal* makes this point bluntly: "The prohibition embroilment is shaping its course as an inevitable class issue. The fashionable rich demand their rum as an inalienable class privilege," crying, "'To hell with the benefits to the poor there may be in prohibition!'"[2]

Despite the etiquette books that, throughout the decade, urged hosts to serve nonalcoholic cocktails and punches at their parties, a strong social undercurrent suggested that to neglect to serve or to drink alcohol at a house party was somehow uncouth, emasculating, or even cowardly. Drinking at cocktail parties was perceived as quintessentially "modern," and a powerful drive existed in the 1920s to be stylishly up-to-date in terms of both manners and morals. As Frederick Lewis Allen notes in *Only Yesterday: An Informal History of the 1920's* (1931), fashionable people turned increasingly to cocktail parties during Prohibition because "everybody wanted to be modern,—and sophisticated, and smart, to smash the conventions and to be devastatingly frank. And with a cocktail glass in one's hand it was easy at least to be frank" (92). Cocktail parties, at their best, combined all the newly established social conventions of the young: mixed company, drinking, smoking, brazen language, daring fashion—all mingling with the celebration of relatively uninhibited sexuality. However, not all observers approved of this modern fashion. More traditionally minded people believed that the drinking of cocktails, particularly by women, was a clear indicator of immorality and a harbinger of scandal—and a double violation of ladylike behavior because it transgressed both legal strictures and social propriety. Yet abundant evidence indicates that many women willingly risked social opprobrium by continuing to indulge in cocktail drinking. "There can be little doubt that the number of women . . . who have admitted the cocktail and 'highball' to personal favour, and who are undismayed by what they see around them, is larger than it was," reported the London *Times*'s Washington correspondent in 1923. "'You know, I hardly ever touched anything at all before Prohibition came in,' is a phrase all too often on the lips of women to prevent a denial of its truth or a closing of the eyes to its significance. The taking of a drink became an adventure, and when time dulled the zest of the adventure, the habit of the beverage itself had taken its place as an incentive" (Barr 151).

The cocktail party frequently appears in the literature of the Prohibition era, and all of these scenes share a few general characteristics beyond the obvious availability of cocktails. Convention dictated that the hosts absorb the expense of throwing a cocktail party (unlike rent parties or other fund-raising events), and thus money for alcohol did not change hands. However, guests were often known to bring their own flasks, either to avoid partaking too liberally of the host's generosity or to avoid having to drink liquor of a possibly inferior quality. Hosts issued invitations to cocktail parties in advance, often in writing, and expected their guests to dress appropriately, in either semiformal or formal gowns for women and suits or tuxedos for men. Music, dancing, or other forms of entertainment such as poetry reciting or oration were often, though not always, provided. The size and purpose of these gatherings would vary, but the liberal enjoyment of alcohol in a mixed-gender setting remained constant, as did the almost absolute certainty that cocktail parties would not be compromised by interference from law enforcement officials.

Just because house parties were seldom raided does not mean that they were universally considered to be acceptable. F. Scott Fitzgerald's *The Beautiful and Damned* (1922) depicts the tension between the reformers and the revelers over the consumption of alcohol; in this case, a wild house party that takes place just before the enactment of National Prohibition essentially destroys the lives of Anthony and Gloria Patch, two young, fashionable moderns whose drinking costs them their happiness and nearly an enormous inheritance. Anthony Patch, a stubbornly idle man, builds a life around waiting for his wealthy grandfather's eventual death, upon which, he assumes, he will inherit enough money to enjoy the luxurious lifestyle he believes he deserves. To pass the time, he and his beautiful wife, Gloria, squander their modest income by purchasing expensive new clothes and entertaining their friends. One summer evening, Anthony, Gloria, and their houseguests fall into their familiar pattern of dancing to phonograph records and drinking to excess. They roll up the carpets, move tables and chairs, and as the alcohol takes control of them, "bedlam creeps screaming out of the bottles" (222) and the partiers become increasingly wild and uninhibited. The once-sedate cocktail party becomes a confusing, swirling concatenation of deafening music, grotesque dancing, inappropriate flirting, and, above all, frenetic drinking. As the mayhem reaches its peak and the story reaches its turning point, Fitzgerald draws the readers' attention to an intruder in their midst, Anthony's rich grandfather, Adam Patch, who had, unbeknownst to anyone in the room, "that morning made a contribution of fifty thousand dollars to the cause of national prohibition" (223). After witnessing for himself his grandson's intemperate lifestyle, the elder Patch disinherits his only living relative from his forty-million-dollar estate.

Adam Patch dies a few months later, and the rest of the novel is largely consumed with Anthony and Gloria's attempts to contest, on tenuous grounds, his will. As the court proceedings stretch from months into years, Anthony succumbs to increasingly debilitating alcoholism, exacerbated by the ubiquitous presence of liquor in the homes he visits. Anthony notices that, during Prohibition, "there was more drinking than ever before. One's host now brought out a bottle upon the slightest pretext. The tendency to display liquor was a manifestation of the same instinct that led a man to deck his wife with jewels. To have liquor was a boast, almost a badge of respectability" (317). Anthony's alcoholism progresses until he can no longer bear to be sober, and time and again he recklessly spends their last few dollars on cases of bootleg liquor or drinks at Sammy's, his favorite speakeasy. Gloria also drinks, which adds to the steadily increasing unhappiness of their marriage. Ultimately, after four and a half years, the court overrides Adam Patch's last will and testament and awards the Patches their inheritance, apparently not because of the strength of their case but "because of the reaction, due to excessive prohibition, that had recently set in against reforms and reformers" (360).

Cocktail parties are also imbued with much social significance in the 1927 hit novella *It,* by Elinor Glyn (the movie version of *It,* only loosely based on the book, led to Clara Bow's immortal reign as the "It Girl"). "It" is a euphemism for sexual magnetism, and the two main characters of the story, the calculating millionaire John Gaunt and the aristocratic but poor Ada Cleveland, are overflowing with "it." The unmarried Ada and her good-for-nothing brother Larry, a dope fiend, bootlegger, and thief, belong by birth to the elite aristocracy of New York but have fallen on hard financial times. A friend, knowing Ada's situation, pushes Ada and John together at a cocktail party, where Ada enjoys a gin cocktail while her male companion, in obvious contrast, sedately drinks tea. The next night Ada and John are seated together at dinner; the narrator notes that "Miss Cleveland was as attractive a modern young woman as ever drank three cocktails before dinner, and a bottle of champagne all to herself at the repast" (26). John falls in love with Ada in no small part because of her delightful, nontraditional behaviors and, through a complicated series of maneuvers, eventually manages to win her heart.

The reader quickly ascertains, through such details as Ada's stylishly bobbed hair, her keen sense of fashion, and her fondness for gambling at cards, that Ada is intended to represent the quintessential young woman of the 1920s. But it is her enthusiastic drinking at the house parties she attends that first tips the reader off to her status as a rebellious, free-thinking flapper. Both John Gaunt and the reader cannot help but notice how Ada drinks her cocktails swiftly and steadily, and Gaunt in particular admires her for retaining her poise and never appearing intoxicated. Despite her impressive tolerance, Ada's socializing does seem to revolve around alcohol. She eagerly accepts glasses of champagne at every cocktail party she attends, and later in the story, when economics force her take a job at John Gaunt's company, she pines for her regular four o'clock cocktail. Indeed, Ada's most difficult adjustment to life as a working woman proves to be neither the hours nor the tasks, but her lack of access to decent liquor. While primarily a love story, *It* also chronicles how women like Ada adapted to the culture of Prohibition by learning to drink with men, and many significant moments of the story, especially John and Ada's evolving courtship, take place over cocktails.

The meanings invested in cocktail parties in Prohibition-era fiction differ somewhat in the works of white and African American writers. While scenes of at-home revelry in both cases provide details about social class and political orientation, the fashionable "modern" lifestyle, and the impulse to transgress against law and order, black writers of the 1920s were faced with different challenges in the literary marketplace than were white writers of the same generation. The New Negro movement, led by Alain Locke, W. E. B. Du Bois, and James Weldon Johnson, among others, promoted in many African American writers a sense of mission that their work contribute directly to the social uplift of the race; in Du Bois's essay "Criteria of Negro Art" (1926), he asserts that "it is the bounden duty of black America to begin this great work of the creation of Beauty, of the preservation of Beauty, of the realization of Beauty" (102). Because all art is propaganda, Du Bois continues, black art ought to be used for the deliberate purposes of securing the rights and freedoms of black people in America. Within the context of Prohibition culture, however, this edict becomes complicated. Were black writers to deny the vibrant, albeit "unsophisticated" African American culture that thrived in the house parties, speakeasies, and cabarets of black communities across the nation? Would the portrayal of a black character violating liquor laws and other social decrees somehow undermine the so-called progress of the race? Would intemperate black characters merely reinforce stereotypes that the racist white world already believed? Many African American writers of the Prohibition era did in fact believe that the lives of working-class black people were not legitimate subjects of literary examination, and that the lives of respectable, upper-middle-class urban black people ought to be highlighted as more accurate representations of African American culture.

African American literature of the Prohibition era was, then, deeply divided in both its goals and its approaches; this schism is readily apparent in the portrayals of party scenes in the novels of various black writers. While many works of Jazz Age African American fiction include some kind of party scene, a handful of representative texts can illuminate how the context of Prohibition influenced the depiction of revelry in African American communities. For example, Countee Cullen and Nella Larsen portray cocktail parties in their fiction as sophisticated and urbane events, despite the drinking that takes place. A number of their characters represent the most privileged of Harlem's black upper and upper-middle classes, and the behavior of these educated, professional men and women closely mirrors the behavior of wealthy white socialites.

Countee Cullen's novel *One Way to Heaven* (1932) depicts the lives of several Harlem residents who occupy a wide range of social and economic positions. The central plot of Mattie Johnson, a pious domestic worker, and her relationship with her one-armed con-man husband, Sam Lucas, competes with the fascinating intersecting plot of Constancia Brandon, Mattie's African American employer, a character of whom the narrator clearly approves: "Constancia Brandon, for whom Mattie worked, was the mirror in which most of social Harlem delighted to gaze and see itself. She was beautiful, possessed money enough to be willful, capricious, and rude whenever she desired to deviate from her usual suave kindness; and she was not totally deficient in brains" (90). Many of the central scenes in the novel revolve around Constancia's frequent and lavish cocktail parties, which "never lacked excitement and verve" and regarding which "there was seldom a week in which the *New York Era* or the *Colonial News* did not carry a portrait of 'Harlem's most charming hostess'" (97).

Cullen uses Constancia's cocktail parties in part to illustrate the breadth of upper- and middle-class social life in Harlem during Prohibition.

Indeed, Constancia delights in bringing together members of distinctly different social and racial groups and allowing them to get to know one another. Like the real-life Carl Van Vechten, the fictional Constancia Brandon acts as if she is oblivious to the race-based etiquette that controls many of her guests' conduct. However, she dispenses cocktails "with a prodigality shocking in a country addicted to prohibition" (158), which in many cases makes it easier for her guests to interact with one another. For example, the narrator describes a humorous moment at one of Constancia's parties in which the hostess forces a black party guest and a white author, Walter Derwent, into a conversation:

> When at one of her parties it was suggested to her in fiery language by a spirited young Negro . . . that a celebrated white writer present was out to exploit and ridicule her, she . . . then [took] the protesting youngster by the hand, piloted him through her groups of chattering guests, and brought him to a standstill before Walter Derwent.
>
> "My dear Mr. Derwent, I want you to do me a kindness. Here is a young man who is laboring under the apprehension that your frequent visits to Harlem have an ulterior motive, that you look upon us as some strange concoction which you are out to analyse and betray. I wish you would either disabuse him of, or confirm him in, his fears."
>
> And she had left them together, both equally frightened. (98–99)

The fact that Cullen's portrayal of interracial socializing takes place at a cocktail party during Prohibition is significant for a number of reasons. Of course, alcohol has been widely and rightfully acknowledged as a social lubricant, and so it is easy to understand how intimate conversations might occur between inebriated people who would otherwise ignore each other if they were to meet on the street. But Prohibition-era cocktail parties also operated on another, more political level. Anyone attending and imbibing at Constancia's party or at any other cocktail party of the era became automatic, if temporary, allies in their transgression against the law and against the puritanical code that condemned intemperance as immoral. The black critic and the white author in the scene mentioned above may have had little else in common, but the cocktail glass in each of their hands indicates that they felt similar disregard for National Prohibition laws.

The mingling of the races always marks Constancia's parties, and so it is not surprising that a cocktail party provides the setting for her most legendary dabbling with uncomfortable racial relations. To amuse her guests, and herself, one evening, Constancia mischievously contracts Dr. Seth

Calhoun, an elderly white southern professor and author, to deliver a talk to her guests entitled "The Menace of the Negro Race to Our American Civilization." Until he arrives at the party, Dr. Calhoun is unaware that his audience is composed almost entirely of African Americans; indeed, the guests themselves have no idea that they have been assembled to hear a diatribe on the evil odors and cultural defects attributed to the black race. Initially her guests are thoroughly scandalized by the white supremacist professor and angry with their hostess, but Constancia calmly demands they pay respectful attention to the lecture. After the talk she hands the professor a "thin glass of scarlet iced liquid" by way of refreshment. When he finishes his cocktail, the ever-gracious Constancia takes his glass and then drops it, as if by mistake, so that it shatters on the hearth and thus prevents her or any of her friends from ever having to drink from his glass. In the context of National Prohibition, even cocktail glasses themselves provide opportunities to express subtle but significant political messages.

Nella Larsen also includes an upper-middle-class Harlem cocktail party in her novella *Quicksand* (1929), at which the guests, unlike those at Constancia Brandon's parties, represent a very narrowly defined stratum of economic and racial backgrounds. The story itself portrays the complicated friendship between Irene Redfield, the wife of a successful Harlem doctor, and Clare Kendry, her childhood friend who has for years been "passing" for white in Chicago but who has returned to Harlem eager to reconnect with her former friends and environment. The drama of the tale lies in Irene's conflicted feelings toward Clare, and the story culminates in a final ambiguous moment in which Clare plummets from a sixth-story window to her death, the result of a suicidal jump, an accidental slip, or even perhaps, the narrator implies, a shove from Irene. This dramatic conclusion takes place at a cocktail party thrown by Dave and Felise Freeland, friends of the Redfields. Although Larsen's explicit goals clearly do not include exploring the implications of National Prohibition, the cocktail party provides a meaningful background for the concluding plot twist.

The guests at the Freelands' cocktail party are members of Harlem's upper class, and although all of them are of African American descent, several of them, including Irene Redfield and Clare Kendry, have complexions light enough in color to "pass" for white. Larsen portrays this group as a close-knit social set; although Irene apparently lacks intimate friends, it is clear that the Redfields and the Freelands' other guests frequently attend the same dances, tea parties, dinners, and cocktail parties. It is also clear that they are all accustomed to drinking together; when Dave Freeland notices that Irene seems quiet and preoccupied, he concludes that she's ready to cry because she does not yet have a drink in her hand. "What'll you take?" he asks, and she requests a weak highball, "a glass of ginger-ale and three drops of Scotch" (237). Irene endures being teased about her watered-down drink; meanwhile, it seems apparent that the rest of the group is heartily enjoying their cocktails. Larsen suggests that members of this set represent the ultimate in social respectability, and yet this respectability is in no way compromised by their quiet rebellion against Prohibition. Attending cocktail parties and drinking scotch is not an indication of immorality or unpatriotic behavior but rather of social decorum.

While some black authors concentrated on depicting the lives of well-to-do, "respectable" African Americans, writers such as Langston Hughes, Wallace Thurman, and Claude McKay felt compelled to write about people who possessed neither money nor a claim to Harlem's elite social circles. Both Thurman and McKay juxtapose the educated middle-class black subject (Emma Lou in Thurman's *The Blacker the Berry* . . . and Ray in McKay's *Home to Harlem*) with the raucous experience of rent parties and buffet flats that were far more familiar to most Harlem residents than was the pretentious cocktail party. By examining the liquor-based relationship between hosts and guests at a variety of Harlem house parties, Thurman and McKay reveal how Prohibition culture helped to define and separate the social worlds that existed for Harlem residents.

Rent Parties

You Don't Get Nothing for Being an Angel Child,
So you Might As Well Get Real Busy and Real Wild.
—From an invitation to a Harlem rent party, 1920s

The Prohibition era coincided with the Great Migration of African American southerners into northern urban centers, including Harlem. But instead of finding plentiful and profitable work in northern cities, many African Americans found relentless economic exploitation by both employers and landlords. Wages for black workers were disproportionately low in New York, and rents in Harlem were exorbitantly high. Harlem apartment owners demanded rents often six times as high as those for comparable homes in southern cities; during the 1920s houses in Harlem rented for up to $250 a month, apartments for about $20 a room, and even the most squalid tenements for about $10 a room.[3] Dire economic necessity sometimes forced two or more families to live in an apartment designed for only one, and each night the floor space would be crowded to capacity with makeshift sleeping pallets. Tenants would partition large rooms into several smaller ones, and even "shift-sleeping," whereby a day worker sleeps in a bed at night and a night worker occupies it during the day, was fairly common. The closed doors that blocked economic advancement in Harlem forced residents to find creative ways to supplement their income, and the combination of desperate poverty, community spirit, and fear of eviction spawned a unique form of economic self-sufficiency known as the rent party.

Hosts of rent parties opened up their homes to friends and strangers alike, charged an admission fee, and offered food and alcohol for sale. Their relatively frequent appearance in the literature, music, and especially newspapers of the 1920s suggests that rent parties were commonplace in urban African American communities, and that these events were reasonably well known even beyond the streets of Harlem and other black neighborhoods. Still, in his short story "The Promised Land" (1927), originally published in the *Atlantic Monthly*, Rudolph Fisher felt compelled to describe these parties for this magazine's largely white audience. Fisher explained, "A rent party is a public dance given in a private apartment. If, after letting out three of your five rooms to lodgers, your resources are still unequal to your rent, you make up the deficit by means of a rent party. You provide music, your friends provide advertisement, and your guests, by paying admission; provide what your resources lack" (48). A 1929 *New York Sunday News* article emphasized the alcohol-drenched atmosphere of rent parties in its comment that "most everyone in the neighborhood is invited to the rent parties, and the usual procedure is to sell a cheap brand of liquor at 25 cents a drink until either the rent is made up or the patrons pass out" (Schoener 84–85). Although the thousands of rent parties in Harlem, Chicago, Washington, D.C., and other black communities saved countless families from eviction, as important cultural events they are often overlooked today. Examining rent party scenes in literary works of the era can help us to understand better these boisterous, drunken gatherings during which families defied Prohibition laws in order to stave off homelessness.

Langston Hughes, who moved to Harlem in September 1921, claims to have been a frequent guest at rent parties, and he remembers them warmly, almost reverentially, in his 1940 autobiography, *The Big Sea:*

> The Saturday night rent parties that I attended were often more amusing than any night club, in small apartments where God knows who lived—because the guests seldom did—but where the piano would often be augmented by a guitar, or an odd cornet, or somebody with a pair of drums walking in off the street. And where awful bootleg whiskey and good fried fish or steaming chitterling were sold at very low prices. And the dancing and singing and impromptu entertaining went on until dawn came in at the windows. . . . Almost every Saturday night when I was in Harlem I went to a house-rent

party. I wrote lots of poems about house-rent parties, and ate there-
at many a fried fish and pig's foot—with liquid refreshment on the
side. I met ladies' maids and truck drivers, laundry workers and shoe
shine boys, seamstresses and porters. I can still hear their laughter in
my ears, hear the soft slow music, and feel the floor shaking as the
dancers danced. (229, 233)

Hughes offers a decidedly romantic image of the average rent party, especially considering that many rent parties included gambling, sex, drug use,
and even instances of violence. However, he does mention an important
fact: many kinds of people who could not afford to patronize expensive
nightclubs attended these parties to dance, eat, and drink.

Hughes's depiction of rent parties in his autobiography also testifies to
his earnest belief—one that he shared with Wallace Thurman, Zora Neale
Hurston, and Claude McKay—that Harlem should be represented hon-
estly in art and literature. Artists should neither overstate the highbrow
nor understate the lowbrow, because the goal of the artist was not explicitly to please or to impress white readers. In his well-known 1926 essay
"The Negro Artist and the Racial Mountain," Hughes explains that for
the black artist to achieve greatness, he or she must conquer "the urge
within the race toward whiteness, the desire to pour racial individuality
into the mold of American standardization, and to be as little Negro and
as much American as possible" (91). Disagreeing vehemently with the
notion that literature should deny the sordid in order to demonstrate the
sophistication of black people, Hughes attempted to portray as authenti-
cally as possible the lives and experiences of ordinary working-class people. Depicting the common rent party was one route by which he con-
veyed to readers the ways in which desperate poverty and relentless
exploitation intersected with eating, drinking, dancing, and lovemaking
in Harlem neighborhoods.

The Prohibition laws inadvertently helped to bolster the popularity of
these rent-raising parties, for these events provided relatively safe places for
people to drink and socialize. But competition for party guests was sometimes fierce; as many as twelve parties to a single block and five to an
apartment building, simultaneously, was not uncommon in Harlem during the 1920s (Kellner 300). In order to draw a good crowd, rent party
hosts devised a number of clever publicity strategies. Of course, invitations
were passed by word of mouth, but even uninvited strangers would often
be lured in by the music they heard from the street and would be made
welcome—after they surrendered their admission fee. Many Harlem hosts
also boosted their prospective guest list (and thus their profits) by circu-
lating what became known as "rent party tickets." Often these entrepre-

neurial hosts turned for help to the Wayside Printer, a middle-aged white man who would daily walk the streets of Harlem with his portable printing press perched atop a small handcart. The jingle of a little bell tied to his wagon announced his approach, and would-be hosts would come down to the street to give him all the pertinent information about their upcoming party. While they waited, the Wayside Printer would lay out his small platen and print the tickets, usually about the size and shape of a business card, for a modest fee. His grammar and spelling were sometimes questionable, but the invitations on those little tickets were perfectly clear.

Although the spoken language of Harlem and the written language of newspapers and other reportage collectively identified these events as "rent parties," the tickets themselves never described them as such. Instead, hosts favored more lofty language, terming their event a "Social Party," "Social Whist Party," "Parlor Social," or "Matinee Party." Other, less elevated terms also occasionally appeared on these tickets, including "Too Terrible Party," "Boogie," and "Tea Cup Party." It was always understood that admission to these events would be charged, even if the invitation did not denote a price. Tickets were often embellished with popular slang phrases, lyrics from current songs, or snippets of poetry. One 1927 ticket, for example, implores: "Save your tears for a rainy day, / We are giving a party where you can play / With red-hot mammas and too bad She-bas / Who wear their dresses above their knees / And mess around with whom they please." Another from 1926 notes: "If you cant Charleston or do the Pigeon Wing / You sure can shake that thing at a / Social Party." Still others reason "If You Can't Hold Your Man, Don't Cry After He's Gone, Just Find Another," and "You Don't Get Nothing for Being an Angel Child, So you Might As Well Get Real Busy and Real Wild" (Reid 145).

Hosts distributed these tickets to neighbors and to strangers they encountered on the street corner, in subway and train stations, in restaurants—wherever large numbers of black working-class people might be seeking excitement and camaraderie for the evening. Sometimes hosts conscripted their children to hand out tickets indiscriminately. Other times, hosts invited only members of a carefully selected population, seeking out particular groups of people such as Pullman porters, interstate truck drivers, and black tourists who probably knew few people in the city and thus might be looking for an evening's entertainment. Some hosts enticed guests from their own apartment building or neighborhood block by tucking the tickets, sometimes printed on brightly colored paper, into the grilles of the elevators or even in their apartment's out-facing windows. Rent parties raged every night of the week in Harlem during the 1920s, but by far the most popular evening was Saturday, since day laborers were paid on Saturday night and usually did not work on Sunday. Thursdays tended to be the second-favorite party night, since that was the evening that most live-in domestic workers were off duty.

Publicity was important to ensure the success of a rent party, but just as important were house preparations. Hosts would clear all furniture and rugs from the front rooms of the apartment, except for the piano (a common fixture even in working-class homes), and sometimes would rent folding chairs from the local undertaker. The regular bulbs in the light fixtures would be replaced with more sensuous red or blue lightbulbs. Private detectives called "Home Defense Officers" (HDOs) were sometimes hired to monitor the party by bouncing unwelcome guests, squelching incipient brawls, and ousting "clean-up men" who would come to such parties to steal guests' coats and wallets or to scope out the apartment in anticipation of a later burglary. Liquid refreshment, usually homemade corn liquor (called "King Kong") or bootleg gin was sold either by the pint or in quarter-pint portions called "shorties" that cost between twenty-five and fifty cents. For a nominal price, hungry partygoers could enjoy southern cooking at its finest. Menus often included some combination of Hoppin' John, fried chicken, chitterlings, mulatto rice (rice and tomatoes), gumbo, chili, collard greens, potato salad, and sweet potato pone. After the meal, dancing would resume until the guests were exhausted or until a noisy brawl summoned the "Black Maria" (the police patrol wagon) to break up the party. It was not uncommon for rent parties to devolve into violence; liquor flowed freely and occasionally guests fought not just with their fists but with razors or revolvers. Nonetheless, the potential for harm was not enough to keep the rent parties from flourishing, giving black families a chance to keep up with expenses when wages were low and work was scarce.

Good dance music was virtually guaranteed at rent parties, sometimes provided by a single piano player or a series of pianists who would pound out jump rhythms and popular boogie-woogie tunes all night long. Often, a three-piece ensemble (usually a drummer, a pianist, and a saxophonist) would jam themselves into a corner and show off their mastery of the latest jazzy dance hits. Even such better-known musicians as Thomas "Fats" Waller and Willie "the Lion" Smith made the rounds at rent parties; they could play their regular stints at a cabaret and still make it to a rent party for a late-night set, especially since most rent parties did not get started until around midnight or even later. These musicians played for the tips they could wheedle from the crowd, and at the same time they welcomed the chance to play for an enthusiastic black audience after performing all evening for white patrons. Some musicians, by choice or by necessity, scraped together a living by playing exclusively at rent parties: they made decent money, often secured meals and a bed from the host, and got the party guests to pay for their drinks.

The only population generally refused invitations to rent parties was white people. Any white man in Harlem could potentially be a revenuer or a cop who would certainly appreciate an invitation to raid a rent party for violation of liquor laws, or to extort money from the hosts in order to keep them out of jail. But even without that threat, black hosts usually did not welcome the presence of unfamiliar white people in their homes, especially since the tremendous influx of curious white tourists into Harlem after the 1926 publication of Carl Van Vechten's *Nigger Heaven.* Langston Hughes remembers, in *The Big Sea,* how black people turned to rent parties not only to make enough money to forestall eviction but also to have a private place to dance, celebrate, and socialize without being observed by intrusive and inquisitive white voyeurs. Black Harlem residents, he remarks, "didn't like to be stared at by white folks," and they relished the opportunity to dance the Black Bottom or the lindy hop "with no [white] stranger behind you trying to do it, too" (229). One African American New Yorker, in a WPA oral history, describes the occasional appearance of uninvited guests at a Harlem rent party:

> Once in awhile a stray ofay[4] or a small party of pseudo-artistic young Negroes, the upper-crust, the creme-de-la-creme of Black Manhattan society, would wander into one of these parties and gasp or titter (with cultured restraint, of course) at the primitive, untutored Negroes who apparently had so much fun wriggling their bodies about to the accompaniment of such mad, riotously abandoned music. Seldom, however, did these outsiders seem to catch the real spirit of the party, and as far as the rug-cutters were concerned, they simply did not belong.[5]

While thousands of white people dropped tens of thousands of dollars at integrated or semi-integrated Harlem cabarets, musical revues, and nightclubs, relatively few ever experienced the rent party firsthand.

Besides the obvious respite from the workaday grind that rent parties provided, part of the reason these events proved so popular and so successful in Harlem and in other black neighborhoods is the sense of community they fostered. Rent parties amounted, essentially, to a grassroots form of social welfare, and surviving first-person accounts of rent parties invariably mention the satisfaction the partiers took in assisting other struggling black families. It is important to remember that the great majority of the guests at rent parties were poor, unemployed, or underemployed black laborers who were struggling to make ends meet. Yet they attended rent parties regularly and did what they could to help keep their friends and neighbors housed and fed, knowing that their friends and neighbors, when called upon, would do the same for them. While they remained powerless to stop the exploitation they suffered at the hands of unscrupulous landlords, Harlemites welcomed the solidarity that rent parties encouraged.

It would be misleading, however, to imagine rent parties as driven solely by goodwill and community uplift; often they served as fronts for more licentious behavior. For a few additional dollars, rent party hosts would sometimes offer couples the private use of back bedrooms. While this was not the case at every rent party, many amorous couples depended upon the availability of these rooms for short periods of time, having no other place to go that was private, discreet, and affordable. Other times, one or more back bedrooms were set aside as havens in which men could play cards and throw dice, with stakes sometimes reaching levels that ordinary working men could ill afford. Back rooms were also sometimes reserved for drug use; while cocaine was too expensive for most working-class Harlem residents, marijuana and opium were cheap, popular, and widely available. Regardless of the activity, historian David Levering Lewis asserts that "many of Harlem's memorable nights took place in houses and apartments" (211) and not in the public spaces of cabarets and speakeasies.

At best, house-rent parties provided downtrodden Harlem residents with much-needed opportunities to blow off steam and temporarily forget their worries; at worst such gatherings became genuinely tragic affairs. Because hosts seldom paid protection money to police in advance (as did many proprietors of the local speakeasies), cops took tremendous satisfaction in breaking up these so-called private affairs and fining the hosts for violating the Prohibition laws, disturbing the peace, creating a public nuisance, and whatever other charges they could drum up. In fact, police raided these parties far more often than they did the local speakeasy or "gin mill" (Ottley 63). Even without police interference, sometimes alcohol and drugs, combined with the frustrations that many wage-earning black Harlemites felt, resulted in vicious lashings-out with knives, razors, or guns. Privately contracted Home Defense Officers did much to avert potentially violent scenes, but they could not prevent some revelers from leaving the party in an ambulance or, even worse, a hearse. An editorial in the *New York Age* remarked, "One of these rent parties a few weeks ago was the scene of a tragic crime in which one jealous woman cut the throat of another, because the two were rivals for the affections of a third woman." The editor wryly noted, "[T]he combination of bad gin, jealous women, a carving knife, and a rent party is dangerous to the health of all concerned" (Reid 147–48).

Rent parties also became the means by which some Harlem residents scammed their neighbors. One WPA interview captures the memories of one former rent-party hustler:

Sure, I used to give rent-parties all the time. And I made pretty good at it till repeal [of Prohibition] came along. . . .

There was plenty of dough in the party racket and it used to be the mainstay of a lot of the boys who needed to make a little extra dough. But the only trouble with staging rent-parties as an out-an-out [*sic*] hustle was the lousy crowd you had to cater to. You put out your cards, hire a piano-player, open your door an' just wait for all sorts of studs and chicks to wander in. If you were lucky, you might get through the night without any major accidents—but I never seemed to have that kinda luck. Some punchdrunk broad was always breaking up my shindigs. First they'd get loaded to the gills with King Kong, start getting rambuncktuous an' wanting to pick a fight at the drop of a hat. Some guy'd get accidently shoved or just naturally get evil cause his ol' lady would dance more than once [with the] same guy. The next minute, he'd be whooping like a wild Indian, waving his blade and threatening to cut anybody who came near him. Well, that'd most likely be the end of my party. Folks would start running in every direction—out into the hallway, on the fire-escape, any-where. One Saturday night I even found a chick bracing herself inside the dumb-waiter shaft, after some Mose[6] went haywire and shot out the lights.[7]

Despite their occasional violence, rent parties formed the backbone of Harlem nightlife for many black residents who wanted to drink and social-ize without spending very much money. Few Harlem residents could afford the expensive cover charges and outrageously priced drinks at the trendy Harlem nightclubs, even if they were admitted. Many other down-town entertainment venues, including expensive Broadway theaters as well as more reasonably priced movie houses, denied black patronage altogeth-er. So rent parties became for many working people the best opportunity to mingle, dance, and enjoy themselves without sacrificing their whole week's pay.

Rent parties, however, became a source of embarrassment among cer-tain Harlem residents. Many devout black families who clung to tradition-al religious beliefs considered blues and jazz music scandalous and saw them, along with their inevitable counterparts, liquor and dancing, as the devil's playthings. In his short story "The Promised Land," Rudolph Fisher gives voice to this attitude toward rent parties through the character of Mammy, an elderly African American woman who has moved from Virginia to Harlem, and who observes a rent party in the apartment build-ing across the airshaft from hers. As she watches the young, wild partiers carousing and dancing the "camel walk," she laments to herself: "But such

a dance! The camel walk. Everybody 'cameling.' Had God wanted a man
to move like a camel he'd have put a hump in his back. Yet was there any
sign of what God wanted in that scene across the shaft? . . . Young girls'
arms around boys' shoulders, their own waists tightly clasped; bodies
warmly fused, bending to the sensual waves of the 'camel.' Where was
God in that?" (49). Some black intellectuals and writers also scorned rent
parties, but for different reasons. Such rowdy displays of passion and
intemperance, they feared, reflected poorly on the black race as a whole;
consequently, they refused to acknowledge the existence of these low-class
social events in their writings. No accounts of rent parties surface in the
works of such well-known authors as Jessie Fauset, Nella Larsen, or W. E. B.
Du Bois, for instance, and in his skewed sociological description of
Harlem, *Black Manhattan* (1930), James Weldon Johnson simply ignores
rent parties and other comparable forms of entertainment altogether.
Instead, he describes "the pleasure-loving people" of Harlem who find
amusement in "things far too simple for other folks," such as strolling
down Lenox Avenue in their nicest clothes and attending their local
churches (161–62). Enthusiastic depictions of rent parties do appear,
however, in the works of Wallace Thurman and Claude McKay.

Wallace Thurman, who was raised in Salt Lake City and briefly attended the University of Utah and the University of Southern California,
arrived in Harlem in September 1925. A social man who loved parties and
drinking, he embraced any opportunity to frequent the speakeasies and
clubs that proliferated above 125th Street. Part of the appeal of rent parties for the alcoholic Thurman was, no doubt, the easy access to cheap
liquor; for a modest price he could go on a bender that might last any-
where from a few hours to a few days. He demonstrates his familiarity
with rent parties in several of his works, including his novels *The Blacker
the Berry* . . . (1929) and *Infants of the Spring* (1932), and a play, cowrit-
ten with William Jourdan Rapp, titled *Harlem: A Melodrama of Negro Life
in Harlem* (1928). In fact, Thurman is easily the most frequent chronicler
of Harlem rent parties. He firmly believed (as did Hughes) that writers are
obligated to portray life as they see it and not as they wish it to be; as a
result, Thurman did not shy away from writing stories that included
details about rent parties that embarrassed and sometimes angered those
who felt, like Du Bois, that African American writers were duty-bound to
create and preserve "respectable" images of black life.

A rent party figures prominently in Thurman's loosely autobiographical first novel, *The Blacker the Berry* . . . , which chronicles the coming of
age of Emma Lou Morgan, a dark-skinned girl miserably ashamed of her
color. In the fourth section, "Rent Party," Thurman uses the event to
demonstrate the cultural chasms that existed between several different

Figure 10
The young Wallace Thurman. Courtesy of the Yale Collection of American
Literature, Beinecke Rare Book and Manuscript Library.

groups of black Harlemites: the rent party guests themselves, portrayed as
fun-loving but animalistic; the African American intellectuals, who
observe the revelers with both sociological detachment and awed delight;
and the conservative Emma Lou, who, like Du Bois, feels certain that such
wild behavior undermines the possibilities for racial uplift and the ultimate

acceptance of African Americans by white people. While Thurman's narrative voice is uncritical of the party scene, Emma Lou is deeply disturbed by the decadence she observes. Thurman's narrator describes, in revealing fragments, what Emma Lou and her companions see and hear as they approach the site of the bacchanalian "parlor social":

> "Ahhhh, sock it." . . . "Ummmm" . . . Piano playing—slow, loud, and discordant, accompanied by the rhythmic sound of shuffling feet. Down a long, dark hallway to an inside room, lit by a solitary red bulb. "Oh, play it you dirty no-gooder." . . . A room full of dancing couples, scarcely moving their feet, arms completely encircling one another's bodies . . . cheeks being warmed by one another's breath . . . eyes closed . . . animal ecstasy agitating their perspiring faces. There was much panting, much hip movement, much shaking of the buttocks. . . . "Do it twice in the same place." . . . "Git off that dime." Now somebody was singing, "I ask you very confidentially . . ." "Sing it man, sing it." . . . Piano treble moaning, bass rumbling like thunder. A swarm of people, motivating their bodies to express in suggestive movements the ultimate consummation of desire. (147–48)

The naive Emma Lou is frightened by the intensity of the party and, more importantly, by the unnerving sensation that "the general atmosphere of the room and the liquor she had drunk had presumably created another person in her stead" who cannot resist succumbing to "the music and to the liquor and to the physical madness of the moment" (149). She struggles to maintain her disapproval of the rent party even as she becomes increasingly intoxicated, both by the corn liquor she drinks and by the wild music and dancing she witnesses in this "dreadful place" (152).

Thurman also examines in detail the various reactions of the black intellectuals and artists who attend the rent party. For most of them, it is their first time at such a gathering. Emma Lou's shiftless "sweetback" boyfriend, Alva, has agreed to act as a liaison between the rent-party hosts and these young black literati who long to experience one of these well-known Harlem events but fear that their "polished manners and exteriors" might isolate them. Alva feels it necessary to play the role of escort because "proletarian Negroes are as suspicious of their more sophisticated brethren as they are of white men, and resent as keenly their intrusions into their social world" (138). Thurman includes satiric portrayals of many prominent figures of the Harlem Renaissance who were also his close friends, including Langston Hughes ("Tony Crews"), Zora Neale Hurston ("Cora Thurston"), Richard Bruce Nugent ("Paul"), Aaron Douglas ("Aaron"), and even Thurman himself ("Truman Walter"). Around 1:00 A.M. the drunken troupe of "niggerati,"[8] along with Alva, his white friend Ray, and the reluctant Emma Lou, arrive at the rent party. Alva is perfectly at ease in this environment, while Emma Lou is utterly horrified. The most interesting element of this scene, however, is the reaction of the black intellectuals to the spectacle before them.

Thurman portrays the black literati as just as condescending and voyeuristic as the white nightclubbers who traveled up to Harlem throughout the 1920s to get a taste of trendy black culture. The intellectuals come across as embarrassing, obnoxious, amateur sociologists doing fieldwork in Harlem; as participant-observers they do a lot more gawking and finger pointing than they do participating. Their pleasure in attending the party is amplified by their obvious thrill at "slumming" in Harlem: "Isn't this marvelous?" Truman, the quintessential voyeur, asks excitedly. Tony Crews confidently declares, "It's the greatest I've seen yet" (149). Their titillation only increases at their discovery of the King Kong and traditional "downhome" food available to paying guests:

> "Do you know they have corn liquor in the kitchen? They serve it from a coffee pot." Aaron seemed proud of his discovery.
>
> "Yes," said Alva, "and they got hoppin'-john out there, too."
>
> "What the hell is hoppin'-john?"
>
> "Ray, I'm ashamed of you. Here you are passing for colored and don't know what hoppin'-john is!"
>
> "Tell him, Cora, I don't know either."
>
> "Another one of these foreigners." Cora looked at Truman disdainfully. "Hoppin'-john is blackeyed peas and rice. Didn't they have any out in Salt Lake City?"
>
> "Have they any chitterlings?" Alta asked eagerly.
>
> "No, Alta," Alva replied, dryly. "This isn't Kansas. They have got pig's feet though."
>
> "Lead me to 'em," Aaron and Alta shouted in unison, and led the way to the kitchen . . . (150)

Truman and Ray's ignorance of Hoppin' John, a common southern soulfood dish and one enjoyed by many people of meager means, indicates the wide cultural and economic chasms that separate them from the rest of the partygoers, and it also helps to underscore the intellectuals' outsider status at the rent party. Theirs was truly, as Truman mockingly calls it, a "pilgrimage to the proletariat's parlor social" (153), and one that Thurman uses to dramatize the vast cultural differences between ordinary Harlemites and the leaders of the so-called New Negro movement.

Thurman's portrayal of the rent party, one of the more extended such scenes in Harlem Renaissance fiction, allows him to assemble members of several disparate populations in Harlem in a plausible setting and comment on the tremendous diversity of their worldviews. White literature, and particularly white newspaper reportage of the 1920s, tended to lump African Americans together under a single monolithic identity without taking into account the wide range of education, professions, economic situations, nationalities, and aspirations they represented. Of course white society recognized the occasional African American outside the narrow boundaries of Harlem—the white press and white audiences enthusiastically applauded entertainers such as Paul Robeson, Florence Mills, Louis Armstrong, Duke Ellington, Josephine Baker, and a few others. But seldom did white writers accentuate the diversity of black Harlem that was represented even at an ordinary rent party; the simple truth is probably that they had no idea that such diversity existed. Even Carl Van Vechten, who was perhaps more widely welcomed at Harlem parties than any other white person in the 1920s, included party scenes in his fiction that were dominated by black characters who largely resembled each other in their proclivities toward jazz, liquor, and licentiousness (of course, Van Vechten attended parties thrown by the black elite; he was not a guest at ordinary working-class rent parties). Thurman's portrayal highlights the inadequacy of this monolithic interpretation of black culture by pointing out that African Americans from various strata of society might attend a single rent party, albeit for very different reasons.

Thurman's fascination with house parties also informs his second novel, *Infants of the Spring,* which portrays a Harlem Renaissance movement awash in gin, dissipation, and self-indulgence. Unlike *The Blacker the Berry . . . ,* which primarily concerns the evolution of a single character's consciousness, *Infants of the Spring* captures the perspective of a whole generation of African American intellectuals and is decidedly more caustic than the earlier novel. The parade of characters in *Infants of the Spring* all represent either a corollary individual (including Thurman himself as well as many well-known Harlem Renaissance figures, some of whom were also portrayed in the rent-party section of *The Blacker The Berry . . .*), or a particular type of person indicative, at least to Thurman, of the wastefulness and vanity of the Harlem Renaissance. But regardless of whether a character can be identified with an actual contemporary of Thurman's, or even with Thurman himself, what *Infants of the Spring* does suggest is that some Harlem Renaissance artists and writers treated life during Prohibition as just one long debauched party.

The subject of *Infants of the Spring* is the Harlem Renaissance itself and, as Thurman sees it, its general lack of success as a unified movement. The artists and writers in the story are self-conscious to the point of paralysis—their art suffers because they struggle with meeting their self-imposed challenge of leading a new social and cultural movement. They also flounder, Thurman suggests none too subtly, because they seldom remain sober enough to do an honest day's work. The novel is set mostly in a boarding house that Thurman dubs "Niggerati Manor," a house essentially donated to a colony of artists, singers, writers, and musicians by a wealthy white female patron of the African American arts in the hope that it would function as both a cultural salon and a productive workplace.[9] Instead, the house serves primarily as a place for the hedonistic residents to have sex, get drunk, and fritter away their time discussing, instead of producing, art. Raymond Taylor (a writer based on Thurman himself) and his complicated relationship with his white friend, Stephen, form the nucleus of the novel, but the many characters in *Infants of the Spring* (and their many alcoholic, sociopathic, and psychological problems) swirl around Raymond and Stephen in scenes of drunken confusion and frustrating aimlessness.

While not mentioned outright in *Infants of the Spring*, Prohibition forms a critical backdrop to the novel. The ubiquity of liquor in the novel is itself both astonishing and revealing, especially in light of the Eighteenth Amendment. The residents of Niggerati Manor swill gin incessantly; Raymond simply cannot do anything without a gin-and-ginger-ale in his hand, and virtually every conversation in the novel begins with something akin to "Let's have a drink." While the action of the novel seldom takes place in the characters' favorite speakeasy around the corner, this watering hole frequently crops up in conversation as either a recent or imminent destination. In the novel, drinking gin tends to intensify latent elements of the characters' personalities—the belligerent become more belligerent, the arrogant become more arrogant. At the same time, drinking excessively seems to offer a way for them to appear artsy, avant-garde, and socially rebellious without actually rebelling against anything but Prohibition laws—hardly a radical position for a crew of so-called radical thinkers. In fact, Thurman robs the residents of any political motivation to drink—they never debate the issue of Prohibition; rather, they seem to drink primarily in order to avoid working toward their professed artistic goals.

The characters in *Infants of the Spring* do not pay rent, but when finances get especially tight they throw a "donation party"—just like a rent party—in an attempt to acquire some much-needed groceries. Two-thirds of the way through the novel, the residents of Niggerati Manor, perpetually strapped for cash, suddenly realize that they have neither money nor food. Since they spend most of their money on liquor instead of food, this can hardly come as a surprise to any of them. Nevertheless, two of the artists-in-residence concoct the grand idea of a donation party, asking guests to bring food instead of paying a standard admission fee. After ten days of preparation (during which time their food source is unclear), the residents host a donation party for dozens of guests, both black and white, who bring bags full of groceries:

> All were convivial and excited. Various persons sang and danced. Highballs were quickly disposed of. A jazz pianist starred at the piano. There was a rush to dance. Everyone seemed to be hilariously drunk. Shouts of joy merged into one persistent noisy blare. Couples staggered to the kitchen to the studio and back again. Others leaned despairingly, sillily against the walls, or else sank helplessly into chairs or window sills. Fresh crowds continued to come in. The Donation Party was successful beyond all hopes. (184–85)

At first glance, this appears to be a triumphant moment, but Thurman instead demonstrates how the donation party, like the alcohol-dependent lives of the party's sponsors, threatens to spin out of control.

Far more debauched even than the rent party in *The Blacker The Berry* . . . , the donation party in *Infants of the Spring* quickly devolves into mayhem. The apparent success of the party cannot eradicate the undertones of despair and disgust that Raymond feels as he grimly surveys the crowd of drunken partiers. Groceries and liquor topple to the floor in a sticky mess, sexual partners of every gender and racial combination covertly take over the upstairs bedrooms, and, despite the enthusiastic gyrations of the dancers to the deafening music, the party takes on a sense of desperation:

> The party had reached new heights. The lights in the basement had been dimmed, and the revelling dancers cast grotesque shadows on the heavily tapestried walls. Color lines had been completely eradicated. Whites and blacks clung passionately together as if trying to effect a permanent merger. Liquor, jazz, and close physical contact had achieved what decades of propaganda had advocated with little success. Here, Raymond thought, . . . is social equality. Tomorrow all of them will have an emotional hangover . . . (186–87)

"Social equality," according to the cynical Raymond, comes from gin bottles and jazz music, and this scene of drunken interracial licentiousness is clearly a far cry from what the leaders of the temperance movement and the authors of the Prohibition amendment intended.

Thurman's detailed scenes of drinking and revelry in both of his novels seem intended to satirize the black intellectuals of the Harlem Renaissance, but to different degrees. In *The Blacker the Berry . . .* , the interlopers at the rent party appear merely silly. They do not belong at the party, but they know too little about the culture of working-class African Americans to realize it. As a result, they have a wonderful time, never once suspecting that their foolish banter about the food and condescending declarations of the scene as "marvelous" force the reader to see them as ridiculous. The satire evident in the story of the donation party in *Infants of the Spring,* and throughout this later novel, is far more bitter. The "niggerati" in *Infants of the Spring* appear pathetic during their highly alcoholic revelry that evening, but in fact Thurman paints them as pathetic no matter what they are doing. The donation party epitomizes their idleness and self-indulgence, and indicates how deeply disappointed Thurman, as Raymond, was with himself and with his talented colleagues who squandered their opportunities and promise. Surveying his friends that night, all of them intoxicated to the point of near incapacity, Raymond repeats to himself in what is perhaps the bleakest moment of a very bleak novel, "This . . . is the Negro renaissance, and this is about all the whole damn thing is going to amount to" (187).

Rent parties often surfaced in Prohibition-era newspaper reportage, and behind the story of the raid or the arrests, these events appeared to offer evidence that African Americans were living lives mired in vice and immorality. Literary accounts of rent parties, however, differ significantly. In the works of Wallace Thurman and Langston Hughes, rent parties are portrayed positively, almost affectionately, although the economic circumstances that make rent parties essential are not forgotten. The hosts and participants are sympathetic characters who come together to drink, dance, and temporarily forget their troubles, while outsiders who "crash" these parties are regarded with contempt. Rent parties demonstrate yet another way that Prohibition culture influenced the literary work produced during those "dry" years, and these scenes offer readers a revealing glimpse of how and why people routinely defied the liquor laws.

Good-Time Flats

> When the cops would come, they'd stalk through the house straight
> back to the kitchen and throw down a half dozen or more slugs of my
> likker and stuff their coat pockets with fried chicken. I was lucky to
> make a profit at all. But what the hell, sometimes I had a good night.
> —Proprietor of a Prohibition-era good-time flat in Harlem, 1920s

Besides the tremendously popular and profitable rent parties and the occasional "donation party," National Prohibition also spawned a number of corollary social gatherings based on the same principle of throwing a dance party, complete with food and liquor, in order to make money. Enterprising and daring Harlem residents transformed their apartments into "buffet flats," "hooch joints," or "barrelhouse flats," and threw parties not just when the rent was due but sometimes every night of the week. These semipublic speakeasies, operating in private apartments, varied slightly in their focus and their clientele, but they all can be subsumed under the catchall term "good-time flat," and all can trace their roots back to the rent party.

The proprietors of good-time flats seldom had the money or the inclination to pay for protection from either gangsters or police, and so at times they were hard-pressed to keep their establishments open. Regular patrons were careful to keep the nature and whereabouts of these party flats a secret from anyone who might pose a potential threat, for as Paul Oliver explains in *Blues Fell This Morning: Meaning in the Blues* (1990), "raids were feared by the bell-hops and kitchen mechanics, truck drivers and domestic cleaners who frequented [good-time flats] and could ill-afford to lose their jobs" (152). When raids did occur, police usually closed down the flat by disposing of the confiscated liquor (by pouring it out, keeping it for themselves, or selling it to bootleggers), boarding up the windows, padlocking the entrance, and affixing a decal proclaiming the premises a "public nuisance" and therefore closed until further notice. Most proprietors, especially successful ones, responded to police raids by laying low for a while and then setting up shop in a different apartment; as one of Claude McKay's characters happily exclaims in *Home to Harlem* (1928), upon discovering that her favorite good-time flat has reopened elsewhere, "White folks can't padlock niggers outa joy forever" (336).

One specific kind of good-time flat that appears in African American literature of the Prohibition era is the so-called buffet flat. Sometimes this term was used to describe an apartment where an ordinary rent party was being held, and the "buffet" in this case might refer merely to the plentiful southern food and bootleg liquor that was available for a nominal price. But most often a buffet flat suggested a party that was overtly sexual in nature. While romantic encounters occurred at all sorts of crowded Harlem parties, buffet flats usually operated more like a combination speakeasy-brothel. Frequently hosted by small-time pimps or madams, these parties would solicit guests by either sending prostitutes to hand out personal invitations to lonely-looking men in speakeasies, or by relying on satisfied customers to bring their friends. Unlike rent parties, which welcomed strangers, visitors to the more exclusive buffet flats generally had to know someone who would make his introduction to the host. Prostitutes of both genders would entice customers into back rooms, frequently entertaining several different partners in an evening, while the band or phonograph player played jazz music in the front rooms so patrons could dance. David Levering Lewis comments in *When Harlem Was in Vogue* (1981) that at the buffet flat, "varied and often perverse sexual pleasures were offered cafeteria-style," suggesting an orgiastic and decadent ambience throughout the apartment (107).

One WPA oral history interview preserved in the Library of Congress tells the story of Bernice, a former Harlem maid who overcame her initial repulsion to ordinary rent parties and ultimately became a successful madam operating a popular buffet flat. She remembers the initial circumstances that led into her new line of work:

> When my husband, who was a Pullman porter, ran off and left me with a sixty-dollar-a-month apartment on my hands and no job, I soon learned, like everyone else, to rent my rooms out an' throw these Saturday get-togethers. I had two roomers, a colored boy and white girl named Leroy and Hazel, who first gave me the idea. They offered to run the parties for me if we'd split fifty-fifty. I had nothing to lose, so that's how we started.

The three of them would chip in to buy gallons of corn liquor from a local bootlegger and then would sell it in small portions to their guests for fifty cents a drink. Leroy was in charge of gaming in the back room, often bringing in close to thirty dollars a night on poker and blackjack—more than double the weekly wages of many domestics. Bernice and her cohosts soon became known in the neighborhood for the gambling that went on; later, gambling gave way to more licentious enterprises:

> And we rented rooms, sometimes overnight and sometimes for just a little while during the party. I have to admit that, at first, I was a little shocked at the utter boldness of it, but Leroy and Hazel seemed to think nothing of it, so I let it go. Besides, it meant extra money—and extra money was what I needed.
>
> I soon took another hint from Hazel and made even more. I used to notice that Leroy would bring some of his friends home with him and, after they'd have a few drinks, leave them alone in the room with Hazel. I wasn't quite sure that what I was thinking was so until Hazel told me herself. It happened one day when an extra man came along [and] there was no one to take care of him. Hazel buzzed to me and asked me if I would do it. I thought about it for awhile, then made up my mind to do it.
>
> Well, that was the last of days-work [domestic work] for me. I

figured that I was a fool to go out and break my back scrubbing floors, washing, ironing, and cooking, when I could earn three day's pay, or more, in fifteen minutes. Then I began to understand how Hazel got all those fine dresses and good-looking furs. From then on, it was strictly a business with me. I decided that if it was as easy as that, it was the life for me.[10]

Bernice eventually left her initial partners, set herself up as a madam in her own buffet flat, and took half of what the prostitutes in her employ made each night. After Prohibition was repealed, Bernice lamented, as did many proprietors of buffet and other good-time flats, that "it was a good racket while it lasted."

Because regular rent parties were often held by respectable, albeit poor, citizens, they were grudgingly recognized by black intellectuals and social leaders as an unfortunate economic necessity. According to these same leaders, however, good-time flats were a vicious business that should not be tolerated by any self-respecting person, nor should they be popularized in print. Nevertheless, a few Harlem Renaissance writers such as Claude McKay and Zora Neale Hurston did not shy away from portraying the seamier sides of Harlem nightlife in their fiction. McKay's popular 1928 novel *Home to Harlem,* which reportedly left W. E. B. Du Bois with the feeling that he needed a bath after reading it, is steeped in the underworld environment of buffet flats, illicit cabarets, and other bawdy Harlem nightspots. McKay unapologetically included what were seen by many critics to be inappropriately graphic depictions of African American carousing; in response to suggestions that he should have tempered his portrayal, McKay proudly asserted in his autobiography, *A Long Way from Home* (1937), that unlike other black writers of the era, "I created my Negro characters without sandpaper and varnish." McKay decried the interloping voyeur in Harlem, black or white, and attacked those who temporarily "slummed" in a futile attempt to gain insight into the collective psyche of the black working class:

I did not come to the knowing of Negro workers in an academic way, by talking to black crowds at meetings, nor in a bohemian way, by talking about them in cafes. I knew the unskilled Negro worker of the city by working with him as a porter and longshoreman and as waiter on the railroad. I lived in the same quarters and we drank and caroused together in bars and at rent parties. So when I came to write about the low-down Negro, I did not have to compose him from an outside view. Nor did I have to write a pseudo-romantic account, as do bourgeois persons who become working-class for awhile and

work in shops and factories to get material for writing dull books
about workers, whose inner lives are closed to them. (228)

Since some Harlem residents did indeed attend buffet flats and other
good-time nightspots, McKay believed that these places deserved to be
included in his fiction.

Home to Harlem chronicles the adventures of Jake Brown, a black longshoreman and army veteran who resides in 1920s Harlem. Jake is a young,
strong, single black man with no money and no personal obligations. He
deserts the army during World War I, but only after he and his black regiment are not allowed into combat but instead are ordered to build huts to
house white soldiers. Back in Harlem, he works at a series of backbreaking
jobs with few complaints, and he refuses to cross the picket lines of strik-
ing workers. Neither will Jake take money from his cabaret singer-
girlfriend, Rose, who offers to make him her "sweetman" and encourages
him not to work. He does, however, spend his money as fast as he can get
it on various social vices, including drinking and gambling, but McKay
does not condemn him for this. In fact, the bulk of McKay's narrative
eagerly follows Jake on his rounds of the various pool halls, dance halls,
speakeasies, cabarets, and good-time flats of Harlem where he throws dice,
dances, drinks bootleg liquor, and seduces women. Contemporary black
critics vehemently objected to these aspects of the novel, but these same
passages offer today's readers fascinating glimpses into the nightlife that
took place in Prohibition-era Harlem.

After much anticipation on Jake's part, he spends his first night back in
Harlem at a typical buffet flat, accompanied by Clarice, a prostitute he
picks up in a cabaret:

> They went to a buffet flat on One Hundred and Thirty-seventh
> Street. The proprietress opened the door without removing the chain
> and peeked out. She was a matronly mulatto woman. She recognized
> the girl, who had put herself in front of Jake, and she slid back the
> chain and said, "Come right in."
>
> The windows were heavily and carefully shaded. There was beer
> and wine, and there was plenty of hard liquor. Black and brown men
> sat at two tables in one room, playing poker. In another room a
> phonograph was grinding out a "blues," and some couples were danc-
> ing, thick as maggots in a vat of sweet liquor, and as wriggling.
> (13–14)

Jake and his female companion are admitted to the buffet flat not only
because the madam knows the girl but also because Jake is black. Since

there were virtually no African American revenue agents and very few
black police officers in New York City, it was a fairly safe bet that a visibly
black customer at a buffet flat or other illicit watering hole would not pose
a security threat.

An important and often overlooked consequence of Prohibition in
Harlem and other black neighborhoods was that the constant suspicion of
white people as possible revenuers influenced the way light-skinned black
people were treated within their own community. McKay dramatizes this
situation in *Home to Harlem,* when three white men manage to weasel
their way into the good graces of Madame Suarez, the hostess of an exclusive buffet flat. The men drink heavily, dance with the women, make
friends with the men, and spend a great deal of money. Then one night,
in a shocking incident, McKay describes how the ecstatic mood of the flat
was shattered by the betrayal of these white undercover agents who
"unmasked as the Vice Squad and killed the thing" (108). The narrator's
outrage at the Vice Squad's bust stems not only from the inconvenient
closing of the flat and the awkward position that many of the guests (particularly the women) are placed in by having to appear in Night Court,
but also by the blow the policemen strike against community cohesion
and trust. "For a long time," the narrator comments, "Negro proprietors
would not admit white customers into their cabarets and near-white
members of the black race, whose features were unfamiliar in Harlem, had
a difficult time proving their identity" (111).[11]

For many working-class men and women in Harlem during
Prohibition, the social scene revolved primarily, if not exclusively, around
the culture of house parties. McKay's *Home to Harlem* explores some of
these party scenes from a distinctly male perspective, emphasizing the
many pleasures to be found in drinking, dancing, gambling, and sex. No
hint of desperation or despair clouds the experience of Jake and his
cronies; the women they encounter in the good-time flats all appear to be
having as fine a time as the men they so ardently entertain. But in
"Muttsy" (1926), one of her early short stories, Zora Neale Hurston
explores this world of buffet flats from the perspective of a naive young
woman newly arrived in the city and terrified of what she finds.

The often-overlooked "Muttsy," which garnered "One-half of Second
Prize" in a short-story contest sponsored by *Opportunity* in 1926, tells the
tale of Pinkie Jones, a young, attractive, African American woman who had
"jus' come in on the boat" from Eatonville, Florida. A dockworker directs
the bewildered, homeless girl to Ma "Forty-dollars-Kate" Turner's buffet
flat in Harlem, where Pinkie encounters, for the first time in her life, a
middle-aged woman wearing makeup and drinking whiskey. Ma Turner's
husband befriends Pinkie and vows, to Pinkie's dismay, to "edgecate" her in

the ways of the buffet flat. The frightened country girl, surrounded by partiers who were all drinking toddies or "shaking shimmies to music, rolling eyes heavenward as they picked imaginary grapes out of the air" (46), suffers dramatic culture shock as she tries to acclimate herself to these rough urban surroundings steeped in gambling, sex, and bootleg liquor.

The men at the buffet flat tease Pinkie mercilessly, until she "hung her head, embarrassed that she did not understand their mode of speech; she felt the unfriendly eyes of the women, and she loathed the smell of liquor that filled the house now" (46–47). Only the auspicious arrival of Muttsy Owens, a handsome gambler and ladies' man, interrupts the men's terrorizing of the poor girl. Muttsy rescues Pinkie from the unwanted attention of the other men (to the consternation of Muttsy's drunken girlfriend, Ada) and embarks on a short but intense courtship to win over the beautiful country girl. Although she condemns both gambling and liquor outright and vows someday to "scrape herself clear of people who took toddies" (45), after a few days Pinkie is worn down by the pressures of her sordid environment and drinks so much whiskey that she slips into unconsciousness. During the night Muttsy visits her room, kisses and fondles her, then slides his diamond ring onto her finger and leaves the room. When Pinkie awakens to learn that Muttsy has been in her room and left her an engagement ring, she leaves the three dollars she has to her name under her pillow, sneaks away from the buffet flat in shame and terror, and disappears into the anonymity of the city.

The denouement of the story, crammed into the final dozen paragraphs, seems markedly fantastical when compared to the realism of the preceding scenes in the buffet flat. When Muttsy finds out that Pinkie has run away, he instantly abandons his gambling, takes an honest job as a stevedore on the docks, and hunts diligently for his lost love. When he does find her, two weeks later, he somehow wins her affection with his newfound respectability and convinces her to marry him. Although Muttsy is pleased at first with his life as responsible husband and provider, the final note of Hurston's story suggests a much less idyllic future for the couple. After only a month of marriage, Muttsy breaks his promise to quit gambling and returns to shooting dice, remarking to his friend, "What man can't keep one li'l wife an' two li'l bones?" (56).

Compared with much of Hurston's later short fiction, "Muttsy" suffers from a serious lack of character development and plausibility. Neither Pinkie's nor Muttsy's motivations ever seem particularly clear, nor does Muttsy's overnight change from champion crapshooter to responsible stevedore seem likely. And alongside Hurston's more accomplished short fiction, including "Sweat" (1926) and "The Gilded Six-Bits" (1933) in which the sympathetic female heroines prevail, the conclusion of "Muttsy" seems unexpectedly brutal for the innocent girl from Eatonville. Nevertheless, despite certain flaws, "Muttsy" offers readers a glimpse into the inner world of a Harlem buffet flat during Prohibition.

Ma Turner's establishment demonstrates all the characteristics of a typical good-time flat in Jazz Age Harlem. She herself was a former prostitute, nick-named "Forty-dollars-Kate" because, as her husband explains to Pinkie, twenty-five years ago "Men wuz glad 'nough to spend forty dollars on her if dey had it" (43). Knowing the business firsthand, Ma Turner understands just how to make her buffet flat profitable. She hires a piano player to pound out blues and jazz tunes "as only a Negro can" (45), offers plenty of whiskey for sale to her guests, and throughout the course of each evening cautiously admits men and women into the flat "after the same furtive peering out through the nearest crack of the door" (45). But, older now, Ma Turner leaves the sexual entertainment to the younger women, who nightly arrive "by ones and twos, some in shabby coats turned up about the ears, and with various cheap but showy hats crushed down over unkempt hair" (45). And, always with an eye to profit, Ma Turner immediately realizes that the attractive Pinkie will make a fine and lucrative addition to her staff of prostitutes.

Pinkie's innocence at first prevents her from understanding exactly what sort of house she has entered and what is expected of her in order to earn her room and board. But she soon notices that night after night, "the same women, or others just like them, came to Ma Turner's. The same men, or men just like them, came also and treated them to liquor or mis-treated them with fists or cruel jibes" (30). The women, who desperately vie for the attention of the men who can afford to buy their drinks and perhaps their sexual favors, appear competitive and even vicious. The ulti-mate goal for each of them is to land a rich man and leave the world of good-time flats, and they all see the unwitting Pinkie as an unwelcome rival for Muttsy's affections.

Although the atmosphere of Ma Turner's buffet flat seems far more threatening than that of Madame Suarez's in *Home to Harlem,* both of them occupy a similar place in the context of Prohibition culture. Urban, working-class men (and women) sought safe havens where they could drink and socialize with impunity; with the saloons closed, their choice of venue was limited. Because good-time flats were far more private than speakeasies, the opportunity for sex (of all varieties) in the former estab-lishments was greater. Women with few opportunities to make their own living prostituted themselves in the hope of meeting a future husband, as is the case with Clarice in *Home to Harlem* and Ada in "Muttsy." Above all, the drinking culture that had been outlawed by the Eighteenth Amendment flourished behind locked doors in these good-time flats, where the law seldom reached.

∞

Because house parties were so common during Prohibition, it is not at all surprising that they appear so frequently in the literature of the 1920s and early 1930s. From Jay Gatsby's glamorous West Egg galas to George Babbitt's modest suburban cocktail party to Harlem's working-class rent parties, the house party, in its many variations, provided opportunities for people to experiment with new social behaviors in a setting more private than a speakeasy or nightclub. House parties during Prohibition were modern, chic, and, contrary to the spirit of the Eighteenth Amendment, almost by definition included liquor. In her 1933 etiquette book, *No Nice Girl Swears*, writer Alice-Leone Moats comments, "There was once a time when a man who got drunk in a lady's drawing room was never invited to that house again. If he showed the same lack of control in another home, he ran the risk of having every door closed to him. Now a hostess who insists that all her guests remain sober would find that she was giving parties to a chosen few, and very dull ones at that. She takes it for granted that the majority of her guests will be wavering before the evening is over" (171). Fiction writers of the Prohibition era thus used the occasion of the drunken house party to demonstrate how firmly people resisted the intrusiveness of Prohibition and how even the most socially respectable individuals often flaunted their disrespect for the liquor laws. Most of all, these parties functioned in literature as symbolic events that reflected those turbulent years when Americans were so deeply divided over the issue of Prohibition.

The Legacies of National Prohibition in American Literature

Prohibition will work great injury to the cause of temperance. It is a species of intemperance within itself, for it goes beyond the bounds of reason in that it attempts to control a man's appetite by legislation and makes a crime out of things that are not crimes. A prohibition law strikes at the very principle upon which our government was founded.
—Abraham Lincoln, 1840

When Abraham Lincoln, a lifelong teetotaler, spoke these words as a member of the Illinois state legislature, he anticipated exactly the sort of political backlash that National Prohibition would create eighty years later. Unfortunately, when the Eighteenth Amendment was sent to the states for ratification, no prophet stood up to warn, as historian Herbert Asbury puts it, of "the illicit breweries and distilleries, the bootleggers and the speakeasies, the corruption of police and judiciary, the hijackers and their machine guns, the gang wars, the multimillionaire booze barons, the murders and assassinations, the national breakdown of morals and manners, and all the rest of the long train of evils" that would result from National Prohibition ("The Noble Experiment" 34). While it is overly simplistic to blame Prohibition alone for all these social ills, federal attempts to eliminate drinking undoubtedly did great harm to the temperance cause, as measured both by statistical studies that charted increased drinking among certain sectors of the population, and by anecdotal evidence that suggested drinking became, to many, a much more desirable behavior after it was outlawed. But even more importantly, by making, as Lincoln put it, "a crime out of things that are not crimes," National Prohibition damaged Americans' faith in their government to such an extent that even now, generations later, that faith has not completely recovered. The Twenty-first Amendment, which repealed National Prohibition in December 1933, may have reopened the breweries, distilleries, and bars, but it did little to restore Americans' confidence that the federal government could be relied upon to look after the private lives of its citizens wisely and fairly.

In 1920, shortly after Prohibition went into effect, Senator Morris Sheppard of Texas, a politician instrumental in the drafting of the Volstead Act, boasted that "there is as much chance of repealing the Eighteenth Amendment as there is for a hummingbird to fly to the planet Mars with the Washington Monument tied to its tail" (Asbury, *The Great Illusion* 316). Although this comment seems laughable today, Sheppard's opinion, generally speaking, reigned as the prevailing wisdom of the 1920s. No constitutional amendment had ever been repealed, and that precedent was enough to convince most Americans that amendments, once ratified, become permanent legal fixtures. Thus, the Prohibition-related literature produced during the so-called dry decade reveals how Americans lived under an unpopular law that nearly everyone believed would, for better or worse, endure.

National Prohibition cast a long shadow over many works of American fiction published during the 1920s and early 1930s, influencing them in ways that are rarely identified or acknowledged by readers or critics. But the influence of National Prohibition on American literature certainly did not subside with repeal; indeed, in the years immediately following repeal, many writers continued to wrestle with the implications and consequences of Prohibition. For example, although novelist and short-story writer John O'Hara knew of Prohibition's imminent repeal as he wrote *Appointment in Samarra* (1934), the psychological and political landscape of 1930 proved to be an irresistible background to his story of corruption, alcoholism, and desperation. The novel tells the bleak story of the selfish and self-destructive Julian English, a wealthy member of the fashionable set, and the ruthless bootleggers and gangsters who control his small Pennsylvania town of Gibbsville. Illegal liquor saturates the lives of nearly all the characters; Julian's alcoholism is only one manifestation of the narrator's observation that "everyone was drinking, or had just finished a drink, or was about to take one" (7). Julian's encounters with the bottom of the bottle increase when the Great Depression hits, and his inevitable suicide offers a revealing comment on how drinking adversely affected the confident men of the post–World War I generation.

John O'Hara was only one of many American authors who revisited the culture of Prohibition in their stories of flappers, bootleggers, and the Jazz Age in the years immediately following repeal. The year 1934 also saw the publication of Langston Hughes's short story "Why, You Reckon?" in which a young black Harlem resident convinces another black youth, the narrator, to help him rob a rich white nightclubber on his way into an expensive Prohibition-era cabaret. The two boys jump a well-dressed

young white man, drag him into a furnace room, and demand that he
hand over his wallet and empty his pockets. Hughes's most interesting
comment comes at the end of the story, however, when the first mugger
absconds with the loot and leaves the narrator alone with the shoeless and
coatless white man, who responds to the robbery by saying, "Gee, this was
thrilling! . . . This is the first time in my life I've ever had a good time in
Harlem. Everything else has been fake, a show. You know, something you
pay for. This was real." The story ends with the white man standing in the
snow in his stocking feet, calmly hailing a downtown taxi, and the bewildered Harlem narrator wondering to himself, "What do you suppose is the
matter with rich white folks? Why you reckon they ain't happy?" (71).
Clearly, critical portrayals of white incursion into black nightspots did not
cease just because Prohibition came to an end.

William Faulkner, F. Scott Fitzgerald, Dorothy West, Carl Van
Vechten, Dashiell Hammett, and Dorothy Parker, among many others,
continued to focus on the people and places that Prohibition engendered
in their fictional works published in the 1930s, 1940s, and in some cases
even later. The genres of gangster fiction and crime fiction that became
popular after Prohibition also owe their existence, in some measure, to the
groundbreaking fiction of the 1920s in which mob bosses and bootleggers
figured prominently. To cite a more recent example, Toni Morrison's novel
Jazz (1992), set in Harlem during the 1920s, is replete with references to
Prohibition culture. It seems likely, though, that writers who did not
directly experience National Prohibition, such as Morrison, would portray this era of American history rather differently in their fiction than
would those who actually lived through the era of speakeasies, bootleg
liquor, and revenue agents. This line of questioning would undoubtedly
prove fruitful for scholars interested in the literary legacy of the
Eighteenth Amendment.

While the deep psychological aftershocks of World War I and the explo-
sion of new technologies irrefutably contributed to the development of a
modern American literature, the controversial "liquor problem" and the
nation's ensuing lawlessness also helped to shape the evolution of American
letters during the years of Prohibition. Unfortunately, National
Prohibition is seldom indexed in critical studies of American fiction of the
1920s, and it is rarely cited as a contributing force in the evolution of
post–World War I literature. Despite its marginal presence in literary studies of fiction written between 1920 and 1933, however, Prohibition exert-
ed a tremendous influence on how American writers conceptualized transgression, rebellion, morality, and even modernity itself. In doing so,
National Prohibition stamped its indelible cultural mark on some of the
greatest works of American literature.

Notes

Notes to Introduction

1. "Bone-Dry Literature Coming," *Wall Street Journal* (April 15, 1919): 9.
2. "Must We De-Alcoholize Literature? How Shakespeare, Rare Ben Jonson, Robert Burns, and Omar Khayyam Will Sound if They Are Revised to Fit Those Sober Days Soon to Come," *New York Times* (March 16, 1919): 77.
3. "Prohibition Won't Produce Great Literature, Quiller-Couch Replies to a Teetotaller," *New York Times* (March 17, 1922): 1.
4. *New York Times* review of *If Today Be Sweet* by Ednah Aiken (November 11, 1923): BR8.

Notes to Chapter 1

1. James B. Morrow, "Prohibition Law Will Be Rigidly Enforced," *Boston Daily Globe,* January 4, 1920.
2. See especially Paula Fass, *The Damned and the Beautiful: American Youth in the 1920's* (New York: Oxford University Press, 1977); Elizabeth Stevenson, *Babbitts and Bohemians: From the Great War to the Great Depression* (1967; New York: Macmillan, 1998); and Frederick Lewis Allen, *Only Yesterday: An Informal History of the 1920's* (1931; New York: Harper & Row, 1964).
3. The "Talk of the Town" section of the *New Yorker* often carried information about the illegal liquor economy; for examples see the issues dated 9/10/27, 9/26/25, 12/26/25, 1/2/26, 1/16/26, and 2/6/26 (among many others).

Notes to Chapter 2

1. "A Novel of the Southern Mills," *New York Times* (September 25, 1932): BR7.
2. See, for example, Joseph R. Urgo, "Proletarian Literature and Feminism: The Gastonia Novels and Feminist Protest," *Minnesota Review* 24 (Spring 1985): 64–84, esp. 71–73.
3. Louis Kronenberger, "Sherwood Anderson's Story-Telling Art," *New York Times* (April 23, 1933): BR6.
4. John Chamberlain, "Dostoyefsky's Shadow in the Deep South," *New York Times* (February 15, 1931): 9.
5. William Faulkner, letter dated September 14, 1950. In *William Faulkner, Essays, Speeches, and Public Letters,* ed. James B. Meriwether (London: Chatto and Windus, 1967), 209.

6. "Harvard Warns Bootleggers to Keep Clear of Dormitories." *New York Times* (January 9, 1925): 19.

7. "Only Suckers Work," *American Life Histories: Manuscripts from the Federal Writers' Project, 1936–1940,* June 14, 2004. <http://memory.loc.gov/ammem/wpaintro/wpahome.html>.

8. "Murdered by Bootleggers" advertisement for the *Ladies' Home Journal. New York Times* (June 1, 1923): 23.

9. "Only Suckers Work," <http://memory.loc.gov/ammem/wpaintro/wpahome.html>.

10. George Schuyler and Theophilus Lewis, "Shafts & Darts: A Page of Calumny and Satire," *The Messenger* 7.8 (August 1925): 295.

11. According to Fisher's "Introduction to Contemporary Harlemese," a glossary included at the back of the novel, *dickty* is an epithet that means "a high-toned person." As an adjective, *dickty* usually appears in a negative, sarcastic context.

12. Izzy and Moe were beloved figures of the Prohibition age, and a number of histories and essays chronicle their remarkable careers. Some of these sources include Edward Behr, *Prohibition: Thirteen Years That Changed America* (New York: Arcade Publishing, 1996), 154–57; John Kobler, *Ardent Spirits: The Rise and Fall of Prohibition* (1973; New York: Da Capo Press, 1993), 294–300; and Herbert Asbury, "The Noble Experiment of Izzy and Moe," *The Aspirin Age, 1919–1941,* ed. Isabel Leighton (New York: Simon & Schuster, 1965), 34–49.

13. Mencken, H. L., "A Moral Tale," *The Nation* 133 (September 23, 1931): 310.

14. Stanley Walker, *Books* (September 13, 1931): 1.

15. *Christian Century* 48: 1145 (Sept. 16, 1931).

Notes to Chapter 3

1. John F. Carter, Jr., "'These Wild Young People' by One of Them," *Atlantic Monthly* 126 (September 1920): 301–4.

2. In 1925 alone almost 4,200 people died from drinking tainted liquor, tens of thousands of people were blinded each year from poisoned drink, and in 1930 more than fifty thousand people were stricken with a paralytic condition called "jake leg" after drinking a medicinal extract of Jamaican ginger. See John P. Morgan and Thomas C. Tulloss, "The Jake Walk Blues," *Old Time Music* 28 (Spring 1978): 17–25.

3. Of course, not every young person in the United States shared these views. Many teenagers raised in more conservative areas of the country or in very traditionalist homes surely believed that drinking alcohol was unwise or even sinful, and that drunken peers were cause for pity and not admiration.

4. F. Scott Fitzgerald, "Bernice Bobs Her Hair," *The Short Stories of F. Scott Fitzgerald: A New Collection,* ed. Matthew J. Bruccoli (New York: Simon and Schuster: 1989), 25–47.

5. F. Scott Fitzgerald, "The Jelly-Bean," *Short Stories of F. Scott Fitzgerald,* 142–58.

6. F. Scott Fitzgerald, "Winter Dreams," *Short Stories of F. Scott Fitzgerald,* 217–36.

7. A hairstyle popular in the early 1920s in which long braids were coiled into two buns that rested just behind a woman's ears, in the fashion of Princess Leia in the original *Star Wars* movie. The "cootie garage" was soon supplanted by the ubiquitous bob.

Notes to Chapter 4

1. The conclusions drawn from this study seem reasonable and are corroborated by a number of other examinations conducted by various researchers and interested parties. But at bottom, the numerous statistical studies of American drinking habits, conducted before, during, and after the years of Prohibition, indicate only that no definitive numbers exist that accurately describe the consumption of alcohol in this country. Conclusions drawn from these studies vary as widely as their foci, and while nearly all of them purport to demonstrate how American drinking increased or decreased as a result of Prohibition, the fact is that none of them can, with any real degree of proficiency, prove anything absolutely. No study could have possibly estimated the volume of liquor smuggled, stolen, or produced illegally in the country, nor could any study take into account the truthfulness of various interviewees regarding their own illegal drinking habits. Thus the statistics regarding drinking habits are inherently flawed. Anecdotally, evidence generally suggests that some people (such as urban working-class men) drank somewhat less because of Prohibition, while others (such as women and college students) drank somewhat more. See also Murdock (94).

2. "Vice Report Scores Dance Hall Evils," *New York Times* (May 21, 1930): 23.

3. Babbitt's experience in the speakeasy would have indicated to readers that Sinclair Lewis himself knew his way around a speakeasy; indeed, like so many other revered American writers of the 1920s, Lewis suffered from debilitating alcoholism.

4. Other public venues in the 1920s also afforded women opportunities to push the boundaries of female propriety, including dance halls and amusement parks. For more extended discussions of these entertainment venues, see John F. Kasson, *Amusing the Million: Coney Island at the Turn of the Century* (New York: Hill and Wang, 1978); Kathy Peiss, *Cheap Amusements: Working Women and Leisure in Turn-of-the-Century New York* (Philadelphia: Temple University Press, 1986); Tera W. Hunter, *To 'Joy My Freedom: Southern Black Women's Lives and Labors After the Civil War* (Cambridge, Mass.: Harvard University Press, 1997), especially 145–86; and Randy D. McBee, *Dance Hall Days: Intimacy and Leisure Among Working-Class Immigrants in the United States* (New York: New York University Press, 2001).

5. "Enright Lectures Vice Squad: Thinks Some Are Grafting," *New York Times* (February 26, 1924): 1, 4.

6. "Night Clubs Found Chief Vice Centres," *New York Times* (October 14, 1929): 1.

7. W. F. White, review of *The Walls of Jericho*, *New York World* (August 5, 1928): 7m.

8. Zora Neale Hurston, "Characteristics of Negro Expression" (1934), in

Within the Circle: An Anthology of African American Literary Criticism from the Harlem Renaissance to the Present, ed. Angelyn Mitchell (Durham, N.C., & London: Duke University Press, 1994), 89–90.

9. This commercial liquor was commonly called "bottle in bond" or just "bond" whiskey, from the distillers' term "bottled in bond," which indicates 100 proof whiskey that has been aged under government supervision for at least four years.

10. "Calls Night Clubs Rendezvous of Vice," *New York Times* (July 15, 1927): 6.

11. W. E. B. Du Bois, Review of *Nigger Heaven, The Crisis* 33 (December 1926): 81.

12. W. E. B. Du Bois, "The Du Bois Literary Prize," *The Crisis* 39.4 (April 1931): 137.

13. Van Vechten defines "creeper" in his "Glossary of Negro Words and Phrases," included at the end of *Nigger Heaven,* as "a man who invades another's marital rights" (285).

14. Leon Coleman also notes that in 1927 the African American revue *Blackbirds* incorporated a cabaret scene inspired by Van Vechten's novel, and in 1928 a popular song called "Nigger Heaven Blues" was published. See Coleman (124).

15. W. E. B. Du Bois, "Harlem," *The Crisis* 34.7 (September 1927): 240.

16. White Rock was a popular soda manufacturer in the 1920s, mostly known for its club soda and ginger ale. In this context "White Rock" probably refers to club soda.

17. Chandler Owen, "The Black and Tan Cabaret—America's Most Democratic Institution," *The Messenger* 7.2 (February 1925): 97, 100.

Notes to Chapter 5

1. "Drinking Accessories," *New Yorker* 5 (December 14, 1929): 102.

2. Qtd. in Paul A. Carter, *Another Part of the Twenties* (New York: Columbia University Press, 1977), 88.

3. By comparison, one study in the late twenties estimated that families in white working-class neighborhoods paid about $6.67 a room. See Osofsky (136).

4. The slang term *ofay* (or *fay*) was often used by African Americans to refer to a white person.

5. Byrd, "Harlem Rent Parties," <http://lcweb2.10c.gov/ammem/>.

6. According to Bruce Kellner's *The Harlem Renaissance: A Historical Dictionary for the Era,* "Mose" was a slang term for a black person and was considered derogatory when used by a white person.

7. Byrd, "'Slick' Reynolds," <http://lcweb2.10c.gov/ammem/>.

8. Niggerati: a term coined by Zora Neale Hurston to describe the black literary circle that she and Thurman were a part of in 1920s Harlem. This term figures prominently in Thurman's *Infants of the Spring,* in which the boarding house where the black literati live is dubbed "Niggerati Manor."

9. This benefactor may be based in part on Charlotte Osgood Mason, the white patron of Langston Hughes and Zora Neale Hurston.

10. Byrd, "Bernice," <http://lcweb2.10c.gov/ammem/>.

11. Another variety of Prohibition-era good-time flat was the "barrelhouse flat," a favorite nightspot for men to drink and gamble. Named for the makeshift bar that would be set up using a plank laid across two or more whiskey kegs, barrelhouse flats were essentially a continuation of the pre-Prohibition saloon. Overwhelmingly masculine, these flats would sometimes forego an official bartender and instead encourage paying guests simply to dip their own cup into the whiskey barrel. Prostitutes would sometimes gather at barrelhouse flats, just as they did at workingmen's saloons before Prohibition, and the back rooms that were not reserved strictly for gambling would sometimes be used for sex. A barrelhouse flat differed from buffet flats in that the primary focus at the former was gambling and sex was incidental; the reverse was generally true of a buffet flat. See Oliver (150–52).

Bibliography

Literary Works

Anderson, Sherwood. "A Jury Case." *Death in the Woods and Other Stories*. 1933. New York: W. W. Norton and Co., 1961.

Cullen, Countee. *One Way to Heaven*. New York: Harper and Brothers Publishers, 1932.

Faulkner, William. *Essays, Speeches, and Public Letters*. Ed. James B. Meriwether. London: Chatto and Windus, 1967.

————. *Sanctuary*. 1931. New York: Vintage/Random House, 1993.

Fisher, Rudolph. "The Promised Land." In *City of Refuge*. Ed. John McCluskey, Jr. Columbia: University of Missouri Press, 1987. 48–59.

————. *The Walls of Jericho*. 1928. London: The X Press, 1995.

Fitzgerald, F. Scott. *The Beautiful and Damned*. 1922. New York: Signet/Penguin Putnam Inc., 1998.

————. *The Great Gatsby*. 1925. New York: Collier/Macmillan Publishing Co., 1980.

————. *The Short Stories of F. Scott Fitzgerald: A New Collection*. Ed. Matthew J. Bruccoli. New York: Simon and Schuster, 1989.

————. *This Side of Paradise*. 1920. New York: Dover Publications, Inc., 1996.

Glyn, Elinor. *"It" and Other Stories*. London: Duckworth, 1927.

Hughes, Langston. *The Big Sea*. 1940. New York: Hill and Wang/Farrar, Straus and Giroux, 1997.

————. "The Negro Artist and the Racial Mountain." In *The Portable Harlem Renaissance Reader*. Ed. David Levering Lewis. New York: Viking Penguin, 1994. 91–95.

————. *Not Without Laughter*. 1931. New York: Macmillan Publishing Co., 1969.

————. "Why, You Reckon?" In *Short Stories Langston Hughes*. Ed. Akiba Sullivan Harper. New York: Hill and Wang/Farrar, Straus and Giroux, 1996. 66–71.

Hurston, Zora Neale. "Muttsy." In *The Complete Stories*. Ed. Henry Louis Gates, Jr., and Sieglinde Lemke. New York: HarperCollins, 1996. 41–56.

Lardner, Ring. *The Big Town: or, How I and the Mrs. Go to New York to See Life and Get Katie a Husband*. Indianapolis: The Bobbs-Merrill Company, 1921. New York & London: Charles Scribner's Sons, 1925.

Larsen, Nella. *Quicksand*. 1929. In *Quicksand and Passing*. Ed. Deborah E. McDowell. New Brunswick, N.J.: Rutgers University Press, 1986. 137–246.

Lewis, Sinclair. *Arrowsmith*. 1925. New York: Signet/Penguin, 1980.

————. *Babbitt*. 1922. New York: Penguin Books, 1996.

Lumpkin, Grace. *To Make My Bread*. 1932. Urbana & Chicago: University of Illinois Press, 1995.

McKay, Claude. *Harlem Glory: A Fragment of Aframerican Life*. Chicago: Charles H. Kerr Publishing Company, 1999.

————. *Home to Harlem.* 1928. Boston: Northeastern University Press, 1987.

————. *A Long Way from Home.* 1937. New York: Harvest/Harcourt, Brace and World, Inc., 1970.

O'Hara, John. *Appointment in Samarra.* 1934. New York: Vintage, 1997.

Parker, Dorothy. *Complete Stories.* Ed. Colleen Breese. Introd. Regina Barreca. New York: Penguin Classics, 2003.

Sinclair, Upton. *The Wet Parade.* New York: Farrar and Rinehart Inc., 1931.

Tarkington, Booth. "The Neck, and Bush Thring." *The Saturday Evening Post* 201 (March 23, 1929): 8–9, 156, 158, 161, 163.

Thurman, Wallace. *The Blacker the Berry . . .* 1929. New York: Scribner/Simon and Schuster, 1996.

————. *The Collected Writings of Wallace Thurman: A Harlem Renaissance Reader.* Ed. Amrijit Singh and Daniel M. Scott III. New Brunswick, N.J.: Rutgers University Press, 2003.

————. "Cordelia the Crude." *Fire!!* 1.1 (November 1926): 5–6.

————. *Infants of the Spring.* 1932. Boston: Northeastern University Press, 1992.

Toomer, Jean. *Cane.* 1923. New York: W. W. Norton and Co., 1988.

Van Vechten, Carl. *Nigger Heaven.* 1926. Urbana & Chicago: University of Illinois Press, 2000.

White, Walter. *The Fire in the Flint.* 1924. Introd. R. Baxter Miller. Athens: University of Georgia Press, 1996.

Other Sources

Adams, James Truslow. "Our Dissolving Ethics." *Atlantic Monthly* (November 1926): 577.

Allen, Frederick Lewis. *Only Yesterday: An Informal History of the 1920's.* 1931. New York: Harper and Row, 1964.

Asbury, Herbert. *The Great Illusion: An Informal History of Prohibition.* Garden City, N.Y.: Doubleday and Company, Inc., 1950.

————. "The Noble Experiment of Izzy and Moe." In *The Aspirin Age, 1919–1941.* Ed. Isabel Leighton. New York: Simon and Schuster, 1965. 34–49.

Barr, Andrew. *Drink: A Social History of America.* New York: Carroll and Graf Publishers, Inc., 1999.

Behr, Edward. *Prohibition: Thirteen Years That Changed America.* New York: Arcade Publishing, 1996.

Bliven, Bruce. "Flapper Jane." In *Essays of 1925.* Ed. Odell Shepard. Hartford, Conn.: Edwin Valentine Mitchell, 1926. 242–48.

Bloodworth, William A., Jr. *Upton Sinclair.* Boston: Twayne Publishers, 1977.

Blotner, Joseph. *Faulkner: A Biography.* New York: Random House, 1984.

Brauer, Stephen. "Jay Gatsby and the Prohibition Gangster as Businessman." *The F. Scott Fitzgerald Review* 2 (2003): 51–71.

Bruccoli, Matthew. "How Are You and the Family Old Sport—Gerlach and Gatsby." *Fitzgerald/Hemingway Annual* 7 (1975): 33–36.

Burns, Eric. *The Spirits of America: A Social History of Alcohol.* Philadelphia: Temple University Press, 2004.

Byrd, Frank. "Harlem Rent Parties." *American Life Histories: Manuscripts from the Federal Writers' Project, 1936–1940.* April 29, 2000. <http://memory.loc.gov/ammem/wpaintro/wpahome.html>.

Calt, Stephen, and Gayle Wardlow. *King of the Delta Blues: The Life and Music of Charlie Patton.* Newton, N.J.: Rock Chapel Press, 1988.

Carter, John F., Jr. "'These Wild Young People' by One of Them." *Atlantic Monthly* 126 (September 1920): 301–4.

Carter, Paul A. *Another Part of the Twenties.* New York: Columbia University Press, 1977.

Cashman, Sean Dennis. *Prohibition: The Lie of the Land.* New York: The Free Press, 1981.

Chauncey, George. *Gay New York: Gender, Urban Culture, and the Making of the Gay Male World, 1890–1940.* New York: Basic Books, 1994.

Clark, Norman. *Deliver Us from Evil: An Interpretation of American Prohibition.* New York: W. W. Norton and Co., 1976.

———. *The Dry Years: Prohibition and Social Change in Washington.* 1965. Seattle: University of Washington Press, 1988.

Coleman, Leon. *Carl Van Vechten and the Harlem Renaissance: A Critical Assessment.* New York: Garland Publishing, 1998.

Dardis, Tom. *The Thirsty Muse: Alcohol and the American Writer.* New York: Ticknor and Fields, 1989.

Douglas, Ann. *Terrible Honesty: Mongrel Manhattan in the 1920s.* New York: Farrar, Straus and Giroux, 1995.

Drowne, Kathleen, and Patrick Huber. *The 1920s.* Westport, Conn.: Greenwood Press, 2004.

Du Bois, W. E. B. "Criteria of Negro Art." 1926. In *The Portable Harlem Renaissance Reader.* Ed. David Levering Lewis. New York: Viking Penguin, 1994. 100–105.

———. "The Du Bois Literary Prize." *The Crisis* 39.4 (April 1931): 137.

———. "Harlem." *The Crisis* 34.7 (September 1927): 240.

Dumenil, Lynn. *The Modern Temper: American Culture and Society in the 1920s.* New York: Hill and Wang/Farrar, Straus and Giroux, 1995.

Engelmann, Larry. *Intemperance: The Lost War Against Liquor.* New York: The Free Press/Macmillan Publishing, 1979.

Erenberg, Lewis A. *Stepping Out: New York Nightlife and the Transformation of American Culture, 1890–1930.* Westport, Conn.: Greenwood Press, 1981.

Erskine, John. "The Prohibition Tangle." In *Prohibition and Christianity and Other Paradoxes of the American Spirit.* Indianapolis: The Bobbs-Merrill Company, 1927.

Fass, Paula. *The Damned and the Beautiful: American Youth in the 1920's.* New York: Oxford University Press, 1977.

Foley, Barbara. *Telling the Truth: The Theory and Practice of Documentary Fiction.* Ithaca, N.Y.: Cornell University Press, 1986.

Gilmore, Thomas B. *Equivocal Spirits: Alcoholism and Drinking in Twentieth-Century Literature.* Chapel Hill: University of North Carolina Press, 1987.

Gray, Richard. *The Life of William Faulkner: A Critical Biography.* Cambridge, Mass.: Blackwell Publishers, 1994.

Hardin, Achsah. "Volstead English." *American Speech* 7.2 (December 1931): 81–88.

Harris, Leon. *Upton Sinclair: American Rebel.* New York: Thomas Y. Crowell Company, 1975.

Jackson, Kenneth T. *The Ku Klux Klan in the City, 1915–1930.* New York: Oxford University Press, 1967.

Johnson, James Weldon. *Black Manhattan.* 1930. Introd. Sondra Kathryn Wilson. New York: Da Capo Press, 1991.

Kellner, Bruce, ed. *The Harlem Renaissance: A Historical Dictionary for the Era.* Westport, Conn.: Greenwood Press, 1984.

Kiser, Clyde Vernon. *From Sea Island to City: A Study of St. Helena Islanders in Harlem and Other Urban Centers.* 1932. New York: Atheneum Press, 1969.

Kobler, John. *Ardent Spirits: The Rise and Fall of Prohibition.* 1973. New York: Da Capo Press, 1993.

Lane, Winthrop D. "Ambushed in the City: The Grim Side of Harlem." In *The Survey Graphic* Harlem Number. Vol. VI, No. 6. March 1925. 692–95; 713–15.

Leighton, Isabel, ed. *The Aspirin Age, 1919–1941.* New York: Simon and Schuster, 1965.

Leonard, Neil. *Jazz and the White Americans.* Chicago: University of Chicago Press, 1962.

Lerner, Michael A. "Dry Manhattan: Class, Culture, and Politics in Prohibition-Era New York City, 1919–1933." Ph.D. diss. New York University, 1999.

Leuchtenburg, William E. *Perils of Prosperity, 1914–32.* 1958. Chicago & London: University of Chicago Press, 1993.

Lewis, David Levering. *When Harlem Was in Vogue.* New York & Oxford: Oxford University Press, 1981.

Lornall, Christopher. "The Effects of Social and Economic Changes on the Uses of the Blues." *John Edwards Memorial Foundation Quarterly* 11 (Spring 1975): 43–48.

Mason, Philip P. *Rum Running and the Roaring Twenties: Prohibition on the Michigan-Ontario Waterway.* Detroit, Mich.: Wayne State University Press, 1995.

McFadden, William J. *The Law of Prohibition: Volstead Act Annotated.* Chicago: Callaghan and Company, 1925.

Mencken, H. L. *The American Language: An Inquiry Into the Development of English in the United States, Supplement I.* 1945. New York: Knopf, 1962.

———. "Portrait of an American Citizen." In *Sinclair Lewis.* Ed. Mark Schorer. Englewood Cliffs, N.J.: Prentice-Hall, Inc., 1962.

Merz, Charles. *The Dry Decade.* Garden City, N.Y.: Doubleday, Doran & Company, Inc., 1931.

Minter, David. *William Faulkner: His Life and Work.* Baltimore, Md.: The Johns Hopkins University Press, 1997.

Moats, Alice-Leone. *No Nice Girl Swears.* New York: Knopf, 1933.

Morgan, John P., and Thomas C. Tulloss. "The Jake Walk Blues." *Old Time Music* 28 (Spring 1978): 17–25.

Murdock, Catherine Gilbert. *Domesticating Drink: Women, Men, and Alcohol in America, 1870–1940.* Baltimore, Md., & London: The Johns Hopkins University Press, 1998.

Oliver, Paul. *Blues Fell This Morning: Meaning in the Blues.* New York: Cambridge University Press, 1990.

Osofsky, Gilbert. *Harlem: The Making of a Ghetto: Negro New York, 1890–1930,* 2nd ed. New York: Harper and Row, 1971.

Ottley, Roi. *New World A-Coming.* New York: Arno Press and the *New York Times,* 1968.

Owen, Chandler. "The Black and Tan Cabaret—America's Most Democratic Institution." *The Messenger* 7.2 (February 1925): 97, 100.

Pauley, Thomas H. "Gatsby as Gangster." *Studies in American Fiction* 21 (August 1993): 225–36.

Pfeiffer, Kathleen. "Introduction." *Nigger Heaven.* Urbana & Chicago: University of Illinois Press, 2000. ix–xxxix.

Powers, Madelon. *Faces Along the Bar: Lore and Order in the Workingman's Saloon, 1870–1920.* Chicago & London: University of Chicago Press, 1998.

Reid, Ira De A. "Mrs. Bailey Pays the Rent." In *Ebony and Topaz: A Collectanea.* 1927. Ed. Charles S. Johnson. Freeport, N.Y.: Books for Libraries Press, 1971. 144–48.

Rogers, Will. *The Cowboy Philosopher on Prohibition.* Stillwater: Oklahoma State University Press, 1975.

Ruth, David E. *Inventing the Public Enemy: The Gangster in American Culture, 1918–1934.* Chicago: University of Chicago Press, 1996.

Schoener, Allon, ed. *Harlem on My Mind: Cultural Capital of Black America, 1900–1968.* New York: Random House, 1968.

Schorer, Mark. *Sinclair Lewis: An American Life.* New York: Dell Publishing Co., 1961.

Schreibersdorf, Lisa. "Radical Mothers: Maternal Testimony and Metaphor in Four Novels of the Gastonia Strike." *JNT: Journal of Narrative Theory* 29.3 (Fall 1999): 303–22.

Schuyler, George, and Theophilus Lewis. "Shafts & Darts: A Page of Calumny and Satire." *The Messenger* 7.8 (August 1925): 295.

Silverman, Joan L. "*The Birth of a Nation*: Prohibition Propaganda." *The Southern Quarterly* 19.3–4 (Spring–Summer 1981): 23–30.

Singal, Daniel J. *William Faulkner: The Making of a Modernist.* Chapel Hill: University of North Carolina Press, 1997.

Stevenson, Elizabeth. *Babbitts and Bohemians: From the Great War to the Great Depression.* 1967. New York: Macmillan, 1998.

van Notten, Eleonore. *Wallace Thurman's Harlem Renaissance.* Costerus Ser. 93. Amsterdam & Atlanta, Ga.: Rodopi, 1994.

Walker, Stanley. *The Night Club Era.* 1933. Baltimore, Md., & London: The Johns Hopkins University Press, 1999.

West, Dorothy. "Elephant's Dance: A Memoir of Wallace Thurman." *Black World* 20.1 (November 1970): 77–85.

Willebrandt, Mabel Walker. *The Inside of Prohibition.* Indianapolis: The Bobbs-Merrill Company, Inc., 1929.

Wilson, Edmund. *The American Earthquake: A Documentary of the Twenties and Thirties.* Garden City, N.Y.: Doubleday, 1958.

Wintz, Cary D. *Black Culture and the Harlem Renaissance.* Houston, Tex.: Rice University Press, 1988.

Woofter, T. J., Jr. *Negro Problems in Cities.* Garden City, N.Y.: Doubleday, Doran and Company, Inc., 1928.

Index

Adams, James Truslow, 26
advertising, 1–2, 13, 20, 84, 133
Aiken, Ednah, 2–3, 65
alcoholism, 75, 103
Allen, Frederick Lewis, 32, 35–36, 67, 133
The American Earthquake: A Documentary of the Twenties and Thirties (Wilson, Edmund), 30–31
American Language (Mencken), 30, 96
American popular culture. *See* popular culture
Amsterdam News (newspaper), 24–25, 108
Amusing the Million: Coney Island at the Turn of the Century (Kasson), 171n4
Anderson, Sherwood, 6, 36, 42–43, 62
Anti-Saloon League, 9, 16, 17
Appointment in Samarra (O'Hara), 166
Arlen, Michael, 81
Armstrong, Louis, 119, 152
Arrowsmith (Lewis, Sinclair), 102
Arthur, Timothy Shay, 31
Asbury, Herbert, 8, 50, 75, 95–96, 98, 165, 166
Atlantic Monthly (magazine), 26, 68, 141

Babbitt (Lewis, Sinclair), 6, 12, 21–22, 33, 41, 88–92, 99–102, 115–16, 163
Babbitts and Bohemians: From the Great War to the Great Depression (Stevenson), 71, 73
Baker, Josephine, 152
Barbecue Bob, 95, 99
barrelhouse flats, 173n11. *See also* buffet flats

barrelhouses. *See* roadhouses
Barron's, 125, 127. *See also* cabarets; Harlem
The Beautiful and Damned (Fitzgerald), 6, 12, 41, 47, 70, 82–83, 86–87, 134–35
"Bernice Bobs Her Hair" (Fitzgerald), 82
"Big Blonde" (Parker), 6, 95, 103
The Big Sea (Hughes), 122, 141–42, 145
The Big Town (Lardner), 13
The Birth of a Nation (movie), 20–21
black and tan joints, 105, 128. *See also* cabarets; speakeasies; Harlem
Black Bottom (dance), 8, 72, 145
Black Culture and the Harlem Renaissance (Wintz), 109, 118, 120
The Blacker the Berry . . . (Thurman), 3, 6, 12, 47, 62, 124–26, 140, 148–52, 155
Black Manhattan (Johnson, James Weldon), 148
Black Maria, 144. *See also* rent parties
"Blind Pig Blues" (song), 95, 99
blind pigs, 7, 30, 96, 107. *See also* speakeasies
blind tigers, 30, 96, 105, 128. *See also* speakeasies
Bliven, Bruce, 69
Bloodworth, William A., 63
Blues Fell This Morning: Meaning in the Blues (Oliver), 113, 156
"Bona and Paul" (Toomer), 126
bootleggers, 4, 5, 7, 9, 11, 12, 14, 19, 27, 28, 32, 33, 34–36, 38, 43–45, 47, 49–60, 66, 75, 114; depicted in literature, 49–60; 130–32
"Bootleggers' Blues" (song), 31